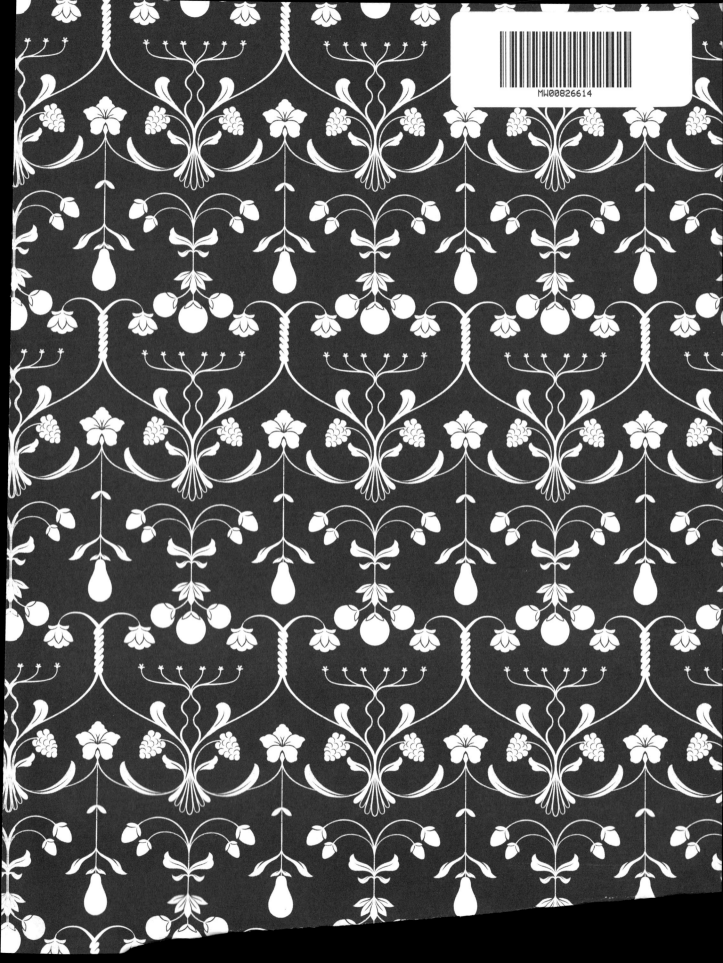

FOR

THE

CULTURE

For the Culture

Phenomenal Black Women and Femmes in Food

Interviews, Inspiration, and Recipes

KLANCY MILLER

Photography by Kelly Marshall
Illustrations by Sarah Madden

HARVEST
An Imprint of WILLIAM MORROW

HarperCollins books may be purchased for educational, business, or sales promotional use. For information, please email the Special Markets Department at SPsales@harpercollins.com.

FIRST EDITION

Designed by George McCalman and Aliena Cameron of McCalman.Co

Photography © 2023 by Kelly Marshall

Illustrations © 2023 by Sarah Madden

Library of Congress Cataloging-in-Publication Data has been applied for.

ISBN 978-0-358-58127-7

23 24 25 26 27 RTL 10 9 8 7 6 5 4 3 2 1

This book is dedicated to my parents, Rose and Isaac Miller, for introducing me to good food, the meaning of hospitality, and for supporting me on my journey.

This book is also dedicated to all Black women and femmes who steward the land, feed us, and bring us together with food and wine.

Contents

Reflections

THE WOMEN ON WHOSE SHOULDERS WE STAND

Interviews & Recipes

WISDOM, INSIGHTS, AND DELICIOUS INSPIRATION

Acknowledgments

I DIDN'T MAKE THIS
BOOK ALONE. IN MANY
WAYS, MAKING THIS
BOOK HAS BEEN ONE
BIG GROUP PROJECT. I'M
DEEPLY GRATEFUL FOR
EVERY SINGLE PERSON
WHO HELPED BRING
THESE PAGES TO LIFE.

To everyone who allowed me to interview them or who filled out my questionnaire, I thank you. Thank you, Zoe Adjonyoh, Mennlay Golokeh Aggrey, Salimatu Amabebe, Myriam Babel, Marva Babel, Mashama Bailey, Ashtin Berry, Lisa Binns, Fatmata Binta, Michelle Braxton, Ardenia Brown, Gabrielle E. W. Carter, Adrienne Cheatham, Julia Coney, Janine Copeland, Jessica Craig, Ayesha Curry, Kia Damon, Kyisha Davenport, Devita Davison, Cheryl Day, Osayi Endolyn, Amethyst Ganaway, Jacqueline Greaves, Jerrelle Guy, Carla Hall, Lani Halliday, Dr. Jessica B. Harris, Shanika Hillocks, Karis Jagger, Sicily Johnson, Adjoa Kittoe, Jillian Knox, Yewande Komolafe, Adrian Lipscombe, Vallery Lomas, Wendy Lopez, Krystal Mack, Meryanne Loum-Martin, Rahanna Bisseret Martinez, Cha McCoy, Kelly Mitchell, Shannon Mustipher, Thérèse Nelson, Zella Palmer, Leah Penniman, Anya Peters, Rāsheeda Purdie, Jamila Robinson, Sophia Roe, Michelle Rousseau, Suzanne Rousseau, Tiffani Rozier, Elle Simone Scott, Georgia Silvera Seamans, Jacqui Sinclair, Joy Spence, Nicole Taylor, Kaylah Thomas, Sarah Thompson, Toni Tipton-Martin, Fabienne Toback, Paola Velez, Korsha Wilson, and Amanda Yee. Each interview with you left me inspired and grateful for your work, energy, and presence in the world. You are all brilliant stars.

To my agent, Jane Dystel, thank you for your thoughtful guidance and for checking in regularly.

To my editor, Stephanie Fletcher, thank you for jumping in with aplomb to edit this book, and for your editorial guidance, patience, and willingness to advocate for this project to make sure it received the necessary resources.

To assistant editor Jacqueline Quirk, thank you for all of your help with the administrative side of this book.

To the sales and marketing team and everyone involved

in this project at HarperCollins, thank you for your expertise and strategy in making this book.

To Jane Cavolina and Amanda Hong, thank you for your copyediting skills.

To editor Karen Murgolo, thank you for acquiring the book!

To the brilliant designer George McCalman, thank you for your crystal-clear vision, creative direction, wise advice, hilarious texts, and advocacy for this book.

To the ever-awesome photographer Kelly Marshall, it was a gift to see you work—and to see you and George collaborate; thank you for your brilliant artistry and for making absolutely stunning images.

To the amazing food stylists Monica Pierini and Alyssa Kondracki, it was a joy to watch you cook. Thank you for being such talented professionals, for making the food so beautiful (and delicious), and for being so much fun to work with.

To visionary prop stylist Martha Bernabe, you made being on set a blast! Thank you for your vision, planning, phenomenal props, and good energy.

To Sarah Madden, thank you for your gorgeous, vibrant illustrations of each interviewee and throughout the book—and cover. Your work is beautiful and you are the absolutely ideal illustrator. I'm so grateful you said yes to this project.

To Aliena Cameron, thank you for keeping this project on the rails and for your attention to detail and positive energy.

To Ali Cayne, thank you for your tremendous generosity and for lending your splendid home for the photo shoot.

I could not have asked for a more gorgeous setting to make the images for this book. To Rosa, Lisa, and Eva, thank you for showing us everything we needed for the shoot.

To the amazing recipe testers Alanna Bass, Martine Thompson, and Alyssa Kondracki—thank you for your detailed notes and photos and recipe testing. To Lauren Campbell, thank you for your research and recipe testing.

To Kathy Martin, thank you for working on the recipes to make them consistent.

To Sarah Neal, thank you for thoughtfully transcribing the interviews.

To Marcus Samuelsson, Bryant Terry, Thérèse Nelson, Korsha Wilson, Krystal Mack, and Zella Palmer, thank you for being generous with your time and sharing your thoughtful reflections on Leah Chase, Edna Lewis, Vertamae Smart-Grosvenor, B. Smith, and Lena Richard.

To Jeff Gordinier, thank you for being my first reader, friend.

To Davis Thompson Moss, thank you for taking photos of the interviews and for checking in.

Thank you to my parents, my greatest cheerleaders—thank you for your love and constant support.

Introduction

WHEN I GRADUATED FROM COLLEGE, I HAD NO IDEA WHAT I WANTED TO DO...

But I was curious about food—having been raised by two restaurant lovers and avid cooks. I got a job in a nonprofit, set aside time to explore my other interests (filmmaking, acting, cooking), and began apprenticing at Fork restaurant in Philadelphia on the weekends to try to figure out what kind of work I'd be passionate about. Amped up by my restaurant gig, I decided to go to culinary school in Paris to become a pastry chef. At the time, I didn't know about the many options available under the big umbrella of food and hospitality. Over the course of several years, I would try on different roles, from baker to supper-club host to restaurant publicist to ghostwriter to cookbook author.

I didn't have a ton of information to guide me. But it didn't have to be that way. Looking back, I wish I'd had more sisterly insights to accompany me on my path. I didn't have this when I was coming up, so I'm giving it to you now, with the hope that it'll help guide future generations that are beginning their paths in the food and hospitality space.

I founded the magazine *For the Culture* because Black women have shaped cuisine in the United States and in many countries, and our stories about our expertise in food do not receive enough attention or admiration. The goal was to create a publication that centers the narratives of Black women and femmes in food and hospitality.

My intention in creating this book is similar, though with a slightly different motivation. I wanted to make it for my twenty-one-year-old self—a person interested in food but completely unaware of all the ways to participate in this space and equally unaware of the Black women and femmes, past and present, doing phenomenal and awe-inspiring work in food, wine, and hospitality. I wanted to ask the questions that a beginner might ask ("How did you begin?"). I also wanted to ask questions about things I am still learning about ("How do you build a team?" "How do you negotiate compensation?" "How do you build community?" "How do you take care of your mental health?").

What you'll find in this book are interviews with sixty-six women and femmes about their careers in food and their lives in general, recipes contributed by the interviewees, and profiles of our culinary matriarch ancestors—the women on whose shoulders we stand and who serve as a collective North Star. My feeling is that if you know and care about Julia Child, you should be equally familiar with Edna Lewis, B. Smith, Lena Richard, Vertamae Smart-Grosvenor, and Leah Chase.

The women and femmes in this book are some of the most generous, brilliant, inquisitive, transparent, hilarious, adventurous, and hardworking people I have encountered. They carry on a rich, sacred tradition that Black women have been at the center of—stewarding the land, educating people about what they cook or imbibe, cooking meals that bring people together and allow our humanity and love to be shared. I hope you will be inspired and energized by their stories and the gems of wisdom they share.

NOTE: THE INTERVIEWS IN THIS BOOK HAVE BEEN EDITED AND CONDENSED FOR CLARITY.

Reflections

THE WOMEN ON WHOSE SHOULDERS WE STAND

Edna Lewis

BORN
APRIL 13, 1916

DIED
FEBRUARY 13, 2006

When I read The Taste of Country Cooking, *I was quite taken by Lewis's emphasis on community, her focus on seasonality, and the personal lens through which she wrote. I saw myself in her: we both came from loving strong Black communities in the South; we both moved to New York City to cultivate our careers; and we both had immense pride in our Blackness.*

—Bryant Terry, chef, educator, author, editor in chief of 4 Color Books; from **Illustrated Black History: Honoring the Iconic & the Unseen** *by George McCalman*

Edna Lewis proved that by preserving your own culture you could shape culture. Her life and work illustrate the power of valuing your own heritage—not taking it for granted, but centering and celebrating what's in your backyard and mastering the skills involved in cooking what is, as she said, the only true American cuisine.[1]

Lewis was born in Freetown, Virginia. In *The Taste of Country Cooking* she describes it as "a community of farming people. It wasn't really a town. The name was adopted because the first residents had all been freed from chattel slavery and they wanted to be known as Free People."[2] Lewis, the grandchild of Chester and Lucinda Lewis, who were among the founders of Freetown, learned from this community everything about cooking, gardening, foraging, and farming that would lead to the foundation of her career.

As a teenager, she left Virginia and moved first to Washington, DC, where she cooked at the Brazilian embassy,[3] and then to New York. There, she worked domestic jobs and became a seamstress whose dresses were in demand by people such as Marilyn Monroe. She also dressed windows at Bonwit Teller, the luxury women's store.[4] Lewis married Steve Kingston, a

1 TONI TIPTON-MARTIN, "A MESSAGE FROM MY MUSE," IN *EDNA LEWIS: AT THE TABLE WITH AN AMERICAN ORIGINAL*, ED. SARA B. FRANKLIN (CHAPEL HILL: UNIVERSITY OF NORTH CAROLINA PRESS, 2018), 38.

2 EDNA LEWIS, *THE TASTE OF COUNTRY COOKING* (NEW YORK: ALFRED A. KNOPF, 1976), XIX.

3 JOHN T. EDGE, *THE POTLIKKER PAPERS: A FOOD HISTORY OF THE MODERN SOUTH* (NEW YORK: PENGUIN PRESS, 2017), 152.

4 FRANCIS LAM, "EDNA LEWIS AND THE BLACK ROOTS OF AMERICAN COOKING," *NEW YORK TIMES MAGAZINE*, OCTOBER 28, 2015.

She was a multi-hyphenate decades before the term was in vogue.

merchant mariner and communist. She worked in the office of the communist newspaper the *Daily Worker*. She was a multi-hyphenate decades before the term was in vogue.

In 1948, she became chef at her friend Johnny Nicholson's Café Nicholson on Manhattan's East Side. She cooked elegant home-style dishes such as roast chicken, cheese soufflé, green salads, biscuits, and chocolate soufflé. Her food made the restaurant a success and attracted celebrities such as Paul Robeson, Marlon Brando, Salvador Dalí, Eleanor Roosevelt, Truman Capote, Tennessee Williams, and William Faulkner.[5] Following her exit from the café in 1954,

she became a pheasant farmer, opened a restaurant in Harlem[6] that was in business only briefly, taught culinary classes, catered, and was a lecturer at the American Museum of Natural History.

Her first cookbook, *The Edna Lewis Cookbook*, was published in 1972. That was the same year she met the renowned editor Judith Jones, who would become the editor for Lewis's most well-known book, *The Taste of Country Cooking*. Both a memoir of her early years in Freetown and a story of the foods she and her family cooked and ate during each season, *The Taste of Country Cooking* is her most iconic book. She also wrote two others: *In Pursuit of Flavor* and *The Gift of Southern*

---

5 LAM, "EDNA LEWIS AND THE BLACK ROOTS OF AMERICAN COOKING."

6 MARY ROURKE, "EDNA LEWIS, 89; CHEF DREW ON FAMILY'S HISTORY IN REVIVING SOUTHERN CUISINE," *LOS ANGELES TIMES*, FEBRUARY 14, 2006.

Cooking, which was coauthored with her friend and protégé, Scott Peacock.

At the age of seventy-two, Edna Lewis became the chef at Gage & Tollner, which at the time was the oldest continuously open restaurant in New York City, having been founded in 1879. Her menu included breaded and butter-fried Ipswich clams, creamy she-crab soup, and catfish stew with scallions and garlic. In 2006, cultural columnist Jeff Weinstein wrote in the *Philadelphia Inquirer*, "I was certain that Edna Lewis' Gage & Tollner was the best place to eat in New York."[7]

Lewis left the restaurant in 1992, at the age of seventy-six, and moved to Atlanta, where she taught cooking and started the Society for the Revival and Preservation of Southern Food.[8] Among the honors she received in her lifetime: being named Grande Dame of Les Dames d'Escoffier International; receiving an honorary PhD in Culinary Arts from Johnson & Wales University; and being inducted into the James Beard Foundation Cookbook Hall of Fame. She was also honored, posthumously, with a commemorative United States postage stamp.

Edna Lewis died in 2006 at the age of eighty-nine. Her life and body of work continue to be a North Star for many people in food and hospitality and beyond. In *Edna Lewis: At the Table with an American Original*, Mashama Bailey encapsulates what countless people feel about Ms. Lewis:

"Edna Lewis's search for taste, as well as her story stuck with me. A Black woman from the South, Miss Lewis moved to New York to start a whole new life, first as a laundress, later as a seamstress and restaurant chef. She was never formally trained, but she had grown up cooking in rural Virginia, was hardworking, and loved wholesome food made with fresh ingredients. This sounded like many women in my family before me. As the opening chef at Café Nicholson in New York in the 1950s, she showcased simple food and was heaped with praise for it. Through Miss Lewis I realized that there was a history of Black women, like me, in professional kitchens, and that I wasn't alone."[9]

---

9 MASHAMA BAILEY, "IT'S NOT ALL FRIED CHICKEN AND GREASY GREENS," IN *EDNA LEWIS*, 195.

---

7 JEFF WEINSTEIN, "SHE WAS A COOK OF QUIET GENIUS," *PHILADELPHIA INQUIRER*, FEBRUARY 16, 2006.

8 NI'KESIA PANNELL, "ALL ABOUT EDNA LEWIS, THE GRANDE DAME OF SOUTHERN COOKING: SIX THINGS YOU SHOULD KNOW ABOUT THE PIONEERING CHEF," DELISH.COM, JANUARY 13, 2022.

Barbara Elaine Smith (B. Smith)

BORN
AUGUST 24, 1949

DIED
FEBRUARY 22, 2020

When you watched her show, she just commanded the camera not only because she was beautiful but just because she was so elegant and poised and seemed naturally just meant to be in this gorgeous home in the Hamptons and hosting people. You felt like you were a guest in her home. That inspires me as a woman and as a Black woman in particular. You can enter those spaces with grace and poise because you were meant to be there, and no one can ever make you feel like you don't deserve to be where you're at.

—*Korsha Wilson, writer and host of* **A Hungry Society** *podcast (page 120)*

The day I graduated from college, my family and I went to eat at B. Smith's restaurant in Manhattan's theater district to celebrate. It was incredibly exciting to me because I saw B. Smith as a role model: Actress, model, singer,[1] television personality, author, magazine editor, cook, restaurateur, and tastemaker, she was a person who exemplified possibilities in a field I found intriguing.

Even though I wasn't entirely sure what I wanted to do next, I felt inspired by all she had accomplished. Eating at her restaurant made me feel like maybe I, too, could create something beautiful and take up space in the world of food and hospitality.

Born in Everson, Pennsylvania, Smith learned to cook from her mother, Florence Claybrook Smith, and her maternal grandmother, Hart Claybrook. Smith's mother was a part-time housekeeper and her father was a steelworker. In her books, she describes her childhood as being filled with numerous family gatherings always supplied with abundant amounts of food, vegetables from their garden, and fruit from their trees. Her mother, grandmother, and aunts cooked often, and her father made homemade wine and root beer for these gatherings.

As a child, Smith was interested in sewing and cooking but felt rebuffed at the local 4-H club (a youth

---

1 JULIA REED, "CAN B. SMITH BE MARTHA?," *NEW YORK TIMES MAGAZINE*, AUGUST 22, 1999, 26.

"I first encountered B. Smith when I was little, and just seeing this fabulous Black woman on TV, who was having these beautiful dinner parties … And I was like, 'Who is this? Wow. I want to do that.'"

development organization), so she created her own home economics club and became its president.[2]

Smith began modeling after finishing high school. In 1969, she won a place in the Ebony Fashion Fair. She later signed with the modeling agency Wilhelmina in New York City and was on the cover of magazines such as *Mademoiselle*, *Ebony*, and *Essence*. In her book *B. Smith's Entertaining and Cooking for Friends*, she wrote, "Helping to create fantasies is one of the reasons I became a fashion model; that and the opportunity to travel. My modeling career took me all over the world, and I loved to sample the food wherever I went. . . . When my modeling career was over, it seemed natural to open a restaurant that would offer the different kinds of food I loved and that would provide a gathering place for the rich variety of people I enjoyed meeting."[3]

Smith opened her first restaurant in Manhattan in 1986. She later opened restaurants in Sag Harbor, New York, and Washington, DC.[4] She met her husband, Dan Gasby, a marketing executive, at her restaurant. He

2 WILLIAM GRIMES, "B. SMITH, MODEL TURNED RESTAURATEUR AND LIFESTYLE GURU, DIES AT 70," *NEW YORK TIMES*, FEBRUARY 23, 2020.

3 BARBARA SMITH, *ENTERTAINING AND COOKING FOR FRIENDS* (NEW YORK: ARTISAN, 1995), 9.

4 REED, "CAN B. SMITH BE MARTHA?"

helped her develop her nationally syndicated television show, *B. Smith with Style*, which she hosted for nearly a decade. Beloved for her glamour, charm, and warmth, Smith also had a talent for interior design, which led her to create a line of home goods under her name—the first product line by a Black woman sold at national retailers such as Bed Bath & Beyond and Macy's.[5] In addition to *B. Smith's Entertaining and Cooking for Friends*, Smith also wrote *B. Smith: Rituals and Celebrations* and *B. Smith Cooks Southern-Style*. In 2013, Smith was diagnosed with early-onset Alzheimer's disease; she and her husband chronicled her experience with dementia in their 2016 book, *Before I Forget*.

In an interview in *New York* magazine in 1997, she responded to being labeled the Black Martha Stewart by the media: "Martha Stewart has presented herself doing the things domestics and African Americans have done for years. We were always expected to redo the chairs and use everything in the garden. This is the legacy that I was left. Martha just got there first."

I asked artist Krystal Mack, one of the women featured in this book (page 132), when she first encountered B. Smith and what Smith meant to her. Krystal's sentiments reflect what many Black women feel about Smith and her legacy:

"I first encountered B. Smith when I was little, and just seeing this fabulous Black woman on TV, who was having these beautiful dinner parties . . . And I was like, 'Who is this? Wow. I want to do that. That's what my mom does with her friends when they have book club and stuff.' It felt like, if this makes any sense—something which I feel like any Black woman hearing this or reading this will understand—it felt like it was an extension of a grown-woman world that I wanted to be a part of. Like, I couldn't watch *Waiting to Exhale* when it came out, I had to sneak and peek through the door. My mom had the VHS and I just remember seeing on the cover of the poster all these beautiful, fabulous Black women that were living life. And I imagine that they had dinners with their girlfriends. And B. Smith was showing how to host dinner. So I was just like, 'Wow, fancy Black ladies, that's my vibe, that's me. I want to be a fancy Black lady.' I think that

eighties babies, nineties kids—we had *A Different World* and *The Cosby Show*, we had a lot of Black representation that was separate from the white gaze. And I think that B. Smith really showed that.

"I didn't think I would always be the consummate host like her, but I knew that if I approached hosting in the way that she did, which I've tried to do even in my time in hospitality—I've tried to kind of keep that solid footing, which was the example I saw with my mom and my grandmother and my aunts when we hosted family gatherings or when they had get-togethers with friends in the community.

"I think if we look back a lot more as we continue to build restaurants and build worlds around what hospitality looks like for Black people in food—Black women, or just people—if we pulled from models like B. Smith, we'd probably have a more nurturing and inviting space to enter into."

5 B.SMITH.COM.

Leah Chase

BORN
JANUARY 6, 1923

DIED
JUNE 1, 2019

When integration came, people said, Leah, you should move, Black people can go anywhere now, they won't come to you. I said, you can't run away from yourself, you are who you are, so you stay where you are and make it work for you. And that's exactly what I did. I stayed right here. All I wanted was a community where people would come, and I have that. I'm still trying to make it a first-class restaurant in this community. That's all I ever wanted. I was on that road, and here comes Katrina, bam, and I had to start over again. I'm never going to give up. I'm going to stay on this battlefield till I die.

—Leah Chase, from Serious Eats, "Leah Chase (1923–2019) in Her Own Words" by Daniel Gritzer

In 2016, I was lucky enough to have a phone conversation with Leah Chase, executive chef emeritus and owner of Dooky Chase's Restaurant in New Orleans, for an interview for *Cherry Bombe* magazine[1] about her appearance in Beyoncé's visual album, *Lemonade*. It was my third time speaking with her for an article—we had spoken before about culinary education and traditional celebratory meals in New Orleans. Besides talking about her music video debut, she also told me how she began in food and about Dooky Chase's Restaurant—which has been in business for more than eighty years.

Chase was born in New Orleans, one of thirteen children, and raised in Madisonville, Louisiana. She said her father wanted his children in Catholic schools, but there were not any available for Blacks, so she went to New Orleans to attend school. She was sixteen when she graduated and went to work as a domestic in the homes of white people. Her first restaurant job was at Colonial Restaurant in the French Quarter.[2]

In 1946, she married musician Edgar "Dooky" Chase Jr. Her mother-in-law had opened Dooky Chase's as a sandwich shop in 1939, then opened it as a restaurant in 1941. In 1952, when Leah Chase's father-in-law became extremely ill, she and her husband began formally running the restaurant. Known as the Queen

1 KLANCY MILLER, "MAMA TASTE, BOW DOWN: A CHAT WITH THE LEGENDARY CHEF LEAH CHASE," *CHERRY BOMBE*, ISSUE 8, 2016.

2 MILLER, "MAMA TASTE, BOW DOWN."

"I loved her. I loved Leah. I'm super grateful for everything that she truly guided me about—past, present, and future."

of Creole Cuisine, Chase became famous for her gumbo, jambalaya, red beans and rice, and trout amandine.[3]

During the Jim Crow era, Dooky Chase's Restaurant played a critical role for activists. It was one of the few places in New Orleans where people of different races could meet to organize for the local civil rights movement. Mrs. Chase told me, "You were not supposed to serve white people and Black people but we did it."

The people Chef Chase fed during the civil rights movement included the Freedom Riders who rode buses throughout the South to challenge segregation laws, James Baldwin, Martin Luther King Jr., members of the Congress of Racial Equality, and more. She was known for saying: "We changed the course of America over a bowl of gumbo."[4]

In the 1970s, Chase started collecting art to display in the restaurant. For poor artists, she would swap art for gumbo. Dooky Chase's Restaurant became an unexpected gallery for Black artists—some of whom include Lois Mailou Jones, Elizabeth Catlett, Jacob Lawrence, Sue Jane Mitchell Smock, John T. Biggers, Samella Lewis, and Chase Kamata.[5]

Chase wrote two cookbooks, *The Dooky Chase Cookbook* and *And Still I Cook*. She was the inspiration for Disney's Princess Tiana in the film *The Princess and the Frog*. She also received numerous awards and honors, such as the 2016 James Beard Lifetime Achievement Award and honorary degrees from Dillard University, Tulane University, Our Lady of Holy Cross College, Madonna College, Loyola University New Orleans, and Johnson & Wales University.

I asked Chef Marcus Samuelsson, to whom Chase was a mentor, about when he first encountered Leah Chase

and what she meant to him, and he said, "I met Leah in the nineties, and it was one of those nights where we all got an award—Sylvia Woods, Leah Chase, and myself. It's like you're an up-and-coming artist and you're sitting at the table with Patti LaBelle and Diana Ross." He went on: "And then the next day she actually came into our restaurant to eat—which for me was so important. Then she really tasted and saw me, you know what I mean? And she's been my mentor ever since that day in ninety-seven. When I came to New Orleans, I didn't even call her. I went straight from the airport to her kitchen.

"I loved her. I loved Leah. I'm super grateful for everything that she truly guided me about—past, present, and future, if you think about how ahead of her time she was. And the balance between raising a family and creating a business—and her business has been in business for eighty years. Think about that! And now her grandson's running it with her daughter Stella and they're on DoorDash. They figured out how to evolve it to make it a true family business. And just her work ethic, right? Think about running a business when you're nineteen until you're ninety-five. Think about the commitment. After Katrina, I called her and I was like, 'This is it, Leah.' She's like, 'What are you talking about? We're going to rebuild.' And they're rebuilding the restaurant, and she was eighty then, and they started again. For me Leah is the highest of highs." He added, "Not a lot of chefs have been a Disney character, in a Beyoncé video, a Beard award [winner], and run a business for eighty years. What more do you want?"

3 "LEAH CHASE (1923–), CHEF," ENCYCLOPEDIA.COM, HTTPS://WWW.ENCYCLOPEDIA.COM/EDUCATION/NEWS-WIRES-WHITE -PAPERS-AND-BOOKS/CHASE-LEAH.

4 MARC H. MORIAL, "LEAH CHASE: 'WE CHANGED THE COURSE OF THE WORLD OVER A BOWL OF GUMBO,'" *NEW PITTSBURGH COURIER*, JUNE 18, 2019.

5 "DOOKY CHASE'S RESTAURANT," BLACK LISTED CULTURE, VOL. II, NO. 19, HTTPS://BLACKLISTEDCULTURE.COM/DOOKY-CHASES -RESTAURANT/.

Vertamae Smart-Grosvenor

BORN
APRIL 4, 1937

DIED
SEPTEMBER 3, 2016

Griot and culinary anthropologist Vertamae Smart-Grosvenor gave us a framework for how to apply our cultural gifts to everyday life. She celebrated our traditions through food, entertaining and place-making, fashion and media. Like my grandmother Artris P. Woodard, she made it fly to be subversive and gave us other ways to protest and disrupt norms that excluded us and our stories. My place in the culinary media world has been carved out by women like her, B. Smith, Ntazake Shange, Cornelia Bailey, Dr. Jessica B. Harris, Norma Jean Darden, Sallie Anne Robinson, and Dori Sanders just to name a few. Their work is a continuation of so many others before them, both free and enslaved.

—Gabrielle E. W. Carter, cultural preservationist (page 128)

The phrase "stay in your lane" could never apply to Vertamae Smart-Grosvenor. She personified the term "multi-hyphenate creative." Smart-Grosvenor was a storyteller, a culinary anthropologist, a poet, an actress, a writer, and an author.[1] She was a National Public Radio correspondent and hosted *Seasonings*, a radio show on holiday cuisines. She was also the host of the television show *The Americas' Family Kitchen*. She was a dancer and space goddess for the band Sun Ra Arkestra.[2] She was in three films: *Personal Problems*, *Daughters of the Dust*, and *Beloved*. She acted on Broadway in the play *Mandingo* in 1960. From 1988 to 1995 she was the host of *Horizons*, NPR's award-winning documentary series. She wrote a food folk opera called *Nyam* [Eat] that she performed in venues throughout the United States. She wrote *Thursdays and Every Other Sunday Off: A Domestic Rap*; *Black Atlantic Cooking*; *Vertamae Cooks in the Americas' Family Kitchen*; and *Vertamae Cooks Again: More Recipes from the Americas' Family Kitchen*.

---

1 MAYUKH SEN, "VERTAMAE SMART-GROSVENOR IS THE UNSUNG GODMOTHER OF AMERICAN FOOD WRITING, *VICE*, FEBRUARY 20, 2018.

2 VERTAMAE GROSVENOR, *VERTAMAE COOKS IN THE AMERICAS' FAMILY KITCHEN* (SAN FRANCISCO: KQED BOOKS, 1996), 192.

Smart-Grosvenor wrote her seminal and autobiographic cookbook, *Vibration Cooking: or, the Travel Notes of a Geechee Girl*, in 1970. Unparalleled for its time (then and now), the book contained more stories and reflections than it did traditionally formatted recipes. She proclaimed, "When I cook, I never measure or weigh anything; I cook by vibration." I asked Zella Palmer, chair and director of the Dillard University Ray Charles Program in African American Material Culture, what the book means to her, and she said, "Vertamae just speaks to my soul. I can't explain it. She was way beyond her years, and still, I still feel like a lot of us don't get it. I mean that vibration cooking cannot be taught. It is an experience. It is legacy. It is rooted in family and roots and just energy. The old folks used to always say, like, 'Oh, you put too much salt in that. You must be in love.' Or all their little sayings, 'Oh, she ain't put no flavor in that. She must be mad.' You know what I mean? And vibration cooking is really a real thing. And for us, that is how we cook. And you ask anyone who cooks constantly and has been rooted in culture, whether it's Creole, Gullah Geechee, Southern regional cuisine, they learned from vibration. It isn't measured. It isn't in a book. It is felt from your soul. I still don't hear people talking about that. I read the introduction to her book *Vibration Cooking* every four or five months just to remind myself why I do the work that I do, because I do believe that it's all connected."

Smart-Grosvenor was born and learned how to cook in South Carolina's Low Country, where the people and language are called Gullah or Geechee. In *Vertamae Cooks in the Americas' Family Kitchen*, she wrote, "We descendants of African slaves in the Low Country have intrigued scholars and anthropologists for more than a century. They call us Gullah, but 'we called weself Geechee.' We say goober or pinder for peanut, gombo for okra, and benne for sesame seed. Bukra means white and can be a white potato or a white person. A skillet blond is a very dark person. We say guinea squash for eggplant and nyam for to eat. I didn't know that people in the rest of the country—or even the rest of the state— spoke differently from us until I left the Low Country to go north. Geechee territory was my home."[3] Smart-Grosvenor and her family left South Carolina when she was ten and moved to Philadelphia.[4] At nineteen, she sailed to Paris, where she would find a community of artists, including expats, that included her future husband, Robert Grosvenor, a sculptor. When she returned to New York, she continued to build a vibrant creative group of friends, for whom dinner parties featured prominently.

Her body of work was and is an ongoing investigation of the ways food conveys culture. In her book *Vertamae Cooks in the Americas' Family Kitchen*, she says, "I was a grown girl across the ocean before I, as folklorist Zora Neale Hurston has described it, looked at home through the spyglass of anthropology and began my exploration into Afro-Atlantic food ways."[5]

When I asked Thérèse Nelson, founder of Black Culinary History, what Vertamae means to her, she said, "When you read *Vibration* in particular, she's saying, 'I'm from this very specific place with these very particular traditions and upbringing,' and she left this country to see the rest of the world, to understand why the lens with which she was viewing the world was trying to marginalize her when she knew the power of who she was and where she was from. And what she found out when she traveled to Europe, when she went to the Continent, when she was confronting not just food but art and other cultures, was that there was a richness and a singularity to her Blackness that was undeniable.

"And her book was this idea about not having to explain yourself or overcorrect for other people's understanding or trying to contort yourself or fit yourself into some sort of box. It was full throated and so irreverent that it gave me permission—I think it gives readers who are reading her carefully—permission to define what it is you want to say at your table, and it deputizes you in a way, which I think is the power of anybody's place in the world. Any kind of culinary art, any kind of artistic endeavor should really empower the consumer to sort of be as open and free as possible. I think she was the first person I read that made me feel like there was power beyond the dishes themselves.

---

3 GROSVENOR, *VERTAMAE COOKS*, 14.

4 SEN, "VERTAMAE SMART-GROSVENOR IS THE UNSUNG GODMOTHER OF AMERICAN FOOD WRITING."

5 GROSVENOR, *VERTAMAE COOKS*, 17.

"She was saying that the laborer–the person whose hands are dirty, their hands are the ones who are creating the culinary world, and they deserve honor."

"*Vibration* is the book that I think people reference the most, but from an industry standpoint—especially from a professional standpoint—I actually feel like *Thursdays and Every Other Sunday Off* is a book that we really need to be celebrating a lot more. She calls it a 'domestic rap,' and I think that language is interesting because this was a time when she would have been immersed in New York culture, especially in the Bronx and Harlem, and she was in community with the Last Poets when they were sort of developing the language of rap music in the mid-to-late seventies. She would have been in community with them as an artist—as a chef, surely, but as an artist as well.

"She uses the language of 'domesticity' because at that point we didn't really have language around 'chef' as a valuable title. She understood that we were, as

domestics, the arbiters of culinary culture, and she was elevating the domestic. I guess in modern parlance, I feel like she was saying that the laborer—the person whose hands are dirty, their hands are the ones who are creating the culinary world, and they deserve honor. They deserve value, and we should be looking at them for best practices."

Lena Richard

BORN
SEPTEMBER 11, 1892

DIED
NOVEMBER 27, 1950

We know so much about Julia Child. We know so much about all these big-time chefs, and we don't know anything about Lena Richard? It's amazing to me. She was part of this African American matriarchal culinary legacy in New Orleans. The legacy of Nellie Murray [a famous nineteenth-century chef] and Rose Nicaud [founder of the first French Quarter coffee stand], all of those formerly enslaved cooks who, after the Civil War, were able to turn what was a horrible situation into a profession.

—Zella Palmer, chair and director of the Dillard University Ray Charles Program in African American Material Culture (page 196)

Did you know that fifteen years before Julia Child's show *The French Chef* aired, a Black woman appeared on television twice a week on her own cooking show, *Lena Richard's New Orleans Cook Book*? I learned that fact from Dr. Jessica B. Harris at a talk she gave in Brooklyn in 2017. Richard was not only (probably) the first Black woman to have her own cooking show, she was also the creator of an empire that included restaurants, retail frozen food, cooking schools, and a cookbook.

Born in 1892, as a teenager Lena Richard began working part time as a domestic worker for the Vairin family in New Orleans.[1] In her own words from a short, unpublished autobiography, Ms. Richard describes the beginning of her work in the kitchen:

"I was born and reared in New Orleans and was fourteen years old when I began working for Mrs. Vairin. I went there to visit a cousin who worked there. While there, my cousin was taken ill and I stayed to help with the work. During this time Mrs. Vairin asked if I would like a little job before and after school and I said I would love that. So it was planned that I would come in and help in the morning, fix the children's lunch and then return after school. I did this for a while and finally Mrs. Vairin's maid left and then I started helping with the downstairs work. Then when summer vacation came along I worked all day. The next year instead of going to day school, I attended night school and continued with my job. At this time Mrs. Vairin's cook left and it was at this time that I started cooking for this family of seven. Mrs. Vairin was amazed that

---

1 TODD A. PRICE, "'FABULOUS' LENA RICHARD: IN JIM CROW TIMES, A BLACK WOMAN CHEF FROM NEW ORLEANS BUILT A FOOD EMPIRE," *USA TODAY*, DECEMBER 16, 2021.

Richard was not only . . . the first Black woman to have her own cooking show, she was also the creator of an empire.

I could prepare such good food since I was so small. I was nineteen years old at that time and I weighed ninety-nine pounds. I was given the responsibility of all the marketing—all the cooks in New Orleans did the marketing. She told me I could buy just what I wanted to. I got a chicken, made stew and had fruit for dessert. From this time on it seemed that no other cook could please her. I was getting $10 a month and was raised to $15. She then told me that I could go to the store and pick out any kind of cooking utensils that I wanted and that she was going to give me cooking lessons and send me to cooking schools and every demonstration. If no other colored woman could get places I certainly could.

"Later I went to Boston and went to school there [at the famous Miss Farmer's School of Cookery founded by Fannie Farmer] for eight weeks. Then I went back to New Orleans. I continued cooking for Mrs. Vairin after I was married until I was twenty-eight and then left and started catering for myself."[2]

Not only did Richard cater, she became quite sought after for her food. Soon after the Great Depression, she worked as chef for the Orleans Club for seven years and then began writing her cookbook.[3] In 1937, she opened a cooking school for Black domestics so that they could enhance their culinary skills and thereby increase their earning potential.[4] She also started a cooking school for brides, bridesmaids, and married women who wanted to learn how to cook well for their husbands. Richard completed and self-published her cookbook, *Lena Richard's New Orleans Cook Book*, in 1939. The next year, Houghton Mifflin bought the book, renamed it *The New Orleans Cook Book*, and published it to wonderful reviews throughout the country.[5] The same year, Richard began working as chef at the Bird and Bottle Inn in Garrison, New York, where she stayed for eighteen months. When she returned to New

Orleans, she opened her own restaurant, Lena's Eatery. Constantly in demand and ever the itinerant chef, she then went to work as chef at Travis House at Colonial Williamsburg.[6] In 1945, she returned home and began a frozen-food business that shipped her famous dishes, such as jambalaya and gumbo, across the country. A few years later, she began filming her cooking show. A year after the show began, she opened Lena Richard's Gumbo House in New Orleans. On November 27, 1950, Lena Richard died of heart failure after working past midnight at her restaurant.[7]

Zella Palmer notes, "She clearly understood the power of food and she was able to maximize everything that she did. Black women mattered to her, right? The fact that she would open up a culinary school to teach domestic cooks dishes so they can make more money, that says a lot. The fact that she understood that, 'I need to help Black women,' is profound.

"She had the wherewithal and the mindset like 'I'm going to build an empire. I'm going to open up a restaurant. I'm going to open up a cooking school. . . .' She saw a need and she filled it."

---

2 PRICE, "'FABULOUS' LENA RICHARD." FROM AN ACCOUNT OF HER LIFE WRITTEN BY LENA RICHARD.

3 PRICE, "'FABULOUS' LENA RICHARD."

4 LILY KATZMAN, "MEET LENA RICHARD, THE CELEBRITY CHEF WHO BROKE BARRIERS IN THE JIM CROW SOUTH," *SMITHSONIAN*, JUNE 12, 2020.

5 PRICE, "'FABULOUS' LENA RICHARD."

6 PRICE, "'FABULOUS' LENA RICHARD."

7 PRICE, "'FABULOUS' LENA RICHARD," AND "'FABULOUS' LENA RICHARD IS DEAD," *LOUISIANA WEEKLY*, DECEMBER 2, 1950, FRONT PAGE.

Interviews & Recipes

WISDOM, INSIGHTS, AND DELICIOUS INSPIRATION

Leah Penniman

CO-DIRECTOR AND FARM MANAGER AT SOUL FIRE FARM
PETERSBURG, NEW YORK

How would you describe your work?

Soul Fire Farm is an Afro Indigenous–centered community farm that's dedicated to uprooting racism and seeding sovereignty in the food system, and we do that in three ways. One is that we care for eighty acres of historically Mohican territory using Afro Indigenous and regenerative farming methods that capture carbon and increase biodiversity, and then we gather up the food and medicine that the earth gives us and provide it at no cost to people who need it in the community.

The second major area of our work is to equip the next generation of Black and Brown farmers, and so we work with youth and adults on farm educational programming and training. We also run a Soul Fire in the City Urban Gardens Program and a North-South Corridor fellowship that provides resources and training for famers who are getting started with their own businesses.

The final area of our work is public education and advocacy, so we're working on institution building and policies that support the earth and the people who care for the earth— things like fairness for farm workers, debt relief for Black farmers, land access for Indigenous people and other people of color, access to food, and so on.

How did you begin in your field?

My first experience with growing food was gardening with my grandmother Brown Lee McCullough outside of Boston as a child, and we raised strawberries and crab apples and made jam together. But I did not grow up on a farm. At age sixteen, I got a position working on a farm near Boston and completely fell in love with this intersection of caring for the earth and caring for the human community, so I didn't stop from there. I worked at several other farms across Massachusetts to learn more in both urban and rural spaces, until I had the necessary experience to start my own farm.

Who are some of your role models or mentors in food, farming, and hospitality?

One of my role models and mentors is Karen Washington of Rise & Root Farm, also the founder of Black Urban Growers, and she's now the president of our board of directors at Soul Fire Farm. During a time when I was disillusioned about having chosen a career path as a farmer because there were so few Black or Brown faces at the conferences and in these farming spaces, she gave me a lot of encouragement by saying that we are not guests here, that in fact Black people have built the farming and food systems of this country and that we would one day have our conferences in the region and have our books and to just hold on.

"To free ourselves, we must feed ourselves."

Malik Yakini of D-Town Farm and the Detroit Black Community Food Security Network is also a huge inspiration for me, as an example of people who are impacted by hunger and by lack of access to green space taking matters into their own hands and building community institutions.

What is an important lesson you've learned about money, compensation, or finance over the course of your career?

A lesson that I've learned is the absolute imperative of making sure that whatever businesses we create (whether they are sole proprietorships, co-ops, or nonprofits) are able to pay a living wage and offer fair benefits and reasonable hours, and that can feel really hard with a start-up (especially in the farming space, where it has become the norm to have extremely low wages and very, very long hours). And the farmers themselves—even the farm owners are often not getting paid or are getting paid very little.

But to do the work ahead of time to figure out an economic model, whether it's having a side hustle like agrotourism or high-end crops or to value-add—in our case a nonprofit organization branch that can do some fundraising. Making sure that there is a revenue stream that can ensure that all the people who are working for the organization are taken care of.

How do you take care of your mental health and deal with the stresses of your work?

Mental health is a very significant issue in the farming community. There are high rates of mental illness and suicide among farmers because—well, for many reasons, but certainly the economic system is set up such that it's almost impossible to make it as a farmer financially, and the debt burden can be very high. With climate change and climate chaos, you can put in long weeks of work planting and then just see your whole crop wiped out by a wildfire, by a hurricane, a flood, a drought, a pest outbreak related to our mistreatment of the earth . . . so that is a really tough situation to be in.

So we have to take care of our mental health. I go on a run most mornings. It's very important to have that quiet time and exercise. I also see a therapist regularly, and have a spiritual practice. I'm a deep practitioner of African traditional religions, including the Yoruba religion and Vodun of the Dahomey region.

What advice would you offer someone who wants to do what you do?

For someone who's interested in farming and food justice, the first step is to find a mentor or mentoring organization who will take you on so you can learn the ropes. Farming is skilled labor, just like being a lawyer or a doctor or an engineer. If you wanted to be a doctor you wouldn't just go into the operating room and say, "Hand me a scalpel." You don't go onto the farm and just say, "Hand me a tractor." There is a learning curve, so taking a couple of years at least to work on farms is a very important first step, and then you find out if you'd like it, what kind of scale you like to work at, what type of crops you like to work with before you invest a whole lot of resources into your own operation.

Another thing that I would say is you really do need to have a passion for it. It is not the easiest career to choose, so find out what it is that's motivating you beyond just the economic considerations—whether it's a passion for being outdoors or a desire to connect with the earth or to feed the community—hooking into what is that aspect that makes you come alive.

Do you have a mission or motto, and if so, what is it?

So our motto is "To free ourselves, we must feed ourselves," and our mission is "Soul Fire Farm is an Afro Indigenous–centered community farm dedicated to uprooting racism and seeding sovereignty in the food system."

What do you most enjoy about your work?

Despite the frequency with which I do public speaking and teaching, I am an extreme introvert and really, really enjoy long, quiet days tending to plants and soil. So I think the thing that I enjoy the most is when I have the rare opportunity to have a day where the only sounds are the birds chirping and the wind rustling through the leaves and the soil critters scurrying about, and I may be tending to pruning some trees or harvesting strawberries. I enjoy that very, very much.

What is the most difficult aspect of your career?

Oh, there are many, many, many difficulties, but I would say that as Soul Fire Farm has risen in visibility and influence, I take really seriously the responsibility that we have as leaders to show up in the ways the community asks us to, whether that's to weigh in on a policy or write a letter of recommendation or make a referral to help with strategic conversations about the direction of the movement. These are really, really big asks that come our way, and sometimes we don't have the capacity to meet them all. So the challenge is wanting to say yes to all of this incredibly worthy work but not always being able to.

What brings you joy, and what would you like to experience more of?

So many things bring me a lot of joy, but I would say that I've had a lot of fun the past couple of years as we've increased the herbal line on our farm. We make teas, salves, spiritual baths, and other products from the perennial herbs. One of the most fun parts of the process is something called "garbling the herbs," where you take the dried herbs and rub them over a mesh screen, and then the little bits of leaf fall through the screen—that's what you use to make the tea. It's this wonderful, dusty aromatherapy that happens when we're garbling herbs. That's really fun, and it's a good activity to engage children with. We had a family here for one of our volunteer events and the kids just had a blast garbling. I'd like more experiences of just being hands-on with plants and animals and soil and getting to share that with young people.

What are some of your favorite things to eat or drink?

Well, I like anything in season. Just last night I made this very simple but delicious tea with fresh-harvested peppermint, fresh-harvested lemon balm—steeped that, and then added honey from our beehives and chilled it and iced it, and it was just the most fresh, perfect, wonderful summer drink.

One of my favorite things to eat to go from summer to fall is Soup Joumou. It is the Haitian national dish, made with a joumou pumpkin (or, in our climate, a kabocha squash)—it is the dish of liberation and independence that was enjoyed when the enslaved Haitians overthrew the French enslavers and declared their freedom and then ate the joumou pumpkin, which was not permitted to the enslaved people by the French. Once they were free, they were able to eat this delicacy.

Soup Joumou

BY LEAH PENNIMAN / MAKES 6–8 SERVINGS

1 pound kabocha squash or Caribbean pumpkin, peeled and chopped

Vegetable oil

Salt

4 garlic cloves, peeled and crushed

1 celery rib, chopped

1 large onion, peeled and chopped

2 potatoes, peeled and chopped

½ pound cabbage, chopped

1 turnip, diced

2 carrots, peeled and chopped

2 leeks, trimmed and chopped

12-ounce can whole coconut milk

1 cup sweet corn kernels, fresh, frozen, or canned

1 tablespoon chopped parsley

1 whole scotch bonnet or jalapeño pepper

1 tablespoon freshly squeezed lime juice

2 whole cloves

4 ounces dried pasta, such as penne (optional)

Freshly ground black pepper

Fresh thyme leaves, to taste

Splash of sweetener such as honey (optional)

For people of Haitian descent, Soup Joumou is the soup of independence, the soup of remembrance, and the soup that celebrates the New Year. The soul-warming dish commemorates January 1, 1804, the date of Haiti's liberation from France. The soup was once a delicacy reserved for white enslavers and forbidden to the enslaved people who cooked it. After independence, Haitians took to eating it to celebrate the world's first and only successful revolution of enslaved people resulting in an independent nation. The squash and hot peppers are essential; all other vegetables may be substituted with similar produce that is locally available.

Preheat the oven to 400°F.

Toss the squash with oil to coat and salt to taste, spread it on a sheet pan in a single layer, and roast until golden brown and tender, 15 to 20 minutes. At the same time in a separate pan, toss the garlic, celery, onion, potatoes, cabbage, turnip, carrots, and leeks in a little oil and salt and roast until golden and tender, 30 to 40 minutes.

When cool enough to handle, transfer the roasted squash to a blender or food processor, add the coconut milk, and process until smooth.

In a large pot, combine the squash puree with 8 cups water and bring to low boil. Add the roasted vegetables, corn, parsley, hot pepper, lime juice, and cloves. Simmer for 15 to 20 minutes to blend the flavors. If you are using pasta, add it about 10 minutes before the end of the cooking time. Taste the soup and season as desired with pepper, thyme, and sweetener. Remove the whole scotch bonnet pepper before serving.

Jerrelle Guy

COOKBOOK AUTHOR, FOOD STYLIST, PHOTOGRAPHER, RECIPE DEVELOPER
DALLAS, TEXAS

How would you describe your work?

I think of my work as art because it's self-expressive and always a reflection of where I am and what I'm liking at the moment.

How did you begin in your field?

A month after graduating college I started *chocolateforbasil*, which was a travel blog at the time. I moved to Dallas and emailed around town to get work as an assistant food stylist, but instead landed a job as a food photo assistant.

What are you most proud of?

Honestly, I'm proud of who I am. I haven't always felt this way, but the internal growth I've had to make to be standing where I am right now and feel solid, it's something people can't see, but I'm proud of myself for it.

What is the greatest regret in your career?

Ultimately, I believe that everything always works out, and whenever I look back after lots of time on something I had judged as embarrassing or bad because I didn't execute in the perfect way, I'm humbled because I see that it led me to a better place, a place I wouldn't have gotten to as quickly without that "mistake."

What is an important lesson you've learned about money, compensation, or finance over the course of your career?

Ask for what you want. Set clear boundaries. Know where you're willing to flex and honor that.

How do you take care of your mental health and deal with the stresses of work?

Journaling is super helpful for me. I get great clarity when I prioritize writing in moments of confusion or overwhelm.

Do you have a mission or motto, and if so, what is it?

Follow your heart.

What do you most enjoy about your work?

The ability to bring the visions I have to life and then share them with the world.

What's the most difficult aspect of your career?

Being my own boss—there's a lot of pressure to lead myself in the right direction!

What is your greatest food extravagance?

Lately I have been investing in quality tools and machines for my studio, like my french-door oven and my induction stove. They make the work I do in the kitchen a lot more efficient. And when I can streamline my process, I feel happy!

What are some of your favorite things to eat or drink?

Key lime Greek yogurt, iced oat milk matcha, and kombucha mocktails.

Baked Smoked Okra Dip

BY JERRELLE GUY / MAKES 5–6 SERVINGS

8 medium okra pods

2 tablespoons olive oil, plus more for drizzling

1 small shallot, peeled and diced

½ teaspoon crushed red pepper flakes

Salt and freshly ground black pepper

8-ounce package cream cheese, at room temperature

½ cup plain Greek yogurt

2 tablespoons mayonnaise (optional), preferably Duke's

1 teaspoon hot sauce

½ cup shredded whole-milk mozzarella

¾ cup shredded smoked gouda, divided

Paprika for sprinkling

Corn tortilla chips or toasted bread for serving

Preheat the oven to 425°F. Have a 16-ounce ramekin or two 8-ounce ramekins at hand.

Trim the tops off the okra and slice them in half lengthwise and then again in half widthwise. Set them aside.

In a medium sauté pan over medium-high heat, heat the olive oil. Add the shallot and cook, stirring often, until soft but not brown, about 3 minutes. Stir in the pepper flakes, okra, and salt and pepper to taste. Cook, stirring often, until the okra just begins to soften and weep some of its slime, 3 or 4 minutes. Remove the pan from the heat and set aside.

In a large bowl, mix the cream cheese, yogurt, mayonnaise (if using), hot sauce, mozzarella, ½ cup of the gouda, and salt and pepper to taste. Fold in the okra and shallots and transfer the mixture to the ramekin(s). Top with the remaining gouda, a splash of olive oil, and a sprinkling of paprika. Bake for 10 to 12 minutes or until the cheese is melted and the top is a little crusty. Serve warm with chips or bread.

Devita Davison

How would you describe your work?

FoodLab came out of a need to support Black-owned businesses and communities that have been traditionally, historically disinvested and marginalized. And the reason we decided to focus on food is because we also understood the intersectionalities between these disinvested, marginalized communities and health.

We thought, if we could start an organization that provided support and mentorship and social capital to food-based businesses, might we be able to do two things: Could we create an infrastructure in the city of Detroit that consisted of food businesses owned by Detroiters? And could those food businesses be healthy, fresh, affordable, accessible businesses that sold culturally appropriate food in our communities—communities ravaged with fast food, bodegas, Detroiters eating out of gas stations, etc.?

People will say that, taken at face value, FoodLab Detroit (and we're also piloting a FoodLab in Chicago)

is an incubator or maybe an accelerator. Some people call us a small-business support organization. But at the end of the day, the real secret sauce and the way I describe my work is that I am a community organizer and activist. At my core, I do this work to empower Black-owned business owners, understanding that in our community we have the opportunity not only to generate wealth in small businesses—we have the opportunity to hire our people, to provide them with good jobs, and to remake the food system, to envision a food system that is not exploitive of our Black bodies.

At the end of the day the goal is power. How do we extract power from this corporately owned takeover of our food system and bring power back into the hands of the people? So that's how I describe my work: I set out to empower folks, and the medium in which I do it is food, and the vehicle is small-business ownership.

How did you become a community activist?

I think I was born to be a community activist. I think it's my rite of passage. I am a daughter and a granddaughter and a great-granddaughter of Baptist preachers, and for me, the Baptist Church is the birthplace of community organizing. That was the place in which our people came together not only to celebrate, not only to worship, not only to love up on one another, not only to pray, but it is where movement building happened—in the basements of those churches.

And so my journey, even though I didn't have a name for it, I couldn't identify it, I didn't have the language behind it, growing up in the Baptist Church, sitting at the feet of Baptist ministers—I think I was born into community activism.

How do you connect it to food? Well, in the tradition of the Baptist Church, my mother and father came out of rural

"My favorite meals are always when I am 'round the table in the company of people who I love."

Alabama. Daddy was born and raised in a small town called Bessemer right outside of Birmingham, and my mother is a child of the birthplace of the Civil Rights Movement, which is Selma, Alabama. And so they migrated—both of them— to the city of Detroit in 1965, and you could take Mommy and Daddy out of Alabama but you can't take Alabama out of my mother and father.

My mother was one of those commandeers of the church kitchen. It was no surprise when I started Detroit Kitchen Connect (which was a network of community kitchens to give entrepreneurs the opportunity to start their businesses out of a licensed kitchen), I started it out of a church basement. It is what I've been around my entire life, how church and food were used to build community, and so that's really how I started.

How have you approached building a team for the work you do?

I don't want to be controversial. My first approach in building a team is to follow Black women. That's it. Rule #1: Follow Black women. Let me tell you something. I know I'm a bit biased when I say that, but the fact of the matter is that my most rewarding interactions thus far in this work have come from surrounding myself in an ecosystem of radical, loving, daring, audacious Black women. And when I say "Black women," I'm not just talking about people who identify or people who were born with a vagina. I'm talking about femmes, too. I'm talking about radical-ass Black women who have pushed me to envision a world that I didn't even think was freaking possible.

Beyond that, it's to understand who you are, what strengths you have, but also the weaknesses you have. So you think about it: What do I have to offer somebody and what can somebody offer to me? You do your own assessment of who you are. A lot of us spend more time working than we do even with our families. I want to build a team of people who also inspire me, and I want to be around people who are also the thinkers, the visionaries.

Because I know who I am—a really big thinker, a big visionary. I can wordsmith the hell out of a grant or a report, but when it comes to those day-to-day tasks, Klancy Miller, let me tell you something. I will do fifteen other things other than do the thing that I need to do. So I'm not that sticky in the weeds, in the numbers, focused on tasks and operational. I know I'm not that, so I have to find somebody who loves that shit, who loves operations, who loves being the conductor . . . and I have that somebody in my life. And so I look at what each individual can bring to a team, their own unique skill set.

I know I'm a bit biased when I say this, but my work is always centered around being in the company of and being proximate to women. The team at FoodLab is all women. The consulting firm that FoodLab has been working with to design and to execute our fellowship is called the Work Department. They're all women. The project that I'm launching right now in Chicago, which is FoodLab Chicago in partnership with Greater Chatham Initiative in the South Shore Chamber of Commerce, all women.

We get shit done. Listen, I'm not discounting the brothers at all. I'm just saying I am my most productive self, I am my most calm self, I am my most happy self when I am in the brilliance and wrapped up in the love and the radicalism of women.

What advice would you offer to someone who wants to do what you do?

This is such a tough question, and I'm just going to speak for my own experience.

Sheryl Sandberg wrote a whole-ass book called Lean In, but for a Black woman, my understanding is you can't have it all. You can't. The kind of work that I do and the way that I do the work, there are sacrifices. You have to be willing to make the necessary sacrifices to do this work. Particularly if you're a small, grassroots, community-led nonprofit, you're not going to get rich doing this work, and so you have to create a lifestyle that does not necessitate you having a whole bunch of money. Not to say that you can't have that, but I am just saying that you are not going to have it all, and that there are sacrifices that you are going to have to make, and it's going to take time.

Be very clear about the path that you want to take, and stay focused. I feel so bad that sometimes these young women compare their lives to the highlights of other people's lives on Instagram. So my advice is stay the hell off social media. Get down to doing the damn work that you want to do.

If you want to do the work that I want to do, you have to be very clear about who you are, what brings you joy, what brings you happiness, and you also have to spend some time alone. Because there are going to be some dark days doing this work. You're going to have to get really, really comfortable with yourself.

You're going to hear—and hopefully, this will get better—but as a Black woman leading an organization you'll get a lot of nos, you're going to get a lot of people who question you. So you're going to have to go into this work being very, very confident about who you are and very clear about what you want to do. And as much as I say, "Spend time alone getting to know yourself," you also are going to have to build and cultivate a community of people who are going to help you, a community of people who are going to love up on you, a community of people who are going to be critical of you when they need to be critical, who are going to hype you up when you need to be hyped up.

And then lastly, what I think I will say is to know your why. Your why will bring you back to the work all the time. It's so important that when you're doing this work, particularly community organizing, activism, leading a nonprofit organization—it is so important for me that you are also a part of the community that you are representing

and standing up for. Please don't parachute into a community that you're not a part of, you're not proximate to, and you just riding the bandwagon on something that you think is popular or can be funded. Understand your why, and be a part of and proximate to the community whose conditions you are trying to improve.

What are some of your favorite things to eat or drink?

My absolute favorite thing to drink is mezcal. I am obsessed with it.

The other thing I love to drink is a good cup of black coffee made from freshly roasted beans, because it's such an experience. I recently went to this coffee shop called Gaslight Coffee Roasters on the North Side of Chicago in Logan Square. And the reason I love Gaslight is because they are a roaster, so they're roasting their beans throughout the day. And when I walk in there—oh, my god. I wish coffee was a fragrance. You know how people say about wine, like, "You drink wine with your eyes, you drink it with your nose, you drink it with your mouth, your ears"? That's the way I feel about a good cup of coffee. I smell it, I'm looking at it, I'm tasting it, and I love when I'm drinking a really good cup of coffee and I can smell the beans roasting in the background.

So coffee and mezcal—the thing I drink in the morning and the thing I drink in the evening.

My favorite food or my favorite dish is one that I will never eat again in my whole life, because my absolute favorite was breakfast mornings at my grandmother's house in Bessemer, Alabama, and my grandmother of course has died. I'll never be able to eat my grandmother's bacon again. I'll never be able to eat her homemade biscuits again, where she rendered that lard and she shaped and molded that dough so lightly with her fingertips. I'll never be able to sit with her on the swing on the front porch, taking the biscuits and literally sopping them up with molasses and butter and having that conversation with Nana.

So it's not so much what my favorite dish is—it is who I am in the company of when I am eating. I love all kinds of food. But my favorite meals are always when I am 'round the table in the company of people who I love.

Julia Coney

JOURNALIST, WINE WRITER
WASHINGTON, DC

How would you describe your work?

My work, to me, is rooted in service. I look at myself as in service to people, particularly Black people, BIPOC people in the wine world.

How did you begin in your field?

Well, that's a very circuitous route. I didn't come to wine like most people. I came to wine when I realized, after ten years of beauty blogging and beauty writing, that I didn't want to write about beauty anymore, and I kept thinking what would be my third act. My first act was being a legal assistant, my second act was transforming a beauty blog into a beauty career, and then the third act was going from beauty to wine. Even though I'm still a beauty junky and I subscribe to all the beauty magazines and I know what's going on, I didn't want to write about it. I love food and wine, but I knew I didn't want to be a food writer. I knew instinctively, as much as I love food and enjoy great meals, I love wine more because wine reminded me of beauty.

When I started really studying wine, I had been drinking wine and visiting wine regions since my late twenties, so I knew about wine. And then my mother (who was living at the time) was like, "You should write about wine. You love food, but you really love wine," and that's when I decided to do formal education in wine studies to tighten up what I knew and actually learn a lot of things I didn't.

Who are some of your role models or mentors in the wine space?

You know the saying "You become what you see": I would not be here without Dorothy Gaiter and John Brecher. I read their *Wall Street Journal* column, "Tastings," and to see this Black woman writer with short hair who looked like me talking about wine as a story and storytelling about wine—because it wasn't just about the wine, it was the story that went with it—I just was like, "Oh, this is fascinating."

So when I thought of wine writers I thought of her first, and then of Jancis Robinson in England—they are two different styles of writing.

What advice would you offer to someone who wants to do what you do?

I would say, first, be nice. Kindness goes a long way. Also, study. Wine is a fascinating career, but you have to study wine. Not just how wine is made and how it tastes, but also the business of wine. Wine is a billion-dollar business.

I always say, there's the sexy and the nonsexy side of wine. The sexy side of wine is me drinking wine and Champagne. That's the sexy side. You see that. The nonsexy side is me understanding French law regarding Champagne, which constantly changes; what's happening with the harvest; how climate change is affecting the wine world. So when I say "study," you have to study all aspects of it.

What is an important lesson you've learned about money, compensation, or finance over the course of your career?

If you start out working for free, you'll never move ahead. If what you ask for doesn't make you shake a little bit and make you nervous, you're asking for too little.

"Wine is a liquid passport."

How do you take care of your mental health and deal with the stresses of your work? And for you specifically, since wine evokes so much beauty and connotes some ideas of leisure, do you even have stresses related to your work?

I'm like everybody else. It's still a job. I still have to meet the expectations of people who send me wine to review or send me to a region to explore. I have private clients for tastings, so I'm beholden to them to make sure that I actually give them value for what they're paying me to talk about.

The way I decompress from work is I play around with facial products. I do a lot of facials on myself. And I am a huge reader. I can shut off anything as long as I have a book—a book that is not anything to do with wine. I mean a very good fiction book, not a book to learn, but a book to escape. So I read a lot. I read Jasmine Guillory. I read Tia Williams. I read Daniel Silva. I'm reading right now *People We Meet on Vacation*. It has nothing to do with wine.

And I listen to music and dance in my house by myself. I really do. I will have a dance party, literally like no one is watching, just because I want to move.

What do you most enjoy about your work?

It keeps me curious. It keeps me on my toes, because every time I think I know something, I realize I know nothing. That's what I always tell people. I don't call myself a "wine expert." I call myself an "educator," because education is a lifelong process. But also, wine is a liquid passport. You can travel around the world with something in your glass. I love travel, but what wine has taught me—and what happened with COVID, because I used to travel so much—was that when I am like, "Oh, I wish I could go to Greece!" I can't go to Greece. But let me go get a Greek wine and Greek food, and I have this moment. I'm tasting the soil from Greece. I'm tasting the food. It can transport you, in a way, if you allow yourself to be open to that.

What's the most difficult aspect of your career?

Wine is slow to change, so the difficult part is an industry steeped in ritual, that doesn't understand the way things are moving faster than they want it to. The rituals are holding them up—the ritual of "We have to present wine in this way," the ritual of "We have to show how it is this way." At a time when you can get people (especially younger people) to really embrace wine, the culture of wine is still seen as snobby, it's hindering the industry.

Wine has a lot of terms. People always like the term "terroir." I find when we change some of the language, it's still the language of wine. If we change "terroir" to say "soil and dirt," how many people comprehend and understand that a little more?

We just need to make wine more approachable in terms of the way we explain it. But also, wine is steeped in European tradition. American wine is considered New World wine. The Old World is still generations upon generations, eight thousand years, of making wine. How do we merge the two?

It's kind of why I talk about Champagne and potato chips, Champagne and snacks. I love foie gras. I love oysters. We can definitely have Champagne with those. But I'll tell people, "Blanc de Blanc goes with Lay's potato chips. Blanc de Noir goes with Ruffles." I don't need a fancy meal. I just need a set of chips. Now, if I want a fancy meal, okay—let me have some rosé Champagne.

What are some of your favorite things to eat or drink?

Oh, it's always going to be sparkling wine. Sparkling wine and crawfish or with barbecue—because I'm from the South, so let's keep it real. For Southern seafood, any of the étouffées, the jambalayas, crawfish, shrimp, fried shrimp . . . and then my barbecue, because I love steak.

Wendy Lopez

REGISTERED DIETICIAN,
COFOUNDER OF *FOOD
HEAVEN* PODCAST *NEW
YORK, NEW YORK*

How would you describe your work?

I work in food media, and as a dietician, I have a background in nutrition and food science. Initially, my work was more focused on the science and the clinical side of food, but as time has passed I'm now more into the culinary side and more of the creative side with recipe development. But it's nice having that science background, and also exploring people's relationship to food as they evolve, and even my own relationship to food. I think it's an interesting perspective as a dietician exploring those things, outside of just cooking and outside of just science.

How did you begin in your field?

When I graduated college I was like, "Oh. It'll be cool to get involved in the farmers' market and just work with the community and do nutrition education demos," and that's how I started working with Jess [Jones, cohost of *Food Heaven*] here in the Bronx. We were providing tools for education and teaching how to incorporate seasonal eating in a way that was culturally relevant to the community we were working with, and I really enjoyed that. I also enjoyed being part of shifting the narrative that people in neighborhoods with not much access or poor communities are not interested in eating fresh fruits and vegetables. After that I decided to pursue my master's in nutrition.

Tell me the genesis of the *Food Heaven* podcast.

That first year we were working together, the farmers' market season ended for the winter, and we were like, "How can we keep providing this education, maybe to a bigger audience?" So we started recording videos in Jessica's apartment in Brooklyn, and we were putting them out on the local channel on BCAT—Brooklyn Community Access Television. And then eventually we were like, "Oh. We should put these online." And then it took off from there.

Jess ended up moving back to California, and we couldn't record together anymore, so we were like, "Oh, let's do a podcast." It was just a way to stay connected, and honestly it's so much easier because you don't have to look presentable on camera. You just show up. Like, literally, sometimes I just roll out of bed and I'm recording.

Who are some of your role models or mentors in the food space, in the food media space, in the health space?

One of my first mentors in this space is a dietician, Lorena Drago. She is Colombian. I came up under her. When I was doing my clinical rotations, she kind of took me on at Lincoln Hospital in the Bronx, and I always looked up to her because she always had a million different things going on outside of just clinical. She was the nutrition director at the hospital, but she also had a private practice, and she did all types of workshops around cultural foods, and I was like, "Oh, my god. This is so cool." I've always been connected to my creative side, so it was nice seeing this older woman killing it. To this day she's still killing it and doing all of these amazing things.

It was really nice working with her in those beginning stages because I was like, "Oh, yeah. I don't have to just do one thing. I don't have to just be in the hospital," which is what we're taught as dieticians. It's like the main career option. I feel like it's similar to chefs. You feel like you have to go through certain prerequisites to finally be able to do what you want to do, and for us that would be clinical work. So it was nice seeing an alternative to that.

What advice would you give to someone who wants to do what you do?

I would say just go with whatever it is that you want to do. You don't have to jump through a million hoops—I feel like especially for people of color, it's like we're taught to think that things have to be extremely challenging and you have to go through so many struggles to do what it is that you want to do. White people are way more fearless in that way, where they don't really ask for permission or seek validation. I feel like we have impostor syndrome much more often, and so I would say just do it—especially working in food media. Just start creating things and see how that goes and reach out to people who are a little more seasoned in that line of work and get guidance from them. You don't need permission from anyone to do whatever it is that you want to do.

What do you most enjoy about your work?

Eating. I always get to eat when developing recipes, or sometimes I'll get invited to check out new restaurants or test out new products. I love trying new foods and always being around food.

What's the most challenging part of your work?

Working within food media and also within wellness, there are these health and beauty ideals that don't align with who I am as a Black person and leave so many people out. So it's challenging working within this space and working with a lot of food brands that just don't really get it, or they're trying to capitalize off diversity but don't really understand how important it truly is and why all of us benefit from it.

Also, just being in the online space. I'm sure you've noticed Instagram being a nightmare and having to constantly keep up with these algorithms and whatever. As a creator, for people who consider this to be their line of work, how they make a living, that impacts the amount of money that you're able to make. So instead of creating from a place of joy and inspiration, you're creating because you want to get more engagement or you want to make the brand happy, and that is really unfortunate.

How do you take care of your mental health?

I spend a lot of time with the people I love and also by myself. I think it's striking a good balance. There will always be work, and so for me establishing strong boundaries is important. I'm just not going to be able to work after a certain time, and that might mean that I make less money because these are my priorities. I have to spend some alone time, I have to make time for friends and family, and that really helps to keep me sane—especially the alone time—like just sleeping enough, feeding myself consistently, all those things.

What are some of your favorite things to eat or drink?

So mac and cheese will always be number one. That's my favorite food.

To drink, I've been doing a lot of mezcal, like different mezcal cocktails, or just mixing it with fresh herbs. It's nice for the winters because there is some heat to it. I like fresh-squeezed juices with it. And also whiskey. I'm loving Uncle Nearest whiskey, which is Black-owned.

Creamy Yuca Mash

BY WENDY LOPEZ / MAKES 4 SERVINGS

2½ pounds yuca, peeled and chopped into 3-inch chunks

4 tablespoons butter

Salt

Yuca is a tropical tuber that's a staple in many African and Caribbean cuisines. It's one of my all-time fave root vegetables. Growing up in a Dominican household, I had yuca all the time—mashed, boiled, in fritters, and in soups. I like to top this mash with red onions sautéed in olive oil and mixed with a little red wine vinegar.

Bring a large pot of salted water to a boil over high heat. Add the yuca and cook, covered, adjusting the heat to a low boil or a simmer, adding more water if needed, until very tender, about 30 minutes. You should be able to easily put a fork through the chunks.

Drain the yuca, reserving the cooking water, and transfer it to a bowl. Remove and discard the fibrous stems from each chunk.

Add the butter and ¼ cup of the reserved cooking water, and mash vigorously. For a creamier mash, add a little more cooking water. Season to taste with salt and serve warm.

Thérèse Nelson

CHEF, WRITER, FOUNDER
OF BLACK CULINARY HISTORY
NEW YORK, NEW YORK

How would you describe your work?

I would say that my work is culinary stewardship. I actively work at filling myself up with the tools to be as effective as possible at creating, preserving, and translating Black culinary culture. That means different things different days. Sometimes it's cooking and recipe development to remain in right relationship to the evolving diasporic pantry. Sometimes it's reading in archives, magazines, and books for clues about Black agency, especially where it wasn't obvious. Sometimes it's writing to share what I'm learning and what I think so that this moment doesn't pass us by without the footprint of some critical analysis.

How did you begin in your field?

In high school I was all set my junior year to be a computer engineer with early admission to college and a very neat future imagined, but I was surrounded by mentors and peers who were way more passionate about tech than I was. I knew that I'd have a successful life in a field I could be effective in, but I also wondered if there was something I could be as passionate about. That moment of reflection made me realize that it was food and cooking, and when I found out it was a viable career choice, that was that. I switched plans, applied to culinary school, and the rest has been a daily love affair with carving out my own space in an industry I love.

Who are some of your role models or mentors in the food and hospitality space?

Role models, I would say: Vertamae Smart-Grosvenor for her gorgeous writing, Norma Jean Darden for her business acumen, Chef Toba Garrett for her culinary rigor, and Dr. Jessica B. Harris for her scholarship—I look to them for inspiration. They have each made their space in food so clear and definitive and done so on their own terms. As far as direct mentorship, I would say that Chef Kristi Brown, Chef Erika Davis, Dr. Leni Sorensen, and Dr. Cynthia Greenlee have provided me friendship and mentorship that have served my work invaluably.

What are you most proud of?

I'm most proud that the core ethos of my work is in the DNA of everything I've ever cooked, written, or shared. I feel proud that I've found a way to stay firmly rooted in my values, my personality, and my ethical code so that everything I do is in service of larger, more abstract goals. They are small, personal, and mainly quiet wins, but it's satisfying to watch intention breed results.

"I feel proud that I've found a way to stay firmly rooted in my values."

What is an important lesson you've learned about money, compensation, or finance over the course of your career?

I've learned to always have a number in mind. I used to do work for experience or for whatever compensation was offered without having a real sense of what was fair. In some things there is an established or standard value for services rendered, but for the most part, the way capitalism is set up, compensation is often arbitrary. My biggest lesson has been that if you don't ask for more you don't get more. You can always accept less if the work ultimately serves you in some other ways, but to not have a number in mind devalues your work and breeds disrespect and resentment on all sides.

How do you take care of your mental health and deal with the stresses of work?

It really depends on the type of stress and the time I have. When I'm deep into research I read romance novels as a literary mental palate cleanser. When I'm having a particularly hectic culinary week I make myself a really complicated, elaborate meal so that I've spent some time giving myself the same culinary consideration I give others. It usually involves duck confit. I've also taken to swimming. It's one of the few times in my life I get to feel weightless, and Lord knows that is a gift spiritually and physically.

What advice would you offer to someone who wants to do what you do?

I would say that culinary stewardship is an active and lifelong practice that requires you to add in as much as you extract. A lot of this work is about absorbing all the best, most disparate information, and finding ways to filter it into a coherent point of view that will hopefully be useful to someone at some point. It's lots of reading, it's being in actual community with folks, and it's about developing skills of discernment, all of which will serve you in life in general. The space of culinary history doesn't have a direct path. It's certainly developing as a discipline, but as of right now it's basically a bunch of curious food people trying to make sense of culture through the lens of food. So just start. Once you do, you are in it, and how deep you go is really up to you.

Do you have a mission or motto, and if so, what is it?

My mission in my work is to honor the past by being useful in my work as an example for the future. I look to the past as a student looking for clues about best practices and intention. I use those lessons to inform how I cook and what I contribute to this modern moment, and the sharing of this praxis is a living and evolving blueprint for folks coming behind to at least have a starting point to draw from. As far as a motto, I live by the idea that everyone deserves radical grace, until they don't.

What do you most enjoy about your work?

I love that every day is a new experience. You show up to the kitchen and what you've done the previous day is over and all that matters is what you create in that moment. Cooking professionally is a test of your mettle every day and it's a beautiful thing to have a space where you can feel complete and perfect doing something you've invested in being good at.

What's the most difficult aspect of your career?

Lately it's been the physical aspects that have been most challenging. I'm getting older and culinary work is hard on your body. While my muscles remember the movements, they are getting weary, and it's a delicate balance of endurance and honesty about your limitations. That dichotomy is hard in a profession that isn't typically concerned with the health and wellness of its practitioners.

On the cultural side I would say that funding for cultural culinary work is a tricky thing to quantify and an area I'm still trying to figure out. We love the idea but don't have very many pathways to funding. A lot of the critical cultural work that's needed goes undone because there is no room for this discipline in cultural institutions with funding or in hospitality spaces that don't see the value. There are points of light, but right now it's definitely a major hurdle.

What brings you joy and what would you like to experience more of?

The air and sea in the Caribbean bring me joy. There is something so beautiful and powerful about the hot sand and clean water in places so Black and so proud that makes me so happy. There's an island in the British Virgin Islands called Tortola that is seventy or eighty percent native occupied. I need some island breezes, fresh fried fish, and feeling weightless in the ocean sometime soon to be sure.

What are some of your favorite things to eat or drink?

I love layer cakes. There is something so gorgeous about the power of a beautifully decorated layer cake as a statement piece. There are few flavors I would reject, although I can tell a lot about a cook by the quality of ingredients used. The type of butter, natural or artificial flavorings, the taste level of the decoration. I could die happy with a simple poured caramel cake ungarnished but love an intricately piped and decorated wedding cake. It's all edible art in its clearest form, and at the end of the day you have cake!

Yewande Komolafe

NEW YORK TIMES
COLUMNIST, COOKBOOK
AUTHOR, FOOD STYLIST,
RECIPE DEVELOPER
BROOKLYN, NEW YORK

Why is it you do what you do?

I'm a storyteller at heart. I think that in every aspect of my work, including recipes, I feel like recipes are a way to tell a story of a place, or a dish, or a culture, or a people. And so I'm really drawn to the storytelling aspect of my work, and I think that feeds into everything that I do, like the writing, the recipe development, the video work I do.

What did you want to do when you were a kid?

I knew I wanted to be in food. I just wanted to be like my mom. I grew up in Lagos, Nigeria, and my mom was a food scientist, and I knew that I was interested in food. I didn't know how or when I would end up doing that. And I always thought of her as a scientist, but she got to play with food, and so I wanted to do something similar. I didn't know exactly what I

wanted to be, but I knew that I wanted to work with my hands and work with food.

How did you begin in your field?

I went to college and I originally thought, "I'm going to be a food scientist just like my mom," so I took all these biochem classes. And I started off as a biochem major and realized really quickly that I did not like chemistry. It was one of the first classes I failed. I ended up with a degree in biopsychology, but I still always felt like I was such a scientist at heart. So after my degree in biopsychology, I went to culinary arts school because I was like, "I'm going to do it the cool way and become a cook or a chef, and I'm going to build all these different pastries."

And so I went to culinary arts school and then I started working in restaurants. And while I was working in restaurants, one of the restaurants where I worked in New York had a program where the cooks could participate in recipe development, and I realized it was something that I was really good at. It felt like I was back in biology or the chem lab, and I was working with food, and so it just kind of merged these two things that I loved.

Once I discovered that it was something I was really drawn to, I started looking for jobs at test kitchens and began freelancing. For some time, I had one leg in restaurants and one leg in the freelance world. And then eventually I was able to leave the restaurant world completely and just focus on recipe testing and food styling.

What are you most proud of so far in your career?

Everything that I've accomplished. I moved here. I had to sort of learn the culture. I'm proud of not being conventional. I wanted to be a creative and I think I've always been a creative, so I'm proud of going for what I

"I take mental health very seriously because I think of my person as a whole being—mental, spiritual, physical."

wanted. I think that sometimes I did have blinders on, but I was driven mostly by my desire to do what I want, and that's something that's stayed with me in my whole career. It's hard for me to listen to other people and how they have charted their path. I think that I'm very much someone who has sort of built my own path. I had this misshapen way of doing things and it's worked for me, and so I'm proud of that. I'm just proud of listening to my inner self and listening to the voice inside me.

What is one of the biggest lessons you've learned about money, compensation, or negotiation in your career so far?

That I deserve it. I deserve to be compensated fairly and if somewhere is not doing that, then they don't deserve me. I trust my work and I trust the value of my work. I trust the quality of my work and I deserve to be compensated fairly.

What advice would you offer to someone who wants to do what you do?

I'm always cautious about offering advice. I think that the best advice I could give someone is to listen to their self, and listen to what they truly want to do. Learn to just hear yourself and quiet the voices around you. Another thing I would say is find someone who's doing what you want to be doing and talk to them. Most people are open to talking about their careers or their journeys.

How do you take care of your mental health and deal with the stresses of your work?

Therapy. I take therapy very seriously. I take mental health very seriously because I think of my person as a whole being—mental, spiritual, physical—and I want every aspect of my person to be whole and to be able to be present in the world as whole. I have very close friends who understand me, who see me, all the versions that I am, and I think that's really important—to surround yourself with people who see you. And my family, of course, is so supportive. I just love being around my family, my immediate family and my extended family. My children bring me so much joy. So I think all of those things work together to keep me as a whole functioning being.

Are there any things that you would like to see in the food and food media industries?

Absolutely. Inclusivity, diversity. I know that those are sort of buzzwords right now, but I really would like to see it. It's been a lonely journey. I started working in restaurants, gosh, in 2003, so the food world has been quite lonely. It's exciting

to see all the different perspectives and voices. And I feel that we can only tell a truly realistic story of the world that we live in, of the cities that we live in, if we're hearing from different perspectives, so I would love to see more inclusivity and more diversity. And not just as a poster, but also support for that, for those new people, true support, because that's also important. Find out what it means to truly support people of color in this work and do it. Don't just hire them or acquire books, but also support their work.

What are some of your favorite things to eat or drink?

I've been craving a lot of spicy foods, so I'm really into Nigerian food that comes with a lot of spice.

Adrian Lipscombe

CHEF, FOUNDER OF 40
ACRES & A MULE PROJECT
SAN ANTONIO, TEXAS

How would you describe your work?

I'm very interdisciplinary. My professional background is architecture and city planning. A lot of that does play into the work I do now. I specialize in and study the attitude and behavior of minorities toward land use and transportation. So as land changes because of gentrification, what is their behavior? What is their perspective? When I decided to open the restaurant, I thought, "If I open a place, what does this community think about it coming into their neighborhood?" I was coming into almost an all-white, two percent Black, low-income neighborhood that doesn't know me, where I have no family, no friends that know me.

We were on the north side, and the north side wasn't really getting any love from the city on beautification, on those types of projects to make it better. I came in saying, "Before I even open my doors, we're going to find out what this community wants." So we had a community dinner and we asked questions and took surveys and brought maps out. I literally did what I would do when doing community outreach, but at a different affair, right? So I am now a community citizen. I'm not the city planner who works for the city. I brought in a couple of professional friends who work in planning and we created a comprehensive plan for the community. So now it's a community going to the city saying, "This is what we want. This is what we need. Here's our voice," and we move forward.

How did you begin your work in the food space?

My mom had me very young and so all her aunts were my aunts, and they all cooked. They'd all learned from my great-grandmother. They all knew how to preserve. They all knew how to bake, and it was just something that we always did. It was always oral until they got older, and when they started moving away from Texas is when they would write one another and call one another and talk about recipes. But a lot of our recipes were never written down, so when I cook, it's always by memory.

In Austin, when I moved there to do my PhD work, people were like, "You should start a business," and I was like, "Well, I am an entrepreneur in a tech city. Can I start a business?" I started a business within less than forty-eight hours. I had a bakery and we focused on traditional and gluten-free, and so whatever you think we made traditional, we found a way to make it gluten-free. We weren't even in Austin, we were in Round Rock, which is outside of Austin. And people started coming to our commercial kitchen. They would drive to our commercial kitchen thinking that we were a bakery to pick up things. So we were like, "Okay, maybe we need to have a face-to-face contact or something." We ended up doing farmers' markets, and probably within three months, we became the anchor of the farmers' market.

"The larger goal is sustaining and understanding how many Black farmers are in the United States and how we can make sure they are successful."

Can you tell me about the 40 Acres Project and how it evolved?

The pandemic started and then George Floyd was murdered. I am two hours away from Minneapolis, so we definitely feel this angst and "What do you do? How do you move forward from here?" It literally felt like you were holding your breath trying to figure out what the next step is. This phenomenon was happening—people started Venmoing money [to Black people].

And one day I go to work and there's an envelope with a check in there. The next morning, I woke up and I had this idea in my head, because I was so worried about farmers at the time . . . because farmers had just planted, they already had contracts with people, but [with restaurants closing due to the pandemic] they had nowhere for this food to go.

Then I started thinking about Black farmers and I was like, "We already have a low percentage of Black farmers, less than two percent." That number is so minute, and I'm like, "Why don't we have more farmers?"

I started calling a couple of people and I asked, "Has anybody said, 'I'm just so inspired to buy Black land?' Is anybody preserving farm legacy through collecting of history, really understanding the techniques of what farmers are doing now, and are we recording that?" The answer was no, and I was like, "Well, I'm going to do it."

Within twenty-four hours I launched 40 Acres with a website and a GoFundMe page. My main focus at the time was very romantic. It was, "Buy forty acres—Black land— and we are going to preserve a legacy of Black farmers and also Black foodways."

As I went forward with this idea, there was another group of people thinking the same thing. David Thomas, Tonya Thomas, Michael Twitty, they all went to Africa right before COVID. They went home to the Motherland and they were seeing Black people owning land, Black people farming, Black people cooking the food, eating the food that they grew. They were like, "We should be doing this too."

Conversations started coming up like, "Well, Adrian has

this focus too, how can we come together and move forward and fast?" So it took a lot of work, a lot of land searches and looking for the right piece of property, talking to the right people, because none of us live there [in South Carolina]. The closest person that lives near there is Mashama [Bailey] and she's about forty minutes away from that . . . And so we came together on this. So we're a little shy of forty acres. We've been telling people thirty-eight, but our surveyors are telling us it's more than thirty-eight, it's about thirty-nine acres. We've been very, very lucky.

We have the blessing of the elders on the property—we got the land blessed by so many different representatives from the Motherland.

Working with the White House and their staff on making a better environment for Black farmers who are across the nation, it's just like, "I was meant to be here. I was meant to be here. I was meant to do this."

How would you describe the goals of the 40 Acres Project and the Muloma Heritage Center?

The larger goal is sustaining and understanding how many Black farmers are in the United States and how we can make sure they are successful. How do you create a successful Black farmer, because they had been left out of the economy for so long? How do we secure them? How can I have a child decide whether they want to be a doctor, a lawyer, or a farmer? How do you create a successful farmer, period, especially small-to-medium size, because so many corporations own a huge majority of the farming and economic market?

So for us, it's like creating that successful farmer and getting more land, because distribution ends up being a larger part in this. They can grow food, they can grow amazing food, but how do you get it to the people? So how do we make them part of the mainstream market? It is a huge question, and that's where my city planning brain comes in. It's like, "How do we connect them more into the community?"

The Muloma Heritage Center is a nonprofit on its own, based on the nearly forty acres of land we've acquired on St. Helena Island in South Carolina. There, we are archiving our food and archiving our work and what we do. I'm trying to have a meeting with a couple of people regarding Black restaurants and especially a collection of their menus, because at this time, it's pertinent that we understand what Black restaurants are really out here. What are we serving? How are we serving, because we don't even know how many have closed since the beginning of COVID?

The center is going to have three different kitchens. They're going to have an African kitchen so people will see and understand how food is still cooked there. Then we will have an antebellum kitchen, and that's Michael Twitty's world right there. Then we're going to have the modern kitchen. We will have barbecue pits out there and the understanding of the barbecue pits, so I'm super excited about that. There will be archival information, from Black farmers, not just recording them or doing video, but really understanding where are they getting their seeds and when they decide to plant.

There's nobody collecting that information, and I think it's really important, especially for us in our culture, to have this information saved, and an archive that different universities can use to really have understanding of our culture of food.

What are some of your favorite things to eat or drink?

A peanut butter and jelly sandwich. It has gotten sophisticated over time. I do make my own jam. Sweet tea—I'm from Texas, so sweet tea is an absolute thing—and then fresh tortillas because I am from San Antonio and we make them by hand.

Calypso Persimmon-Baked Chicken Wings

BY ADRIAN LIPSCOMBE / MAKES 4–5 SERVINGS

CALYPSO PERSIMMON SAUCE

1 tablespoon olive oil

1 onion, peeled and chopped

2 garlic cloves, peeled and chopped

4 habanero or scotch bonnet peppers

Juice of 1 lime

2 ripe persimmons, seeded

2 tablespoons brown sugar

2 tablespoons rum

1 teaspoon salt

½ teaspoon dry mustard

1 teaspoon ground allspice

¼ cup apple cider vinegar

½ teaspoon celery seed

CHICKEN WINGS

4 pounds chicken wings

2 tablespoons baking powder

1 teaspoon ground cumin

1 teaspoon garlic powder

1 teaspoon paprika

1 teaspoon salt

½ teaspoon freshly ground black pepper

I always make this recipe during the fall and winter. Persimmon season represents the peak of fall, and they gain so much flavor when the temperature drops. Persimmon has the flavor of honey and melon and it brings a brightness to a calypso sauce. They are sometimes hard to find in Texas. In the peak of the fall, we spend a day breaking down whole chickens to store for winter meals. At the end of the day we take the wings and prepare this dish.

For the sauce, heat the oil in a skillet over medium heat, add the onion, and sauté for 3 minutes. Stir in the garlic and cook until the onion is translucent, about 2 more minutes. Set the pan aside off the heat.

Wearing gloves to protect your hands, stem and seed the chili peppers. Transfer them to a blender along with the cooled onion mixture, lime juice, persimmons, brown sugar, rum, salt, mustard, allspice, vinegar, and celery seed. Blend until smooth and set aside.

For the chicken wings, preheat the oven to 425°F. Line a sheet pan with parchment paper.

In a shallow dish, mix the baking powder, cumin, garlic powder, paprika, salt, and pepper. Press the wings into the mixture to coat evenly, shaking off the excess.

Arrange the wings on the prepared pan, spreading them out evenly. Bake for 30 minutes. Using tongs, turn the wings over and bake for 15 minutes more, until crispy and fully cooked. Remove the pan from the oven and increase the temperature to 500°F.

Transfer the wings to a large bowl and drizzle with ½ cup of the Calypso persimmon sauce, tossing to coat them evenly.

Return the wings to the pan and bake for 8 to 10 minutes, until the sauce is bubbly and caramelized. When the wings are cool enough to handle, serve them with the remaining sauce on the side.

Sophia Roe

COOK, TELEVISION HOST,
PRODUCER *BROOKLYN,
NEW YORK*

How would you describe your work?

Well, titles I would use—I'm a cook, I'm a host, I'm a producer, and I am a local welfare advocate so I work really, really deeply within my own community. Those are the things I do.

What did you want to do when you were a kid?

When I was a kid—you know, I didn't see myself as an adult as a kid.

I had a really bizarre childhood, and I kind of just knew what I *didn't* want. Opportunity wasn't something that I thought I'd ever be afforded the ability to have or to hold on to, so I never really was a big dreamer because I just didn't think it was possible. I just was like, "As long as I'm not homeless I'll be good," or like, "As long as I don't end up like my mom I'll be good." I think I was fine—my eight-year-old self was like, "Yeah, I guess I could work at Dunkin' Donuts," you know? I think I wasn't a big dreamer like that. I definitely was a big daydreamer in general, like in a creative sense. But growing up, what I wanted to do when I grew up was just be alive. That really was a focus, I think—which is sad, which is sad to say. But it's true.

How did you begin in your field in the work that you do?

So I began cooking at nineteen years old. I've said this story a million times, but I just really needed a job. I dropped out of college. I just couldn't keep college together. I didn't have any support. I didn't have any assistance. Even with financial aid, I couldn't afford a nine-hundred-dollar textbook. I didn't have a car to drive to school, and I couldn't ride my bike ten miles to get to campus. So I needed a job. I just lied at this Vietnamese restaurant—I lied and said I knew how to use a knife because they were hiring in the kitchen, and I thought it'd be a great job because it was close to where I lived.

They promptly found out that I in fact could not use a knife. So instead of firing me, I was just a dishwasher, and then I learned how to use a knife, and it never crossed my mind that I'd be a cook or be a chef. That wasn't even—I was just happy with a flippin' paycheck.

I only ever worked in food. I've never done anything else. My first job ever, I worked at Subway. I was fifteen years old. That was fun. I scooped ice cream at this place called the Village Coffee Pot. It really didn't cross my mind to do anything else because I'd never done anything else.

What advice would you offer to someone who wants to do what you do?

I think right now we're in this very strange, TikToky, weird moment. I think that a lot of young chefs are like, "Oh, I'll just make a bunch of content, and then I'll be this Instagram chef, and then I'll get famous and then be a caterer," and it's like, "Well—no." I always think you might see someone on Instagram that's got millions of followers and has really cool content, but they couldn't cater a party for ten to save their life because it's not what they do. If you want to be someone who caters, then you should go work for a catering company, because that's a different thing. Do you want to be a sommelier? Do you want to do pop-ups? Do you want to be someone who has a restaurant? That means you need to be good at math and be good at budgeting and management. Or do you want to just be someone who makes food content on Instagram?

That's its own thing. I just think it's really important to take stock of what you actually want to do and do that thing. Making a bunch of food stuff and making content isn't going to help you become a better restaurant chef.

I think people get blindsided by this idea of what's happening on social media or what's happening on TikTok. For me social media is just an extra, fun, really great thing that is a way for me to express myself, because I already did all the work to be able to do that, to make content. I already worked in a restaurant. I already did the catering. I already was a private chef for six years. I already did that. People need to not be scared to just put the phone down and actually work.

What do you most enjoy about having your own show, and how did you go about creating it?

Well, I most love that my show is not about me. That is the best thing about the show. It's not *Sophia's Home Cooking*. It's not a show about me at all. It's a show where we get to talk about things that I think we should be talking about relative to food, people, culture, the planet—so that's pretty awesome. I get to center a bunch of people that should have been centered a really long time ago or a bunch of ideas that should have been centered a really long time ago.

The way the show happened is kind of funny. It was already kind of in the works in terms of deployment. There were already some news packages shot, and then the pandemic happened. And the pandemic sort of just blew a hole in everything because it really exposed how weak our value chains and global supply chains are and just made it feel like, "Wow. This show is more important than ever."

Initially, the vice president of Vice—she follows me on Instagram, and she just thought I was funny. So it does pay to have a presence on Instagram. But she's like, "You're funny, but also I feel like this is personal to you because you know firsthand what it's like to just not have things."

So I don't know that they initially thought, "Soph knows as much as she does about this." I don't think they actually realized that I was as nerd alert as I am, and some things were hard. Like, I said I wanted to do a mushroom episode, and everyone thought that was really weird, and now mushrooms have taken over the planet, and I'm like, "You're welcome." I started out as just a host, and then they were like, "No, we want to make you a producer," which was a little scary because you're just so involved. With TV, people will send you a DM and just be like, "I just want you to know, I hate your teeth," and I'm like, "Cool. Awesome."

The best thing about having a TV show like this one is

that I really do feel like it actually creates imagination, and I think imagination is what you need to be revolutionary. And I feel like [working with] Vice TV also means I can make what I need to make . . . There are a lot of other networks that would not let me speak to the people that I'm speaking to and wouldn't get it.

So for now, I'm really grateful. I love my network. I love my executive producers. They're great. I'm just grateful that they've really let me make the thing I think we need to make.

How have you gone about building a team that supports you, your work, and your vision?

I was actually taking a break from cooking because I got very burned out, which is something that happens to a lot of people who cook. I took a little hiatus. I took a job at this makeup company, Milk Makeup, because they were taking the company vegan, and I knew a lot about plant-based food, and that was in high-high-high request but also still kind of niche, and they needed someone to talk to that [veganism and vegan makeup]. And it turned out I was pretty good at talking directly to a camera.

And this woman—her name is Marissa Caputo—she sends me an email, she saw me on the Milk Makeup Instagram and she wanted to be my manager. And I was like, "Manager? For what?" I did not get it. I was like, an idiot.

I was scared—really scared. I thought, "Oh, my god. Now I'm not even a chef anymore. What the hell am I going to do?" And my manager was like, "You know, you have this great story, Soph. You should do a panel," and I was like, "A panel? Okay. I'll do a panel. I don't even know what a panel is," but back in the day there were tons of panels and tons of events.

So a Club Monaco panel [of speakers] is my very first job that Marissa ever got me. She told me they were going to pay me twelve hundred dollars to go and talk, and I was like, "Wait. They're going to—what? They're going to pay that?" I did not understand it. I was like, "Why are they going to do that?" and she was like, "Well, that's the job." I did not get it. I remember this funny moment where she was like, "Okay, they're going to send you a car," and I'm like, "Send me a car?" I walked there. I just had no concept.

And Marissa—it was the best thing I ever did for my career. She's like my big sister, and I could not have the career I have without her. She listens. She asks all her talent, "What's your dream?" It doesn't matter how seemingly big, she just wants to know, and we don't do anything that doesn't support what that dream is. If I want to write a book, she finds me a literary agent, or she helps me and supports me in that—and then I realize I don't really want to write a cookbook yet. I'm not feeling called to do that yet, but I do want to write something else. Or TV was my huge dream, and not only do I have a show but I had a show nominated for an Emmy and I was nominated for an Emmy.

So she's really important, and open communication is important. She's the one who told me, "Soph, you have to get a personal assistant. You cannot do everything," and I really pushed back on that, and then finally I was like, "Oh, my god. She's right. I don't need to be sitting on emails all day. I have actual work I need to do." So I got my assistant. My assistant supports the ins and outs, the day-to-day stuff.

And your accountant is also so important, and I can't stress that enough—particularly as Black/Brown/Indigenous folks. We are so often very, very triggered by financials, and I know for me I'm still very deeply triggered. Even where I live now, I wake up sometimes in my home and don't think I deserve it, even though I've worked my whole life for it. I still wake up in my own house and feel like, "This is too nice for me." It took me six months to buy a bed frame because I slept on the floor my whole life.

So I think the biggest thing with your team is understanding that you need one. Understand that every single person out there who is killing it has one, so if you think "I'm alone. I'm solo, and I'm killing it," you'd be ten times more killing it if you had some help. It takes a whole-ass village to make really beautiful shit and actually make a difference. You shouldn't feel insecure or ashamed about that.

What's the biggest lesson you've learned about money, compensation, or finance so far in your career?

I am someone who hires other people. I have vendors. Particularly prepandemic I used to do events, so sometimes I'd be doing a demo and I would hire another chef to come in and actually do the pass-arounds or do the food prep for everyone else because I can't do both. So I have vendors, florists, videographers, photographers. You must pay people, and if you cannot pay them then you shouldn't do the project.

I have to work really hard so that I can afford to pay my team. This idea that everyone wants to be a bad-ass boss bitch—I'm sorry. Being a bad-ass boss means I pay. I cut checks constantly. Constantly. Twenty percent goes to my management. I've got to pay my PR. I've got to pay my assistant. I've got to pay the photographer. I've got to pay the florist. I've got to pay my audio team for the podcast that we're coming out with. Everybody needs to be paid, so the biggest thing is you have to sort of reframe yourself. You have to make your business. This is a business, so if there's a partnership or a brand or something, you have to make sure

that whatever that fee is, you can allocate resources properly to your team. That is so important.

And it's very important to be transparent with brands (particularly brands, because they're the ones typically with certain rates) where their money is going. This is not for Soph to just buy what she wants. There are people that I actually have to support as a business owner, and they need to know that.

Do you have a mission or motto, and if so, what is it?

My mission is to encourage imagination, because I truly do feel it's what's necessary to revolutionize the system that we have, to revolutionize the planet, and to revolutionize the way that we think about saving the planet. It's absolutely necessary, and I'm really worried because there's so much anxiety around saving the planet. There's so much anxiety about making the right decisions and what the right things are, and that anxiety and fear really stunts imagination.

That isn't what young people need. If you have a five- or ten-year-old, they're the ones who are really going to feel the weight of where the planet is right now, and they don't need to hear how hopeless it is.

They need to hear, "No. We can create something new, something that doesn't exist yet, and really change things and create a world where conservation is important. Species conservation is important. Water conservation, planet conservation—that can happen. Just because it doesn't exist doesn't mean it can't happen."

What are some of your favorite things to eat or drink?

There's this thing about olives. I don't care what anyone thinks—and I know that you either love them or you hate them—but I swear to God I could just eat pints of green olives. I just love them deeply—deeply. I love olives to my core. I love oysters too.

My favorite decadent thing—which is maybe a little trashy of me—but just a big bucket of the butteriest popcorn in the world. Like, sign me up. I don't give a shit—ghee, butter, both—salt. Let's go. That's it. Salty stuff! I don't have a sweet tooth.

And my favorite drink in the world is just a cold glass of Beaujolais, which is showing my age. It's just very much showing that I am in that natural wine era, but I love it, and I like my wines young.

Jacqueline Greaves

WRITER, COOK, SALON HOST
NEW YORK, NEW YORK

How would you describe your work?

My work is fundamentally that of feeding people, of feeding their minds and their bodies. The table is a place around which people come to talk, exchange ideas, and my food allows them to feel relaxed, cared for, and nourished, allowing them to open up and creating open conversation. Essentially, I am introducing to them the food from my kitchen that is mainly Italian and Jamaican with a sprinkling here and there of other cultures. I come from an extremely mixed family ethnically and culturally—West African, Chinese, German, English, Scottish, and Irish are the ones I am fully aware of, there might be others, besides being married to an Italian—and so my food reflects that mix and the adaptation that comprises the immigrant kitchen. I want people to appreciate their own kitchens, but to open themselves up to other culinary cultures, recognizing them and appreciating them. I want people to recognize how essential food is as a pillar of our culture and tradition, and not just a way of taking in nutrients.

How did you begin in your field?

Having people in our homes for meals was a constant in both my upbringing and in that of my husband. There was always plenty of food prepared, and a variety of it, because you never knew who or how many would show up. Put a Jamaican and an Italian together and it is natural to want a full table of delicious food and interesting people. My husband works in the field of culture, primarily film and literature. Our home in New York became a place that Italians visiting New York City for work found that they could get a good plate of pasta and could just sit around talking about politics, soccer, music, or just gossip. Later, because of his work, we extended invitations to Americans, writers, actors, directors. Eventually we began bringing the two groups together. It became quite international. We went from Sunday lunches to dinners and then parties. Before COVID we had two or three large parties a year. I think the largest was for 150 people. Slowly people began asking me for my recipes, and then of course my daughters insisted I should start using social media. I enjoy exchanging ideas with others, and I love that people around the world like my recipes and the restaurants I talk about.

What are you most proud of?

I am most proud that I have been able to feed a lot of people, a lot of important people, my home cooking, because that is what is on offer. Feeding people is important, and you shouldn't ever feed people you don't like, because they can't appreciate the love that is in the pot, and so they can't appreciate the culture behind it. I am proud that I don't compromise in my food and that my cooking I think is honest and reflects who I am. I only do recipes or use ingredients that I feel comfortable with. That doesn't mean that I won't eat something. It just means that if it doesn't feel like part of me, I just can't cook it. I really have to feel it in the spiritual part of me.

How do you take care of your mental health?

I love to bake when I am stressed. My husband is like, "Why are we paying so much for flour?" But baking bread or cookies helps me a lot. Yet I am intolerant of flour, and so it isn't the healthiest practice for me. It is a form of meditation that allows me to produce at the same time. I don't like not moving, and only if I am reading do I ever like to sit down. I am slowly teaching myself to do low-impact exercise, without weights and standing up. I hate exercise, and now that I made my two rules, I find that I am enjoying the thirty to fifty minutes, depending on my day, that I dedicate to that practice. I also read. I love to read. I study French. And I have a group of incredible and fabulous friends in New York as well as Italy. I even finally found a wonderful talented enclave of beautiful Black women in Rome—a huge percentage from Texas, for some reason—mainly American. I pick up the phone and vent with them if we can't get together for a meal and a good bottle of wine. I am very lucky, and I can say it is only in the last decade that I have begun to value the importance of women as friends and as a source of support.

What is an important lesson you've learned about money, compensation, or finance over the course of your career?

I can tell you that I am rarely compensated for my work. Of course, when I have catered for others I was paid, but basically only covering the expenses. I don't think I ever made any money catering. It was my fault that I didn't want to be thought as overcharging. I stopped catering as I was basically cheating myself. This is in part a cultural thing, coming from a tradition where money is considered dirty and you don't talk about it. I am probably the worst person to ask this question. Now I am trying to get the courage to say pay me for my articles.

How have you approached creating a team for the work you do?

My team is fabulous, as it consists mainly of my two daughters, who give me advice on social media and send me links to recipes or new ingredients that they want me to try. I have a group of people who work with me when I have dinners and parties, and some have been working with me for over a decade, maybe even more. It's a mix of people who rotate in and out. Most of them work in the catering business and have a great deal of experience. We have a very

"My mission is that everyone at my table feels that the meal was created with them in mind."

happy kitchen, and that is how I like it. We talk, we laugh, swap stories, ideas, experiences, family stories, and recipes as we work together. We share our culinary traditions, and we learn from one another. I want my team to feel like family, because we are preparing food that should reflect our love for one another and the joy that we have in cooking for others. Each of us must feel the importance of what we are doing. Giving joy is a responsibility. Cooking, feeding, and serving people are all arts. Experience is very important, but so is the comradery while preparing a meal.

Do you have a mission or motto, and if so, what is it?

My mission is that everyone at my table feels that the meal was created with them in mind. They must feel welcomed and celebrated.

What are some of your favorite things to eat or drink?

I travel a lot and eat in a lot of restaurants, and yet at the end of the day give me a plate of Jamaican rice and peas with oxtail, or anything fried, but the best is Jamaican escovitch fish. Nothing better. In terms of drink, I am a lover of a rich, not-too-robust glass of red wine, or a tall glass of water with ice, mint, and slices of lemon. Although lately I have been loving in Italy the summer iced tea with lemon granita.

Caribbean Green Shrimp

BY JACQUELINE GREAVES / MAKES 6–8 SERVINGS

GREEN HERB SAUCE

1 scallion, trimmed and roughly chopped

1 medium garlic clove, peeled

1 thumb-size piece fresh ginger

1 cup fresh mint leaves

1 cup fresh cilantro leaves

¼ cup olive oil

Salt and freshly ground black pepper

SHRIMP

1 teaspoon ground ginger

4 tablespoons freshly grated ginger

1 teaspoon ground allspice

1 large garlic clove, peeled and minced

2 scallions, trimmed and minced

1 sprig fresh thyme or 1 teaspoon dried thyme

1 tablespoon honey

1 tablespoon soy sauce or coconut aminos

Grated zest of 1 lemon

1 tablespoon coconut oil, plus more for frying

Salt and freshly ground black pepper

2 pounds medium shrimp, peeled and deveined

I serve this lively shrimp dish over rice or pasta and garnish it with lemon zest and minced parsley or a mixture of mint and cilantro. The green herb sauce came about because a couple years ago I realized I liked mint. I had used cilantro in fish dishes, but I had always associated mint with being sick. My grandmother in Jamaica would make tea from the mint growing in the garden. I loved the idea of combining the two aromas that made me think of Mexico. I added the ginger, scallion, and coconut oil for a Jamaican feel.

For the green herb sauce, place the scallion, garlic, ginger, mint, cilantro, and oil in a food processor or blender and process until smooth. Season to taste with salt and pepper. Refrigerate in a tightly covered container if not using right away, for up to one week, or in the freezer for two weeks.

For the shrimp, place the ground ginger, fresh ginger, allspice, garlic, scallions, thyme, honey, soy sauce, lemon zest, 1 tablespoon coconut oil, and 3 tablespoons green herb sauce in a medium glass bowl. Mix well and season to taste with salt and pepper. Add the shrimp and mix to coat. Cover and refrigerate for at least an hour, ideally overnight or as long as two days, stirring a few times.

Drain the shrimp, reserving the marinade. Heat a couple of tablespoons of coconut oil in a large skillet over medium heat. Working in batches, fry the shrimp, turning once, until they are just opaque, about 2 to 3 minutes. Do not overcook; you want the shrimp to be firm and moist, not dried out. Transfer the cooked shrimp to a serving dish large enough to hold them in a shallow layer.

When you are done frying, add the reserved marinade to the pan along with 2 teaspoons green herb sauce. (Reserve extra sauce for another use.) Bring this gravy to a boil for 2 to 3 minutes, stirring and, if necessary, thinning with a little water, then lower to a simmer for 2 to 3 minutes. Pour the hot gravy over the shrimp. Serve immediately.

Pasta di San Lorenzo (Tuna Pasta)

BY JACQUELINE GREAVES / MAKES 6–8 SERVINGS

¼ cup extra-virgin olive oil

6- to 7-ounce jar Italian tuna in olive oil, drained and oil reserved

1 garlic clove, peeled and minced

2 scallions, trimmed and minced

½ cup minced parsley, stems reserved

2 tablespoons pine nuts

10 large pitted green olives, cut into slivers

2 tablespoons golden raisins

2 tablespoons salt-packed capers, soaked in hot water for 15 minutes and drained

10 bay leaves, divided (preferably fresh bay leaves, but dried is okay)

2 or 3 cinnamon sticks

1 teaspoon red pepper flakes

14- to 15-ounce can whole Italian cherry tomatoes (or other canned tomatoes)

1 pound pasta (farfalle or penne rigate)

Salt

Grated zest of 1 small lemon

Grated zest of 1 small lime

Freshly ground black pepper

Pasta di San Lorenzo is a particular favorite because my mother-in-law introduced it to me, although years later she said she never did it with a red sauce, but with a white sauce. In later years she did indeed make it with a white sauce, adding milk. However I prefer the strong, rich, earthy tomato version. This recipe has its roots in Sicily (olives, capers, and pine nuts) and the Jewish tradition (sweet and sour—the golden currants; and the spice—cinnamon). Toasted bread crumbs are a nice accompaniment to this or just about any pasta, and making them is a great way to use up leftover bread. Mix 2 cups freshly ground bread crumbs with 1 teaspoon dried oregano, spread on a baking sheet, and toast in a 350°F oven for about 20 minutes, stirring often. Store in the freezer and bring to room temperature before using.

In a large skillet with a lid, combine the olive oil, reserved tuna oil, garlic, scallions, and parsley stems. Sauté over medium heat for a few minutes. Add the tuna, breaking it up with a fork, and sauté for 2 to 3 minutes.

Add the pine nuts, olives, raisins, capers, 5 of the bay leaves, cinnamon sticks, and pepper flakes to taste. Add the tomatoes and half the parsley. Bring the mixture to a simmer, and cook gently, covered, for 15 to 20 minutes, stirring occasionally to prevent sticking.

Meanwhile, bring a pot of water to a boil, add the remaining bay leaves and plenty of salt, and cook the pasta al dente according to package directions.

Just before serving, stir the remaining parsley into the sauce along with the citrus zest. Remove and discard the cinnamon sticks and bay leaves. Taste, adding salt if needed (the capers may make it salty enough) and plenty of pepper. Drain the pasta well, top with the sauce, and serve immediately.

Kia Damon

CHEF, FOUNDER OF KIA
FEEDS THE PEOPLE PROGRAM
BROOKLYN, NEW YORK

How would you describe your work?

I am a chef, and—because there are so many hats at this point, it's just like—I'm a food girl. I do recipe development, dabbling in consultation and such as well, and focusing my energy into mutual aid work and food access. That's where a lot of my focus is now.

I'm the chef and founder of Kia Cooks Inc. and a food organizer for mutual aid. I think that's the best way I can describe that.

How did you begin in your field?

Way, way back. Growing up in Orlando, it was just natural to get a hospitality job. There's lots of restaurants, and then there are also amusement parks, so I just found myself in one of those jobs. And I'd always been interested in what was going on in the kitchen, in the back of house, because my family cooked a lot as well. I worked at Universal in food and bev, but then eventually I got a few food jobs at cafés and worked at Chipotle for a while. I knew that I wanted to cook, and that's what I enjoy doing. It was just a matter of how to actually get there and how to actually do that on a larger scale or

a more professional scale. School was out of the question moneywise, but I just moved away to Tallahassee to try to do it on my own. I was like, "Bobby Flay did it." (Though, when I did further research later on, I was like, "Oh, wait. That's not quite how it happened.") But I was like, "Bobby Flay didn't go to school. He didn't even graduate high school, so maybe I can blah, blah, blah." (But no. Different story for Bobby and me . . .)

Tallahassee proved to be very difficult, being a really still-small town, still pretty racist and misogynist, to be honest.

Even when I was in the back of house, I had to prove myself consistently. But I was good at what I did. Regardless of people being racist, misogynist, trying to discriminate against me because of health reasons. I was still easily one of the best cooks in a lot of the kitchens that I went to, and if not the best I was right under management as far as skills.

Eventually I started to break off into my own cooking, exploring what it would be like to cook and post things and do recipes, or do dinner parties. That's shortly after I named myself Kia Cooks on Instagram, which I just did because of the consonant sounds of "Kia Cooks." I started the Supper Club from Nowhere, and I think that's when my food went from cooking or just whatever to thinking more about my impact, or more about the history of Black women cooking and what they're cooking for.

It wasn't just about putting food out anymore, which felt like a really powerful shift in my life. I did that for a bit and gained some attention. That's when I realized, "Well, I've done everything that I can do here. I need to go somewhere else and be challenged and grow naturally in my work." It was between New York and Atlanta. If I went to Atlanta, I was hoping to work for someone who was a private chef for musicians or celebrities and then go the private chef route. And if it was New York, I was applying for the James Beard Women in Culinary Leadership Program. Neither one of them panned out, but I made friends in New York.

Next thing you know, I'm in New York City as a sous-chef for Lalito, where [Chef] Gerardo [Gonzalez] had started. From there—this has been a very fast and chaotic and rewarding three years of my life. I started as a sous-chef, became an executive chef, quit twice—the second time was for good—rebuilt myself and tried to rediscover what I loved about cooking, and then jumped back in the river with everybody else to pave my own path forward.

What are you most proud of?

I am most proud of myself. Career aside, everything aside, just me and the fact that I really did it my way. I remember, there was a very specific conversation I had in Tallahassee, and it just felt like a shifting kind of time. I remember sitting with some friends, and I was like, "You know what? I don't want to live a mediocre life. Whatever that means for me, I just hope that it's not mediocre. I can't fathom doing that."

And somehow, I have made that happen for myself, and people were surprised. I didn't talk a whole lot about the things I wanted to do growing up. I was supposed to be good at school, and then I wasn't. I was super depressed—I almost went into the military. But I never really talked about things I wanted to do for real for real, so when I told people that I wanted to cook, a lot of people were like, "Really? I just never have seen you—it didn't seem like that would be a path that you'd be taking." Prodigies are like cooking and doing all kinds of cuts when they're like ten years old. And that just wasn't me, so a lot of people really were confused by that.

Going through all these kitchens and all of that was very difficult, but I always felt—I just don't want to live a mediocre life, and I want to go after my dreams and my desires to the utmost of my abilities, so as long as I'm happy then I'm good. And now I look up—it's been three years since I moved to New York, but it's been damn near over a decade of pursuing this. I'm twenty-seven now, and I'm proud of myself. I've built a beautiful life, friendships, connections, experiences both sad and rewarding off this pursuit of food. That's why when I try to think about what I do and what my hats are, it's hard to quantify. It's hard to name it because I just feel like, at this point, wherever there's food and if I'm excited about it, I'm doing it, I'm into it. And I think my life is so beautiful because of it, and I'm very proud of myself.

What is an important lesson you've learned about money, compensation, or finance over the course of your career so far?

Be wary about going into restaurant businesses with people who don't have money. That is scary stuff, especially when you specifically really don't have the money, and the people who have any kind of money—

there's a power imbalance there. I've learned to be more diligent about that.

Thinking about compensation—as someone who has to give compensation to others, when I'm in that position, you need to do what you can to make sure people are paid fairly. That is the top and the bottom line. If that means you get paid less, so be it. The people you are compensating need to be paid. You can move the money around, you figure it out—but you give them their money, period.

And then as someone who has to receive compensation sometimes, be transparent with your peers about what you're making. Ask them what they have been making. Try to shake off that shame and secrecy around money because that's what creates the atmosphere for people to be exploited, for people to not speak up for what they deserve, for people with power and money to try to run game.

Try to be mindful of what money trauma you're bringing over from different parts of your life, especially if you want that growth and you want that security for yourself. But yeah, I would say transparency, clarity, checking your money trauma, and doing what you need to do to pay people their living wage—especially people who are working to help you get to your next step. There is no way that you can't be paying them.

How do you take care of your mental health and deal with the stresses of your work?

I say no a lot. I take inventory on "Am I saying yes to something that is fulfilling that I will enjoy, or am I saying yes because I think I will never get another job again?"—and if you move like that, then you have no room to do the things that you really care about and do the things that you love. And then because I eat for joy and also cook food for money, I make specific blocks in my days or in my weeks where I'm like, "Okay. This food-centered thing is for joy," or maybe, "This joy time has nothing to do with food," either way.

So I try to remember that the work that I'm doing and the legacy that I want to leave is not dependent on if I'm saying yes to everything, if I'm putting out content the fastest, if I'm releasing projects the fastest, if I'm doing da da da da da.

I make those boundaries, and I remind myself that there's a difference between "Kia Cooks" and Kia Damon. People think, "Oh, Kia Cooks. Kia Cooks." I'm not Kia Cooks right now. She clocked out. I'm Kia Damon, and I'm going to leave and walk to Williamsburg and get gelato and mind my business.

Do you ever feel like you're in a creative rut, and what do you do when you need inspiration?

I'm oftentimes in a rut, and usually that means I have not gone out and lived life. Whenever I'm in a rut I'm like, well, yeah. How can you be inspired when your dirty clothes are overflowing in your closet and your clean clothes are on the floor, the dishes are dirty, there's no toilet paper, there's no tissue or paper towels? You got *Downton Abbey* playing in the background and you're in emails all day—like, well, yeah. Of course you are not inspired. Of course you are in a rut.

So then I get up, I shut it all down, and I go breathe some air. I go live my life. I hang out with a friend and watch a movie—I go be a person, because it's life and the experiences of life that bring you joy and inspire you. A lot of my great ideas come from when I have interactions with people. I just see happenings in the world, and I'm like, "Oh, my god. Someone is growing bitter melon on my block," which I saw yesterday. "Oh, I haven't tried a Caribbean recipe in a while. Oh, now this. Oh, now this," and now I'm having deep thoughts about the relation between the Caribbean to the South and what foods are similar there, and then I'd probably go eat some Caribbean food, and then—you're living life and being inspired by that.

So yeah, whenever I'm in that rut, I'm like, "Sounds like you have not gone out in the world to be a person in a while."

How do you define success?

My definition of success is being able to go to sleep at night, being pleased with what you've done. I think that's a success. If you can go to bed and be like, "Hmm. I did that. Hmm. I made it through this tough day. I had this goal that no one has known about since I was seven years old, and now I did it." I think that's success: living a life that you can be pleased with. If you can be pleased with yourself and pleased with what you've done—you, without the validation of others, without anything else, just you being pleased, I think that's successful. You really have to figure out what that looks like for yourself every day; otherwise, measuring your success based off the standards of others or what we project others to think or what they project onto us, then you will always feel like a failure. Always.

I have little awards and accolades and things all over my house, even a whole Forbes 30 Under 30 plaque in my office on my wall, and I'll be freaking out because of this one thing, and I'm just like, "Oh, my god! Argh! I'm a failure. Ugh." And then I'll go sit on my couch, and I look in my office, and I'm just like, "Girl, stop. Stop measuring it against everything else. Take a breather. What did you accomplish? What is

this? Do you feel good about your life right now?" Yes—then that is a success. "Do you feel better than yesterday?" Yes. "Do you not? That's okay, but did you try today?" Yes.

And that's success because then you'll end up in these situations where you have all the things, have done all the things, and you never feel satisfied. You never feel happy—you're always green with envy. It's always something else. And then when you hopefully live a long life and your body can't even quite do the same things you did, then you sit and you marinate in all these little things that have happened along the way that you never gave yourself credit for. But it's too late then, Boo—you about to kick the bucket. It's too late in this moment because you're old! Do it now. Do it now. Find success and peace in your life now because if Lord forbid something happens in the next moment or the next day, you really just lived your whole life feeling like a failure, chasing something unattainable, chasing the success of others and not the success of yourself, and that's sad. I don't want to live like that. I'm twenty-seven. Like, girl—I got so many decades. I got to chill out sometimes. But I'm happy. I'm glad. I feel successful.

What are some of your favorite things to eat or drink?

My brain is sifting through so many delicious things. I love me a good fish sandwich—not a fancy fish sandwich, but I mean fried whiting on the cast iron on a piece of white bread, mustard, hot sauce, another piece of white bread. Eat it. Boom—delicious.

Ooh, boiled peanuts.

I love to eat boiled peanuts. I have not been able to find out just yet where to get the raw peanuts from out here to make them for myself maybe next summer. But I will settle for the ones in the can—in that yellow can that are so full of sodium, but it's so delicious, and I have to have some kind of soda, which isn't really quenching the thirst. Just some kind of soda to drink with my salty canned boiled peanuts. It's just fun. And then people see it and they're like, "What the hell? Ew!" And I'm like, "Don't mock it until you try it, buddy," and then they try it, and they're like, "Wow!" That's one thing I miss about home. You could just drive some of the side roads and somebody got boiled peanuts. But yes, boiled peanuts and a catfish sandwich or whiting sandwich.

Salimatu Amabebe

CHEF, MULTIMEDIA ARTIST,
FOUNDER OF BLACK FEAST
PORTLAND, OREGON

How would you describe your work?

In general, I would say that I make multimedia art. A lot of it is food based and sculptural interactive work around Blackness. And for Black Feast, I would say that I make a food art event that centers a Black audience. It's for Black folks by Black folks, and it's about celebrating Black artists and writers through food.

Can you tell me about the genesis of Black Feast and Love Letters to Black Folks?

I studied film and photography for my undergrad and I was planning to go into the art world, and I moved to New York after I graduated from school. Well, I should go back—after I graduated from school, I needed to make some money so I could move to New York. So, I started working as a line cook and then I moved to New York and I was like, "I'll never work as a line cook again, that was awful." And so I worked at an art gallery and then I sort of was going back and forth between food and art. And a lot of

times making food and working in kitchens was just a way for me to make money and was something that I knew I was good at and that I could do anywhere.

And then I had an artist residency in Berlin. It was based on food, art, and ecology. I was working with other chefs and artists who were kind of in this in-between of making food and making art, and it opened up so many doors of possibility for what dinners can be and how to look at cooking and serving food as an art form and as part of your art practice. And then with Black Feast, I moved to Portland, Oregon, and I was hosting plant-based Nigerian food pop-ups. I grew up eating Nigerian food. So I thought I'll do a pop-up with Nigerian food and it was so wildly popular.

I was doing them out of my house. But the first dinner I did, I very naively just put my address on Facebook. So I was looking at the reservations or how many people were interested and it was forty-five people. I was like, "Okay, well, no forty-five people are going to show up at my house. It would probably be maybe fifteen people," but forty-five people showed up at my house and it was so fun. We had people sitting in corners of the house and everything was sliding scale, which is just kind of by donation, come in, grab a plate. Eventually I moved into a restaurant space that was designated specifically for pop-ups and for independent chefs. So I was hosting them once a week and it was a really different audience.

Would you consider Love Letters to Black Folks as kind of a specific-moment-in-time series? Or is that continuing?

It's something that continues, but with maybe less intensity than I did in 2020. You know, it came from Black Feast, and at Black Feast there's so much work that goes into every event. And every time I do it, I'm thinking, "There's no way I can do this again, this is so hard." It just blows my mind how much work you can put into one event. But I have a lot

of people who offer really incredible help and their vision and their talent to Black Feast, one being Annika Hansteen-Izora, who's one of my collaborators, and once they moved to New York, we would travel to do Black Feast events. We did one in New York in, I think, January 2020. And we had plans to keep doing Black Feast throughout the year.

That couldn't really happen with the pandemic. And so at the height of the protests [in the summer of 2020] Annika and I wanted to figure out a way that we could collaborate and do something with our distance. I think we started really considering Black Feast to be a type of care work that we could offer. And so sort of leaning more into that, we did Love Letters to Black Folks, which was Annika writing poems, which were Love Letters. And then in collaboration I would create desserts, and then we made them free and people could sign up and pick them up once a week.

We did that for ten weeks. We did five weeks in the Bay Area, we did five weeks in Portland, and then we also took donations. We had a bunch of flower donations, so we were able to give out flowers, and then it kind of kept building. And we were able to give out these care packages to folks, with body products, skin products, and it kind of just got bigger and bigger. And most weekends we were serving between seventy-five and two hundred people.

What are some of the things that you've learned about hosting pop-ups?

When we started out doing Black Feast, we really didn't have any money. We were as broke as imaginable. So we didn't have a lot to invest in that project other than just our time and energy. And I mean, when it first started, it was just me. I was designing the menu. I was hauling everything in my rental car. I didn't have a car at the time. And something that I learned was the power of collaboration. I think that a lot of times, artists and creators and people with a strong vision often want to do things themselves and take on all the jobs, because you know that you can do all the jobs, and you know you can do them in a way that you want to see things get done. And learning to just let go of some things and let other people step in and be open to collaboration, open to other people's vision, is the thing that made Black Feast grow exponentially.

It's really easy to burn out when you're trying to do all the jobs. So I think that the power of collaboration is one thing that I learned. And a part of that umbrella is also just asking for things that you need. When we started out a lot of the spaces we were using were donated, and it was through contacting event spaces and saying, "Hey, this is our project, this is our vision, do you have a lower price that you can

offer?" because we couldn't afford to be renting out two-thousand-dollar spaces for a dinner that didn't even make two thousand dollars.

I think it's sometimes hard to offer advice specifically around pop-ups because Black Feast has kind of a different model in terms of how we do our finances, because we're offering meals on a sliding scale or by donation for Black folks. And so we don't always have an idea of how much money something's going to bring in. Now how we make things happen is through grants and through donations and contributions, but at the time we didn't have that.

Also: This isn't something that I've learned, but something that I really put into practice—just paying people. We're able to pay people well above minimum wage.

What's an important lesson that you've learned about finding, building, and caring for community?

I think that it's very good to ask people what they want and really listen to people, be open to feedback and open to critique and just be willing to change and shift your model.

How do you take care of your mental health and deal with the stresses of your work?

I don't. I mean, it's a constant struggle. So much of this work is reminding Black folks that we are deserving of all these things and we can have this and there isn't a shortage.

And it is so much work to remind myself of that in the way that I prioritize my own mental and physical well-being. I've heard from other Black friends as well, this idea that we're not going to last that long, like personally. And I think that I have a sense of that, like I may not survive this. So I'm going to do as much as I can in the time I have because I don't know how long that'll be. And I am slowly learning that I want to and I need to try to sustain this body for a long haul.

The biggest way that I take care of myself is probably getting into my physical body, lifting weights. Honestly, lifting weights is a really important thing for me because it's time that I give to myself multiple times a week and then also I take care of myself by really keeping in touch with my close friends.

What are some of your favorite things to eat or drink?

The first is egusi. Egusi and fufu, specifically made by my dad. The second thing that I love to eat is tacos, tacos with fresh handmade tortillas, absolutely. And to drink, I honestly drink way too much kombucha. I drink like three kombuchas a day. So I guess I have to put that and probably water because it makes me feel good about myself.

Red Palm Nut Cheesecake

BY SALIMATU AMABEBE / MAKES 8–10 SERVINGS

CRUST

¼ cup coconut oil plus 1 teaspoon for the pan

1 cup gluten-free oats

1 cup raw walnuts or pecans

½ cup coconut sugar

¼ teaspoon salt

FILLING

4 cups cashews, soaked overnight and drained

1¼ cups maple syrup

½ cup red palm nut cream (I use Praise or Ghana Fresh brand)

1 cup nondairy milk (I use oat)

1½ teaspoons pure vanilla extract

¼ rounded cup arrowroot powder

2 teaspoons sea salt

There are very few Nigerian desserts—so when I was doing Nigerian food pop-ups, I wanted to figure out a way to do a Nigerian dessert based on the ingredients. There's this soup called bongo soup, it's made with red palm fruit cream and it's super rich and fatty. And I thought, "Oh, this should be in a dessert." So I made a red palm fruit cream cheesecake. It's cashew based with red palm fruit cream. It's best to make this cake a day ahead so it can chill and set completely in the refrigerator. A slightly tangy topping is the perfect complement to its sweetness and richness. You can buy red palm fruit cream already prepared and canned, online on Amazon.

Preheat the oven to 350°F. Grease a 9-inch springform pan with 1 teaspoon of the oil and wrap the bottom and sides tightly with aluminum foil so there are no cracks. This will protect your cake in the water bath.

For the crust, place the oats and nuts in a blender or food processor and grind to a fine powder. Continue grinding until the nut oils begin to bind the mixture together. Add the coconut sugar, salt, and remaining ¼ cup coconut oil and process until well blended and sticky. Press the mixture evenly into the prepared pan, building up the sides to about 1 inch. Set aside.

For the filling, combine the cashews, maple syrup, palm nut cream, milk, and vanilla in a blender or food processor. Blend until smooth. Add the arrowroot powder and salt and blend until incorporated. (The cake will be creamy; for a firmer texture, blend in another rounded tablespoon of arrowroot powder.)

Bring a kettle of water to a boil. Place the springform pan inside a large, deep baking dish, and scrape the filling into it. Place the baking dish in the oven. Pour boiling water into the baking dish so it comes 1 to 2 inches up the sides of the springform pan.

Bake the cake for 60 to 70 minutes, until there is little to no jiggle when you move the pan. Turn off the oven, open the oven door a crack, and let the cheesecake cool completely.

Once the cake reaches room temperature, refrigerate it for at least 4 hours and ideally overnight before slicing and serving.

Toni Tipton-Martin

JOURNALIST, AUTHOR,
EDITOR IN CHIEF OF
COOK'S COUNTRY
TEXAS

How would you describe your work?

I would say that in addition to just good solid journalism, I see myself as an advocate. My work might not fall into the traditional model of advocacy, and I've certainly seen remarks about whether it's actually activism. But I have used my work to disrupt the system, the food system as it was. And so I'm very proud of that.

How did you begin in journalism?

My original intention was to pursue hard news, meaning the daily news section of the paper. I never intended to be involved in creative writing or in what we used to call the soft news in the paper. I really was always a just-the-facts kind of girl, but I had an opportunity at a local weekly newspaper to write about food—or actually to just take over the recipes section, it wasn't writing about food—and discovered that it was a way that I could get into the newsroom. And then the hope was that I would move over to the news division and not get stuck basically in the social pages.

How and why did you start collecting Black cookbooks?

Well, from a very young age, I noticed disparities. I was severely wounded as a little girl by Hollywood's depiction of African American women in the kitchen. I never really knew what to do with any of that energy. It's just that . . . that quiet voice that bubbles around inside of your soul and helps inform who you are. And so being involved in the food world, having access to an enormous library of cookbooks, made it logical to me to consult real voices in the food industry as primary sources, and recipe books were one of the few ways that I could have access to real people.

Who are some of your favorite and most meaningful people you've encountered in the cookbooks you've collected? If you were to name a few people, who are they and how do they stand out?

Well, I generally refer to Malinda Russell as among the most important. She was a single mother of a challenged child, thriving in an oppressive environment. She signals to me and to other women the idea that life is hard, but we can make it. We don't have to let down our barriers and give up on self-care in order to thrive. We have to make it so that the next generation can make it.

Freda DeKnight is another compelling figure in this whole collection for me, because she was a journalist, and I was able to see the power of her voice in crying out on behalf of the privileged class. At a time when so much of the history and the focus and the storylines are about survival and poverty and overcoming and making do, she stands up and says, "Wait a minute, there's another side to who African Americans are and it's an elegant side."

She wasn't the only one and she wasn't the first one. The first cookbook in the collection that I was determined to have was a cookbook from 1936, published by the Negro Culinary Art Club of Los Angeles. And just their title was a driving force for me. I had to see what kinds of delicacies a group that identified themselves that way would leave behind.

But what Freda does is elevate the conversation. She uses her platform and, obviously, her platform is *Ebony* so I'm not naive. That was their goal. But I'm just saying even within that, she elevates the storyline for the privileged class without making us feel like we think we're better or bougie or any of those other negative portrayals that we have been saddled with.

But when it comes to Black people, there's a criticism all the way around. And she does a really good job of neutralizing some of those critiques in her recipe choices and definitely in her language. So she validates for me the use of language as a tool to change minds.

Can you tell me about the path to writing *The Jemima Code* and *Jubilee*, and what motivated you to write both of those books?

As a journalist, I still did not see a story unfolding as I was collecting cookbooks because I was only getting one or two here, there, and they weren't really exposing a full story. The story that I was observing was primarily being told at Southern Foodways Alliance and the desire for equity and inclusion that we were pursuing in our annual gatherings there. But that tended to be a lot of scholars, the work of scholars, and I was trying to find my own way and voice within their space. And so I decided to do a lot of research and study of African American foodways, Southern foodways, women and gender studies, so that I could find a narrow lane for myself. Because the interaction that PhDs have, the practice of defending a dissertation, was really new and startling to me as a reporter.

I mean, I knew that defending my work was going to be important if I was going to start to occupy their space. And so leaning back on my journalism skills was really important for me to be able to feel confident in their arena, but also to try to find my own thing. And so the cookbooks started to take on a life of their own as mentors to me in finding my voice in a world that was just starting to be engaged in foodways studies.

Do you have a mission or motto, and if so, what is it?

I love that question because it's part of my memoir that I don't talk about very much, but I do have a mission, a purpose statement, and it derives from Scripture. It's from Proverbs 13:17. The summary of it is a good reporter brings good health. "A reliable reporter brings healing" is kind of the actual words that are there, depending on which version you read.

That Scripture cried out to me in this period after the loss of my father. And while I was trying to figure out how to be a scholar without getting a PhD, I'm very clear about roles. I have never wanted anybody to call me a chef. I never wanted anybody to call me a historian. I've been really rigid about journalism and the promoting of it. And that could be a dying message, because first-person writing and essays and blogging seem to be the new way.

What advice would you offer to someone who wants to do what you do?

I have a recent graduate student who is serving as an intern and an assistant to me right now, and we talk a lot about this because I'm a shotgun blast. I have a lot of projects; I have a lot to keep track of. And being organized, being focused and disciplined, those are really important skills to develop. I'm working with her on strategies for how to do that, whether it's color-coding your files or setting alarms so that you arrive at meetings early. But the kinds of things that the ancestors in the early days included in their cookbooks and/or shared while preparing meals, they always conveyed some kind of wisdom besides how to make great biscuits.

And we have dismissed their wisdom at the same time that we were conflicted about their imagery and about food service and the food industry as extensions of servitude.

I also really encourage her and anyone else to have a very close and strong circle of support. Besides my faith and my family, a very select small group of women in the food industry have kept me going and helped me achieve this level of . . . whatever I've achieved. Acclaim.

What do you most enjoy about your career?

There is a saying that writers hate writing and love having written. That fits me to a tee. I love the research process. I love discovering truths. I love interviews and conversation

"A reliable reporter brings healing."

and discovery, and I do love sharing them in ways that they can be embraced and heard. But the writing process can be hard when there's so much else going on in life. Like, when I was lecturing or speaking, conversations were more natural and free flowing. I could just share my information at the table, at the lectern, wherever we were in a social setting over food.

Once I'm in research mode, I don't want to come out, which I think might be how I've arrived at this idea that these cookbook authors I've studied are my friends. In the early years I was calling them "the ladies" (and a few gentlemen). And they had personas. But very much like when you're a novelist you're immersed in the world with your characters and you love them and you know them and you vocalize for them, that's what my work allows me to do. So sometimes I don't want to come out with the rest of the world. I just want to continue to explore their worlds and their era and find out more truths. And at some point, you have to draw the line and say, "Okay, that's enough research. Now, it's time to share it with someone else."

What are some of your favorite things to eat or drink?
I am a chocolate chip cookie fiend. I have a T-shirt with a little snippet from a Peanuts cartoon strip that appeared years and years ago where chocolate chip cookies are following Snoopy down the sidewalk. I've been treasuring this little T-shirt. It's been rags almost, but I have it. And I love to drink red wine.

Kyisha Davenport

FOUNDER OF BarNoirBoston;
BEVERAGE DIRECTOR
FOR COMFORT KITCHEN
BOSTON, MASSACHUSETTS

How would you describe your work?

Typically, I describe my work as hospitality activism. But to put my work in a sentence or elevator pitch, I try but I really can't. I use the joy and creativity in hospitality to create physical and spiritual space for us, solidarity and safety among us, return what is owed to us.

How did you begin in your field?

I started bartending at eighteen. I originally planned to move to Chicago and work in AmeriCorps, but my mom was like "oh hell no," ha-ha. So I asked her for six hundred dollars to go to bartending school and to this day, it's the most surprising yes I've gotten from her. I thought I'd bartend for a little while, just to make some coin. It was my side job while I worked in after-school education, some finance, and political canvassing. It wasn't until I was twenty-one that hospitality and activism merged, when I started organizing my coworkers at the Barclays Center, where I was also a bartender.

Who are some of your role models or mentors in the food and hospitality space?

My big sister Lexi LaGuerre was one of the first people to mentor me in the bar world, despite me having been in it for nearly a decade when we met. She was the Boston brand ambassador for WhistlePig, and one of the first Black general managers in the North End, a historically Italian neighborhood in Boston. I was just closing my shift when Lexi came into my job—at a place where I wanted to bartend, but was only allowed to serve—and I made a beeline for her. I asked, "Where'd you get your braids done?" I think she read me instantly, because she basically adopted me from that point on. Meeting Lexi was a major turning point for me living in Boston. She was really the blueprint for how to be a beautiful, talented Black girl in the bar world.

What are you most proud of?

I grew up in the hood. Brownsville, Brooklyn. Didn't go to college. I made a lot of choices that people did not understand, didn't respect. Leaving New York City, splitting from organized labor, turning down a city job, opening a restaurant, leaving a restaurant. I don't know which ancestor I came back here as, but I'm grateful to inherit their free spirit, their excitement for the future, their ability to dream. It's brought me through darkness I never thought I would survive, to this place I am in now—100 percent committed to transmute, to evolve, to thrive.

What is an important lesson you've learned about money, compensation, or finance over the course of your career?

I hope you can hear my hands clapping when I say closed

mouths don't get fed! I spent so much time short-changing myself in my work. Some of that comes from being raised to be humble; I'm a middle child in a working-class family. But a large part of it is constantly being told that Black women are not valuable. That's a lie. Nine times out of ten, Black women are the biggest asset in the room, period. So I've learned to come with that energy when I name my price. And it's equally important to keep it pushing if it can't be met.

How do you take care of your mental health and deal with the stresses of your work?

I'm learning to be a little more selfish. I used to never take time off. I would always be the one to speak up, do the physical and emotional labor, fall on the sword. I'm over it. Now, I book the flight. I prioritize what I want. I say no. Yeah, I saw your email . . . and I went back to whatever I was doing.

What advice would you offer to someone who wants to do what you do?

Come through! There is plenty of room for you. In the bar world, you really have to know yourself. You have to know your limits and trust your judgment, as people and situations aren't always how they appear. Take the bar seriously. Learn your basics and your technique. When your foundation is solid, you can have so much fun. I don't think any other industry gives it up like we do. And the more people bringing our culture to the front and center of hospitality, the better.

Do you have a mission or motto, and if so, what is it?

No liberation without libations—that's the motto. It applies in many ways. Literally, as a nod to our bar ancestors who made enough money in hospitality to purchase their families out of enslavement. Acknowledging that at the center of every good march or movement, there was space for celebration and joy. A reminder to myself to find a balance between the two. And an affirmation of the power of Black people and Black culture . . . there is nothing like it!

What do you most enjoy about your work?

I love to listen to, create, and share stories! I had no idea twelve years ago that this would be my work, that this would be the way. But I've always loved storytelling, so it makes sense. BarNoirBoston [a network for Black people in the hospitality industry] is about developing the people who have stories to tell and creating places where they can be shared. Admittedly, I'm a bit nostalgic. So I love this idea that right now, I can tell a story through cocktails. I can pay tribute to my people, my culture. I often feel this urgency to create, to preserve, because

so much of what is ours has been lost, been stolen. Generations from now our descendants will have the stories, taste the recipes. They will know themselves in a way we were unable to. Hospitality really holds and houses the culture.

What's the most difficult aspect of your career?

Access is still the prevailing challenge in our industry. Who gets the grants to study? Who gets the better deal on a lease? Who gets liquor licenses? In Boston, only eight Black-owned establishments have liquor licenses, out of twelve hundred licenses in the city. These are a few of the many roadblocks to success for my community. Sometimes I feel overwhelmed with how much has to be done.

What are some of your favorite things to eat or drink?

Cheese, charcuterie, and wine me down all day! As for a drink, my go-to is usually something funky and bright— think a Tom Collins, but with baijiu. Nonalcoholic, I love a not-too-cold, not-too-carbonated seltzer water . . . the Black girl motto is to drink water and mind your business, after all.

Mudslide aka "With Love from the '90s"

BY KYISHA DAVENPORT / MAKES 1 SERVING

1¼ ounces black cardamom–infused bourbon (see note below)

½ ounce Averna Amaro liqueur

½ ounce heavy cream

¼ ounce Vanille de Madagascar liqueur

2 dashes chocolate bitters

1 dash pure vanilla extract

Dalgona whip (see note below)

Cacao nibs, to garnish

This retro cocktail is a small tribute to Rita Hester, who made the Boston neighborhood of Allston her home. For Rita, life was clearly for living, and it was here that she felt able to live freely as a trans woman. Her style both glamorous and punk, she found community in Boston's rock scene and had a boa constrictor for a pet. Her neighborhood bar was the Silhouette Lounge, where she likely enjoyed what friends say was her favorite cocktail: the popular '90s confection known as the Mudslide. Devastatingly, Rita was murdered on November 28, 1998, just two days shy of her thirty-fifth birthday. Her unsolved murder and subsequent misgendering in the media inspired Boston's first Transgender Day of Remembrance. Twenty-three years after losing Rita, I frequent the Silhouette. Though the chances of grabbing a Mudslide there these days are slim, I've created a version that I imagine Rita would have enjoyed.

NOTE: For the bourbon, gently press 2 or 3 black cardamom pods in a jar and add 8 ounces bourbon (I use Maker's Mark). Let it infuse for at least 3 hours, swirling the jar occasionally and tasting every hour or so. When the bourbon turns darker brown and the flavor is intense, strain it into another container. If you leave it too long, the flavor may become too bitter. For a longer infusion process, leave the cardamom pods whole.

For Dalgona whip, combine 2 tablespoons instant coffee, 2 tablespoons sugar, and 2 tablespoons boiling water in a clean bowl. Beat with a handheld electric mixer or immersion blender, or whisk until thickened. Chill in an airtight container in the refrigerator and use within 1 week.

Combine the bourbon, Averna, heavy cream, Vanille de Madagascar, chocolate bitters, and vanilla extract in an ice-filled shaker. Shake vigorously for 15 to 20 seconds. Using a mesh strainer, double strain the cocktail into a chilled Nick and Nora, coupe, or small martini glass. Using a spoon or pastry bag, layer Dalgona whip on top. Garnish with cacao nibs and serve immediately.

Meryanne Loum-Martin

OWNER OF JNANE
TAMSNA HOTEL
MARRAKECH, MOROCCO

How did you jump from being a lawyer to being a hotelier?

Well, before going to law school, I went to architecture school. Since I was a child, I wanted to build and design, and I had what they call "le baccalauréat," which is the end of senior high school exam, I had it very young, and then I went very young to college. I was sixteen when I went to architecture school, and I was very happy. All of the creative topics were where I was at ease, and I had very good grades in everything that was creative, but to get into third year you needed to have minor credits in physics, chemistry, and math—which was an impossible thing for me, and because of the rigidity of the French system I had to stop.

Then I went into law school and I still thought, "Oh. I will not take the bar exam." Even though on my mother's side I'm fourth-generation lawyer and on my father's side second, I always thought, "Okay. I need a degree, so I'll go to law school, but I'm not going to be an attorney." Then I realized always—because of how the French system is rigid, when you have a law degree, if you're not a lawyer they want you to be in a legal department in the corporate world, and for me it's not possible. It's not what I am. I'm way too creative to be dealing with politics in a company and all of that.

So reluctantly, I took the bar exam, and I got it, and I realized how interesting it was to be an architect. But inside me was saying, "Oh, you need to design. You need to build."

And so it happened because my parents wanted to have a holiday house that would be three hours' flight from home but on the African continent and in an exotic place with all sorts of exciting things to do and discover. And on Sunday lunches it was always, "Well, one day we'll have a place," and then one day I told them, "Look. If you're serious about it, it looks like Marrakech is a place matching all of your requirements." I had a friend who had a house in Marrakech, and I called him, and I told my parents, "Okay. If you're serious about it, I'm going to go and look for land, but I want to be in charge of the project from A to Z."

As you know, I'm a frustrated architect, so they said, "Fine. Go and look, and we'll see if it's worth it." So I came in December 1985, fell in love with the place, found a really nice piece of land (which is not where I am now), and I had the most fantastic time here because I had someone who opened the doors. And I came back in

"What I most enjoy is meeting extraordinary people."

January with my parents, and they also fell in love with the place, and they bought this land. I built and designed a house for them, and while I was doing it I realized that there was a niche market to create for people who wanted to have different types of holidays that were not happening in 150-bedroom hotels where you have a crowd and music around the pool.

This was at the end of the '80s, at the same time the boutique hotel concept was starting to come with luxury offerings like the Aman Resorts.

And it worked so well. People would rent a whole villa or two, and it was very stylish—the décor was magnificent. I had tons of press in top magazines. Also, the lifestyle coming with the houses was so unusual that it was packed all the time. At some point, you couldn't get a place before eighteen months. It was completely packed, and my mother would call me hysterical, saying, "When can I go on holidays in my own house?" And I would look at the books, and I would

say, "Well, maybe in seven months. We have three nights between people—but don't miss your plane because I can't do anything for you if you miss the plane." And it was crazy, but to a degree I had never imagined.

We started having very, very famous people coming, to the point that Tom Cruise's assistant tried four times before we could find space for him.

These people were used to five-star hotels, where everyone recognized them unless they stayed in a suite and never came out. Here, they had the whole place to themselves, with excellent food, a gorgeous setup for tables, beautiful excursions tailor-made, where they wouldn't bump into people.

So this thing, little by little, took over my life. I was still a lawyer in Paris. I was running this separately. I had trained very good staff in Marrakech, and I would just come from time to time.

I would come back from the law firm in the evening, and

there would be miles of faxes in my apartment with people asking to book, and I would answer all the faxes.

In the French system a lawyer is not allowed to have a business. I was having too much press, and I didn't want them to put two and two together, and so I resigned, and I dedicated my time to developing more things in Marrakech. But this hospitality thing was a coincidence. If I had not liked to design and build, I would never be doing this.

What do you most enjoy about being a hotelier?

What I most enjoy is meeting extraordinary people. We used to do a literary salon here for many years. We'd have the house full with guests and friends, and for a long weekend it would be a creative writing workshop and then the author (who would be the guest) would do readings and direct the creative writing workshop and could give out fabulous conversations, and I'm so excited that one of our guests recently got the Nobel Prize for Literature—Abdulrazak Gurnah. He's a Tanzanian author. And I remember, I think it was in March 2007 that he was our guest here.

These are the kinds of things I love. I love organizing cultural events. Now my daughter is also on board, and she's launching a festival—the first female-founded festival of short films. She received films from all over the world. She started this with a friend, and they did a brilliant selection. This is what I like about hospitality, the buzz.

What do you most enjoy about being based in Marrakech?

What I love about being based here is the many things that you can do.

I was asked to create a lifestyle concept for this man who owns a lot of bazaars and antique places in the old part of town. I'm designing new things to be mixed into elements that I created from their enormous inventory. So where else in the world I would be able to do this, I don't know. And we have a very interesting African modern-art scene happening here too, and we also have now all sorts of amazing chefs doing the most beautiful food.

Marrakech is the ultimate crossroads of all sorts of exciting influences and cultures, and I'm three hours' flight from Paris, and the connections are very easy, and the place is bubbling with creativity.

What advice would you offer to someone who wants to be a hotelier?

I'm often asked this question, and people even write to me on Instagram, "I'm dreaming of being you." I say, "Mm-mm-mmm. What are you doing now, and what are your natural skills to change your career without taking a risk which is too big?" I didn't take the risk immediately. I was still a lawyer, and I had this backup plan that if it didn't work my parents would sell a house and then they would just have the holiday house. In fact, people think that I totally changed my life, but the risk was not that huge.

And then I tell people there's such a competition. If you want to become a hotelier, what I would probably personally do now that social media exists (which did not exist when I jumped from the bar to being an innkeeper)—I think that I would try to create my own style on social media, like on Instagram, and try to start creating a look inspired by what you like, and have followers. I think that what I would do is create a strong social brand first before opening a hotel.

People want to be in hospitality, but for what, exactly? What is their vision? What are they going to bring that is not already on the market? It could be food, it could be culture, it could be all sorts of things.

Keep the present job you have, and then if your vision makes sense people are going to follow you. Once people follow you and you can find a way to build or manage or take over something that you really like, then the risk is a bit different because you already have a base of clientele. I wouldn't do it otherwise if I was a young person, I think.

What are some of your favorite things to eat or drink?

I love wine. I love Champagne. I love margaritas, whiskey sours. I love my alcohol.

And to eat, there are a lot of things I like. I really enjoy good Mediterranean food. I love exquisite Vietnamese food, Japanese food. I love food and alcohol. I'm definitely a bon vivant.

Janine Copeland

WINE PROFESSIONAL
BROOKLYN, NEW YORK

How would you describe your work?

A work in progress. I feel like—I used to call myself a wine educator, a hospitality professional. I wanted to do consulting and that sort of thing. And now, I'm like, "What do I want to do? And how can I pivot in a way that feels like I'm not going to have to grind myself?" I feel like the food and beverage industry . . . the whole culture is built around stay up late, and you're out all the time. We don't take holidays off, we don't do sick days, and that's just not appealing to me anymore. I feel like I'm valuing my health and my sanity more.

I definitely still think of myself as a true hospitalitarian of sorts. I like to make people feel comfortable. I like to create space for people. I would love to have a space—not a bar or restaurant, but just a space with food and beverage where people can come to take a break. With all the beauty that's in the world, there's also just so much ugly, and there's really no outlet or room for a pause—which we realized during COVID. It was like, "Oh wow. I didn't realize how fast I was going or how much I was doing." We don't really have those little moments, and I feel like being able to sit down with a glass of wine or settle down with a good meal causes you to really sit in your body and connect. So I want to create space for that, but I don't know what it's going to look like. It's still figuring itself out.

How did you begin in your field?

After I dropped out of college my senior year—financial things—I started working in restaurants. It was supposed to be temporary. I worked at this pizza place called Matchbox, and it was kind of casual—but fancy casual. Then I started working as a cheesemonger at a cheese place. We used to do plates, we had wine and beer and cider, and we would do these pairings and classes and things, and I was like, "Oh. I'm in. This sounds dope." That was the first time I encountered natural wine.

That's a long time ago. So from there I got exposed to more fancy, fine dining–style restaurants, and everything took off from there. I left the cheese shop; cheese is not a very lucrative business to be in, so I ended up leaving there and joining Rose's Luxury, which is the hot girl of DC at the moment. It's won all of the awards—Bon Appétit, James Beard, Michelin, like all of the things—and I got my Level 1 for the Court of Master Sommeliers.

Shortly after that, I left there (another slightly toxic place) to go manage Dio, which I feel like was a defining part of my career.

That was the first natural wine bar in DC. That's when I had a name to put to it, because at Rose's and at the cheese place we were dealing with natural wine and artisanal-based goods and farming and that from-the-land aspect. But it wasn't until Dio that I had a name for it and was able to find the natural wine community.

"I learned that fancy food isn't really fancy."

Who were some of your mentors and/or role models in the food and hospitality space?

I think some of the people who have had the greatest influence on me are my peer mentors, who are Ashtin Berry and Krystal Mack. They were my Instagram friends at first, and just people I hold in really high regard because they're not much older than me, but they've been able to carve out this space for themselves within this industry that's not in a restaurant, that's not in a bar. They both left right when I was hitting my stride, and it was like, "Oh wow. I can leave. I don't have to do this to be successful. I can create what I want to." Both of them have very different approaches to that. They've both been very radical in the way that they move, and I think that's so inspiring to say, "Okay. I can literally do whatever I want."

Do you have a mission or motto, and if so, what is it?

I tell myself, "Don't stop, get it, get it," a lot when I'm feeling kind of down. Or when I'm feeling myself, I'm like, "Don't stop, get it, get it. Don't stop." I'm definitely very much, like, you gotta get something to keep you pushing. It's like, "You got this."

What do you most enjoy about your career?

In all aspects of this world, I feel like it all ends up with somebody enjoying something beautiful or something pleasurable. That's been the most rewarding part of it, especially when I was working on the floor with people being like, "Oh, this is the best meal," or "I was having a terrible day, and it's all turned around now." There are a couple of particular tables that come to mind where they were celebrating something or mourning something, and you get to just be a little bit of light in somebody's life, even if just for a moment. I think that's such a rewarding thing to be able to give people, just a moment, a chance to breathe.

I remember this one table I had: there was a pregnant lady, a woman who was going for her last chemo treatment before she let life take its course—oh, and the birthday. Three different stages of life—one celebrating their fiftieth-something birthday; this person literally ushering themselves out and celebrating the life and choosing, essentially, to move on to the next stage; and then this pregnant lady bringing in new life. I was like, "We have to comp their meal," and they were so happy. First of all, I started sending them all this stuff, and they're probably looking at me like, "Oh, my god. How am I going to pay?" I'm like, "Just do it. Just go for it," and I'm convincing them. And then I gave them the meal for free.

I still get giddy thinking about that moment, and a little emotional thinking about being able to celebrate life in that way for these people, and I don't know them from Jack, you know what I mean? But being able to give somebody a moment is exhilarating.

What are some of your favorite things to eat or drink?

This is simple, but it's also one of my first fancy things (but I also learned that fancy food isn't really fancy)—summer tomatoes with burrata cheese.

After that . . . Okay. So my dad is from North Carolina, and they do chopped barbecue, and my dad's chopped barbecue is the best barbecue.

Spiced Nuts

BY JANINE COPELAND /
MAKES 4 CUPS NUTS
PLUS ABOUT 4 CUPS
ADDITIONAL SPICE BLEND

I once managed a wine bar where I had to come up with snack items to pair with the wines. I really enjoyed developing these simple recipes. The spiced nuts are great on their own, with wine or beer. The spice mix can be kept for months in a tightly sealed container.

SPICE BLEND

1 cup coriander seeds, toasted and ground

⅔ cup kosher salt

⅔ cup ground cinnamon

⅓ cup turmeric powder

⅓ cup smoked paprika

⅓ cup sugar

⅓ cup ground black pepper

⅓ cup ground nutmeg

¼ cup Arbol chili powder

⅛ cup garlic powder

NUTS

4 cups raw almonds

2–3 tablespoons olive oil

Preheat the oven to 350°F.

For the spice blend, combine the coriander, salt, cinnamon, turmeric, paprika, sugar, pepper, nutmeg, chili powder, and garlic powder in a large lidded mason jar. Shake vigorously to combine. You will have 4⅜ cups.

Place the almonds in a bowl, drizzle with olive oil, and toss to coat. Sprinkle with ¼ cup of the spice blend and toss again to coat evenly.

Spread the nuts on a sheet pan in a single layer. Bake for about 8 minutes, stirring several times, until toasty and fragrant. Set the nuts aside to cool. Taste and, if desired, sprinkle with a little more spice blend. Store the nuts in an airtight container at room temperature for 2 weeks, in the refrigerator for 1 month, or in the freezer for up to 2 months. Store the extra spice blend, tightly covered, in the freezer for future use.

Fancy Grilled Cheese

WITH RED ONION JAM

BY JANINE COPELAND / MAKES 1 SERVING

Two ½-inch-thick slices Italian semolina bread

About 2 tablespoons mayonnaise

1 tablespoon whole-grain dijon mustard

2-ounce slice gruyère cheese

1 tablespoon Red Onion Jam (recipe follows)

1-ounce slice cheddar cheese

2 tablespoons duck confit or 1 ounce speck (optional)

RED ONION JAM
MAKES ABOUT 4 CUPS

2 tablespoons canola or other neutral oil

8 large red onions, julienned

2 tablespoons mustard seeds

½ cup brown sugar

½ cup heavy-bodied red wine such as Cabernet Sauvignon

2 tablespoons chopped fresh thyme or rosemary

NOTE: Rather than using a skillet, you may toast the sandwich in a toaster oven at 400°F.

The second snack item I added to the wine bar menu was a classic—a warm and comforting grilled cheese with red onion jam. This recipe makes a large quantity of onion jam that can be stored in a sealed container in the refrigerator for up to two weeks. For other uses of the red onion jam, I recommend spreading it on sandwiches, or on toast or crostini with goat cheese; it also goes well with rotisserie chicken.

Heat a large, well-seasoned cast-iron skillet over medium-high heat.

Spread one side of each bread slice with mayonnaise and place it, mayo side down, on wax paper. Spread the top of one slice with mustard and top it with gruyère. Spread the other slice with jam and top with cheddar. Add duck confit or speck to each slice if using.

Place both pieces of bread, mayo side down, in the hot skillet and cook until the cheese begins to melt, about 1 minute. Close the sandwich and cook until golden brown, turning once, about 5 minutes total. Cut in half on the diagonal and serve warm.

For the red onion jam, heat the oil in a large, high-sided skillet over medium heat, tilting the pan to coat the bottom. Add the onions and reduce the heat to medium-low.

Cook the onions, stirring occasionally. When they begin to brown, stir in the mustard seeds and brown sugar. Cook, stirring occasionally, until the onions are soft and golden brown, about 1 hour. If they begin sticking, deglaze the pan with a little water.

Add the wine to the pan and stir until the onions have absorbed it—simmer as needed until wine is absorbed. Remove the pan from the heat and stir in the fresh herbs. Refrigerate, tightly covered, until needed, up to 2 weeks. The jam can be kept in the freezer, tightly sealed, for up to 2 months.

Paola Velez

How did you begin in your field?

My mom was an accountant by day in a restaurant, and a hostess at night in the same restaurant. So I would go after school and I would have one booth reserved for me. That booth looked directly into the kitchen, and I said, "I want to be just like the men in that room." My mom was not okay with that. She wanted me to become an engineer, and I still do quite a lot of crafty work, or mechanical, technical work in the kitchen, because we have kitchen tools and we have to fix things. But I just fell in love with the kitchen and everything that it meant to everyone. That was probably the only place that I saw majority Black and brown people—not understanding that was the divide between front and leadership, and then back of the house. So hopefully we're changing that now.

Tell me about the beginning of Bakers Against Racism.

I had finished a month-and-some-change-long donut pop-up that benefited undocumented immigrants in the culinary workforce. I was broken, I was crying, because we lived in Virginia and we've experienced racial inequity and tension. Nobody's ever asked me, "Are you Dominican?" They're just like, "Black." I was scared for my husband's life, for our well-being in this climate [the spring and summer of 2020]. DC was torn apart.

And Willa [Pelini, cofounder of Bakers Against Racism] reached out to me and was like, "Do you want to do one more bake sale?" And I was like, "No, it's not enough. As much as I want it to be enough, if we just do this, we're patting ourselves on the back and moving on, and I don't want to do that." So I told her, "Give me some time to think about it." That was on Friday. All of Saturday, I put all of the resources together for Bakers Against Racism. I made the website, I made the Instagram handle, the hashtag. I got everything together and put it in a Google folder for people to read. Then on Sunday, she was like, "I'm so sorry, is everything okay? I didn't mean to overstep. And I didn't realize that could have been seen as insensitive, because I was asking you to activate for yourself."

I was like, "No, it's cool. Because in my tiredness and anger, I was able to do something—do something like this." So I presented it to Rob [Rubba, cofounder of Bakers Against Racism] and Willa, because I reached out to Rob because he does graphic design. And that's how it all came together. Willa was able to give insight to other women who are white, and give them resources, things that I can't particularly talk to. That's how we were able to come together.

We launched on June fourth or sixth and we went viral, not expected, not intentional, but timely, because I think that a lot of other people were feeling the same way Willa was feeling, but didn't have the resources to do something about it. So we gave them weapons to be able to fight in a battle that a lot of people didn't even know they had to fight in. I think really it went viral because of the timeliness of it.

But also my voice was beginning to be trusted a little more because of the James Beard nomination. So it added a little weight to what I was saying. Then on the heels of the pop-up, in DC locally, it made sense, and all of DC activated. Not just bakeries, not just pastry chefs. I'm talking about restaurants, I'm talking about breweries.

"Knowing my worth and establishing my worth took me such a long time."

But it was good, and it is still going very strong. There are chapters all around the nation and the world that are baking still, they're activating because really the main focus of Bakers Against Racism wasn't to activate once and then be done. Because what if I pass away from COVID? I intentionally made everything so that it wouldn't have a head, someone telling people what to do, that people had the resources and the autonomy to make these decisions. Then I just asked them, "Keep yourself accountable. If you are a baker and you are baking and you need to raise funds for yourself because you're unemployed, then donate what you can, but be honest about it and tell people, 'This is for my rent, but also this portion of the proceeds is going to

this organization directly.'" And people were wholeheartedly honest about it. It was the most truthful I've seen people behave in a long time.

What is an important lesson you've learned about money, compensation, or finance over the course of your career?

Before any of the awards, before anything like that, I didn't realize that people were getting compensated for things that I thought were paying my dues. Now what I do, I make sure that I talk to others about it so that they know that they should be getting at least an honorarium for certain things. I think I have gotten a little more bold in my negotiating power. I just tell them, "Hey, this is what I'm worth. If you think I'm worth it, let's collaborate. If you don't think I'm worth it, that's a shame, and it goes against what you just pitched me. But I'm happy to leave." More times than not people are like, "Oh, I didn't mean it that way." And I'm like, "No, it's okay. But that's how it came across."

But there are things that I don't charge for. If it's an organization that's 100 percent fighting for childhood leukemia, I'm not going to ask them for a check. But if you're a Fortune 500 company—then we have to talk. But knowing my worth and establishing my worth took me such a long time. That's the biggest awakening, wake-up call—that I was not being valued despite all of the richness that I would bring to the table when I was seated at the table.

How do you take care of your mental health and deal with the stresses of your work?

I don't, I am very honest about it, but I wish I was better. I've started to openly talk about my struggles, so that people don't think that it's all rainbows and sunshine and butterflies, just because I'm super uplifting, and I care about the community and I always am there to help others. It does not mean that I always know how to help myself. I'm still learning how to take care of me. I'm learning how to honor my husband in these struggles when I'm going through it. Because when I'm going through it, he's going through it, because he wants to be there with me.

Then also is the realization that I can stay who I am, regardless of all the awards, regardless of all the nominations, regardless of all the, I don't know how to . . . in Spanish we call this *pelusa*, the meringue, the fluff. I have to remember that I can only take on what I can take on. Regardless of all the things that are coming, I can only accept what I can bear. So as I progress through all of this, again, I am grateful that I am humble enough to realize that I'm just human. I'm not this giant celebrity. I don't have to be somewhere that I'm not. Wherever I am now, I'm content in it, because it's light-years away from where I was five years ago.

What advice would you offer to someone who wants to do what you do?

Oh Lord. Be prepared not to sleep, be prepared to work even during your vacations. Be prepared to say no when you have to say no, regardless of how good the opportunity looks. Be prepared to read and study and practice more than you could have ever imagined, because you will not be viewed as someone who is a master of their craft regardless of how long you've been doing this. So you have to make sure that you're able to prove whoever it is wrong every step of the way.

Humbly, of course, with grace. Not mean, don't be a jerk about it, but if you look like me, if you grew up in my type of situation, if you are a daughter or a child of an immigrant, we are not afforded the same flexibilities as some of our peers. We are not afforded the same opportunities. In order for us to really get in the room, we have to be beyond what we humanly think we can be, and then more.

What do you most enjoy about your work?

I like making cool stuff.

What's the most difficult aspect of your career?

Having to be the peer that holds the ones that aren't doing the right thing accountable.

What are some of your favorite things to eat or drink?

My favorite thing to drink on planet Earth is something with really fresh ginger in it. So usually if it's rum and ginger, that's my favorite. I think different types of rum too. A golden rum with fresh ginger tastes like cotton candy to me.

And then to eat, I think anything that is comfort. In the DMV [DC Metro] area, we don't have a lot of Dominican restaurants. We have a few, but we don't have a lot. When I'm really trying to feel comfort, I turn to other African diaspora foods, and I try to find something that, I'll be like, "What makes me feel like I'm at home?"

Jacqui Sinclair

FOUNDER OF *NYAM & TROD* *KINGSTON, JAMAICA*

How would you describe your work?

I will say it's very eclectic, because I do several things. I'm not somebody you can put in a box. I just tell people I'm a food media professional versus chef or writer or scientist or all those things that I do. I never wanted to open a restaurant. I never wanted to cater. I just wanted to be more of a storyteller about food and its culture. It's always been very global, eclectic.

How did you begin in your field?

It was accidental. Growing up I thought, "I'm going to be an international journalist, a diplomat, or an archaeologist." Food was not in my career path, but I did always enjoy food because my parents were big food lovers. I don't want to say "foodie" because they're not the era of "foodies." They were gourmands. They loved food. Hospitality is in my blood, so the irony is that even though food was not in my career path, being the daughter of hoteliers—hotels and nightclubs in the UK, and here too, there are always restaurants in there—so growing up, I've always been amongst chefs and bartenders.

Hospitality is in my DNA because of my parents. My dad was a prominent businessman back in the 1970s and '80s in the UK—a Black businessman, well regarded. Every ambassador from Jamaica to the UK, my parents would host them. Of course, some of these ambassadors would bring their other diplomatic friends from other countries, so growing up it was not unusual at our table to have people from around the world. And then my mummy used to belong to this supper club—not supper club in the sense of how we do supper clubs, but it was more like a cookbook-supper club, where they would get cookbooks from around the world, and she would cook from those cookbooks. So I've always had a developed palate.

I did my first degree in the States. I went to the University of Miami because we have a home there too, so Miami is like a second home. There used to be a Publix across the road. So I used to call my mum and say, "Okay, mummy. How did you make this? How did you make that?" and she would email me recipes and stuff like that. When she would come, she would teach me. But then I actually started to experiment.

In our dorms, we had two kitchens, on the sixth and seventh floors. I used to go up and cook. Next thing you know, I was involved with different organizations on campus and stuff, and they're like, "Okay, Jacqui's going to cook!" and I started cooking for everybody. It was so surreal for me because I was coming from a background where I didn't have to cook because I was spoiled. So I started cooking for everybody, and I realized I really loved it.

So I came back to Jamaica and started to research, because I knew I wanted to go back to the UK to do my master's, and I came across Le Cordon Bleu. I said, "Okay.

I'm going to take a gap year at Le Cordon Bleu between my bachelor's and my master's."

I started at Le Cordon Bleu, but got very, very sick, and I had to drop out. And then while I was sick and recovering I started my master's course. Then, when I got a bit better, I took a pause on my master's and I did the full Le Cordon Bleu, and that's how Preeti Mistry and I became friends, because we were classmates there.

So it's so funny that even though my life has not been on the straight and narrow, it's been very organic. But everything that I have studied—politics, diplomacy, journalism, whatever—it's all actually formed what I am today, and it has formed my global outlook.

These incidental things happened. For example, Denise Spencer-Walker. She used to work at Le Cordon Bleu. She's a food stylist in the UK—one of the UK's first food stylists. She's brilliant. She was working at Le Cordon Bleu at the time, and she told me about food styling as well.

I remember the first project I worked on—it was different types of sugars and making pastries and stuff with the different sugars, so that was an education for me too on the job, and I'm like, "I like this. I prefer this environment to the kitchen environment." Because I always knew—like I said, when I went to Le Cordon Bleu as my gap year, it was just more for my appreciation of food, and I wanted to know more about food from a formal sense.

I thought it would be something that would be useful to my family business in hospitality in terms of, like, "One day I will take over for my father at hiring chefs," and stuff like that, because I always said I wanted to improve the restaurants of our hotels.

Then Preeti and I, we used to do private cheffing on the side—you know how you do to make money. And we used to cook for Michael G. Wilson, the producer of James Bond movies as well. We used to cook for him and his wife.

There were these guys from the London Film School, and they wanted somebody to do some food styling for them and catering, and I was like, "Oh, I'll do it." And then through them I met other production people, so I started working on these different productions—either catering on the side or helping out with a little food styling.

When I came back to Jamaica, I'd come, actually, to plan my daddy's seventieth birthday. And I just fell in love with Jamaica again, because I hadn't really been here in a while. And then we had a family friend, Novia McDonald-Whyte, who is the lifestyle editor at the *Jamaica Observer*, and she remembered how well I used to write and stuff, and she was like, "Jacqui, while you're here, could you write some food articles for me?" I

said, "Sure," and they became so popular. So even when I went back to Paris, wherever I traveled, I would write weekly, and what was supposed to be this temporary thing—I moved back to Jamaica—became six years of my food column.

Tell me about *Nyam & Trod.*

Nyam & Trod is my duality. So I have my JuicyChef name [on Instagram]. My motto for JuicyChef was "Cooking global, eating local." That was my whole motto, behind my column and everything: use local foods in international ways. "Nyam," of course, is our patois for "eating," or "to eat," and then "trod" is Old English for "to trod a path; to travel," so Jamaican patois with Old British English. That's the duality too. *Nyam & Trod* is me as a British Jamaican—*Nyam & Trod* as traveling through the palate. It's those dualities that I work upon . . . This is a way that I could dabble in travel writing as well as my food writing.

I started a podcast, and again it was people within my circles because I said . . . I wanted to also show that Caribbean people—we're world travelers. I call it *Drink & a Natter*—again, my British Jamaican. (In England, to have a conversation is to have a "natter.")

So that's how *Nyam & Trod* came to be. I'm my own boss now. I write what I want. I do what I want.

Do you have a mission or motto, and if so, what is it?

Food is love and should be shared. I think everybody has the right to eat well, and I think part of my mission here on the island was to show people (a) that you don't have to cook the same things all the time, and (b) how to cook the humble farmers' market vegetables.

I have a Caribbean Harvest, where I take each typical fruit or vegetable grown here and create something around it. People have this image that food has to be expensive to be beautiful, and I want to show that those humble farm ingredients at the market can make a beautiful dinner.

What are some of your favorite things to eat or drink?

I have just so many. I love wine. For nonalcoholic a good, old-fashioned Jamaican lemonade. It's really limeade—just good ol' lime, sugar, water. It's so refreshing in this heat. And I'm still very British. I love my tea. Even though I'm in coffee country, and of course we have the best coffee with the Blue Mountains. For food now, I love Mediterranean food in terms of Turkish and Lebanese [cuisines]. For Jamaican food, I love a good oxtail. For beverages let me go back. I love sorrel. Sorrel is our Christmas beverage. You can get it year-round commercially, but it's just not the same as homemade Christmas sorrel.

Pickled Green Banana Salad

BY JACQUI SINCLAIR / MAKES 4–6 SERVINGS

Half of a lime

12 green bananas

1 cup olive oil, plus more for the boiling water

1 cup white cane vinegar or apple cider vinegar

1 large onion, sliced

1 scotch bonnet pepper, left whole

1 teaspoon ground allspice

2 large garlic cloves, crushed

2 bay leaves

2 sprigs thyme

2 sprigs marjoram

Our Caribbean neighbors, St. Lucia and Puerto Rico in particular, use green bananas in salads. In St. Lucia it is known as fig salad, and in Puerto Rico, guineos en escabeche. I enjoy both of them tremendously. I have Jamaicanized my adaptation, leaving out the green olives and adding thyme, marjoram, allspice, and fiery scotch bonnet pepper. Jamaica was a former Spanish colony, and the Spanish Jews fleeing the Inquisition who settled on the island brought this style of cooking with them. The green bananas are generally easy to find at Caribbean or Asian grocers and at chain supermarkets. Make sure the bananas you pick are hard to the touch and bright green.

Bring a big pot of water to a boil, adding a squeeze of fresh lime juice and a dash of oil.

Rinse the bananas, trim the ends, and slit the skin lengthways, leaving the bananas in their skins. Add them to the boiling water and cook for 20 to 25 minutes, until fork tender.

In a large, nonreactive saucepan, combine the oil, vinegar, onion, scotch bonnet, allspice, garlic, bay leaves, thyme, and marjoram. Bring the mixture to a boil over high heat. Reduce the heat and simmer until the onions have slightly caramelized and the liquid is reduced by half, about 30 minutes. Set the mixture aside to cool to room temperature.

Peel the bananas, discarding the skins, and cut them into chunks. Add them to the cooled oil mixture and toss to coat. Refrigerate, covered, to marinate for at least 2 hours or overnight, stirring a few times. Serve chilled or at room temperature.

Pine & "Ginga" Punch

BY JACQUI SINCLAIR / MAKES 12 SERVINGS

3 cups pineapple juice

3 cups (one 750-ml bottle) pinot grigio

1 cup dark Jamaican rum

½ cup orange liqueur

2 cups fresh pineapple chunks, preferably sugarloaf, plus more for garnish

10 mint leaves, preferably Jamaican Black, plus more for garnish

2¼ cups ginger beer

Ice, for serving

Pineapple and ginger drinks are traditional in Jamaica, and my boozy version is fun for a crowd. When sugarloaf pineapples are in season, I gorge on the fruit and make the classic pine and ginger drink with the pineapple skins. Nothing goes to waste! My cocktail is perfect to pair with a jerk feast.

In a large pitcher, combine the juice, wine, rum, liqueur, pineapple chunks, and mint. Stir to mix. Set in the refrigerator to infuse for at least an hour.

When ready to serve, top with ginger beer. Pour punch into tall, ice-filled glasses and garnish with pineapple and mint.

Nicole Taylor

WRITER, COOKBOOK AUTHOR
*ATHENS, GEORGIA &
BROOKLYN, NEW YORK*

How would you describe your work?

I like to say first and foremost that I'm a master home cook. When one of my real-deal chef friends who've been trained or worked in kitchens comes to my house, they're always amazed, because I have everything they need to make me food. But the core of who I am started with me cooking really early, as a preteen.

So first and foremost I'm a home cook, and then secondly I like to say I'm a storyteller. Yeah, I write. But over the years, when I look at my body of work, I've been able to push stories and narratives through more than just words.

How did you begin in your field?

I paved my own way. Basically, when I moved to New York City is when I really got serious about being in food media, being a food media professional. I would make this long list on a piece of paper, and I had a subway map (a paper subway map!), and I remember not wanting to upgrade my phone. So I had an old phone that didn't have a map, so I had to use this old-school way of learning the city, and I had this list of all these restaurants I wanted to go to, and I would just pay my own way. I didn't have a media pass; I wasn't media then.

And I would basically take all my money and my paycheck and go to freaking restaurants, and buy cookbooks. That was my life: buy cookbooks, go to cooking classes. I'm self-taught in every way around food media. I would say it's funny because a lot of people say, "Oh, did you model yourself after Jessica Harris?" I respect Jessica, and she is the fairy godmother of Black foodways, but for me it's Melissa Clark: I paid very close attention to everything that she was doing, because at the time she was a columnist for the *New York Times*, she was cowriting books. Actually, one of the first books that she collaborated on was Sylvia's cookbook—*Sylvia's Family Soul Food Cookbook*—and a lot of people don't know that. I was obsessed with her, so she's kind of my early blueprint of how to be more than one thing in the food world.

The thing that probably helped me the most in food media is having a podcast on Heritage Radio Network. And it's funny, looking back now. Everyone's in a podcast. People didn't really understand them back then, and I was blessed to be able to interview people before they got really huge, before people on the national scene were talking about them. From Karen Washington—I've known Karen Washington since I moved to New York. From Michael Twitty to Fany Gerson when she first started Dough—so many people. And sometimes I forget about them, and every now and then Heritage will do a newsletter and they'll put in one of my old podcasts, and I'm like, "Oh. Does this still hold up?"

I would say, for sure, Heritage Radio Network gave me the platform, but there are also so many things that I did on my own.

What do you most enjoy about your career?

I think one of the things I most enjoy is that every story and every project that I work on, I learn a little bit. It still makes me happy to know I'm researching a story about sweet potatoes and I find out some little factoid that I didn't know, or I interview someone I don't know (or maybe I do know them), and I get a little gem or become inspired by them. I still get high off that.

What is the most difficult aspect of your career?

Chasing them invoices down. I think the most difficult part is the business part. Yeah, I'm a creative—writing and being creative and coming up with storytelling. But I think the other part of the job now is basically being self-employed, being a business manager, being a project manager. It's a lot of work, and there are skills that you have to cultivate on that side of your brain to get shit done. So that can be a little tiring sometimes. With that comes invoices. With that is finding an assistant or finding a recipe tester, and you're spending a lot of time with email and stuff like that and typing fucking Google Docs. I mean, I don't enjoy it, but I realize that it's a part of my work for now.

What advice would you offer to someone who wants to do what you do?

Don't quit your day job.

Listen! So many people call me, young people all the time, and I always say this, like "Listen. I have a partner who pays the rent." There is no other way I could be in New York.

Sadly, I literally try to give thanks and pray to George Floyd's family for healing, because if it wasn't for him, the opportunities that I've had in the last eleven months? They wouldn't exist! This is the first year that I've ever made a hundred thousand dollars—which we know in New York City you can live on, I guess, comfortably or semi-comfortably as a freelancer. And people do it—don't get it twisted. But I just tell people, "Keep your job and ease into this world. It's hard, particularly if you're living in a metropolitan city. This is not an easy thing, so keep your day job but also don't be afraid to get a roommate. Don't be afraid to be like, 'I'm going to work on a farm and they're going to pay for my housing.'" But I guess I would say . . . instead of saying, "Keep your day job," really think about what you want to do that's going to give you a roof over your head. Now I sound like an old person.

I think the other piece of advice is a support system—who is your circle? Who is your circle of people that you can go to for advice? And they don't need to be all the time in the food world.

So (1) don't quit your day job; (2) create your circle, create your brain trust of five people—no more than five—that you can go to about money, that you can go to about relationships that may affect your career, people who you can go to straight up who can read your essays and edit before you turn something in. This is all shit I learned later in my career and not at the beginning—sadly. If I had known these things before, I think things might have gone a bit easier.

And I will say, lastly, cultivate advocates. You need people to advocate for you and say your name when you're not in the room, and those people being very clear about it—not they're saying your name because they're looking for a token Black person, but because Klancy fits the bill for this, or Nicole is perfect for that. You need advocates, and that means true relationships with people. And an advocate is, in my opinion, different from a mentor (though an advocate can be a mentor), and it's different from a role model.

How do you take care of your mental health and deal with the stresses of your work?

I see a therapist every other week. I remember the first time I saw a therapist in my twenties, and I thought it was just like a one-check thing, like "You go, you go for a few weeks and they fix the problem," and I never really even thought about going to see a therapist ever after that. But pre-pandemic, I was seeing a therapist—actually at the recommendation of my Reiki person—my spiritual adviser, as I like to say. I do Reiki sessions. I do flower essence.

And I very much pray. I will say that. I grew up rooted in the Christian faith, but I've evolved. I think there's more than one way to connect to a higher being. And for me, that means pausing and getting my energy right with a person who I feel—who does lightwork [energy body work], you know? So I do a flower essence once a quarter.

And then I will say being outside. I love being outside. I grew up being outside. It brings me the most joy and the most inspiration, 100 percent.

What are some of your favorite things to eat and/or drink?

I will walk to the end of the earth for a good french fry. Literally. Waffle fries, cottage cut, shoestring—you name it. I love a good french fry, for sure. It's very comforting.

And I love, love, love desserts. On my birthday I had Champagne, dessert, and french fries. That is my death row meal.

"Cultivate advocates. You need people to advocate for you and say your name when you're not in the room."

Marva & Myriam Babel

CO-OWNERS OF ODE TO BABEL *BROOKLYN, NEW YORK*

How did you decide to open your bar, Ode to Babel?

MARVA: I always wanted to do my own thing. I went to school for interior architecture, and while I was doing that I did it for corporate retailers. And I loved it, but I also realized that I still wasn't really having the voice I wanted in corporate, so I always said, "Okay. I know when the time is right, I'm going to pick up and do my own thing."

This actual space was here, so I said to my husband, "Reach out to the owner of that property and find out what's the story." So he told me that she's interested, and it can be retail or something that is going to have a commercial tenant, so I said, "Okay. Sign me up." My daughter was six months old, and I said, "Sign me up. I'm not going back to work. I'm taking on the space." And initially, the space's

concept was going to be mixed-use. It was really going to focus on home goods, products, and celebrating local independent creatives. I was simultaneously also taking a small-business course, because I had no business background.

MYRIAM: We took it together.

MARVA: As we were taking the course, we started doing the math and realized that's when retail was taking a nosedive. So we had a little panic and decided, "All right. Let's put a little bar inside the space so if someone doesn't really feel like shopping they could still come over and feel communal. People can just chat over a beer or wine, and that would be it." And it's this mixed-use space.

MYRIAM: We also decided to incorporate coffee—like espresso. It was supposed to be a day-night vibe, where it turns from day [with] coffee or light beer and wine into evening [and] more heavily in the beer and wine . . .

Marva and I said we need to have something to help people come in and understand that this is an art space and a space to converge and create.

All of my background is very different. I have a science background. I'm an RN, but I don't really do face-forward patient care. I'm more middle management and logistics. So I knew that's not my calling, my passion, but I'm okay with where I am in my life. My station in life is secure. I was in the midst of a divorce at that time, and it was rough for me, and I needed something that was going to help fill me up in my creative space because I'm more creative.

So I just jumped in, and I said, "Marva, whatever you do, you know I'm with you," because we're always a package. We're

just like, "Whatever you decide, I'm there." So it was Marva's baby brainchild, so to speak, but then we know that we always give each other a hand and we go together.

And then just a quick fast-forward. Our hunch was right; retail wasn't doing as well as we we'd like because it's on a side street and people just weren't shopping. So we were getting a lot of requests to have events here—launch parties, book parties like yours, and just general birthday groups and everything—and that kind of was taking off, big time.

MARVA: So in our true fashion, Myriam and I, we were not married to just being this one thing. We kind of began to pivot, just because we knew we didn't have the financial cushion to let it flounder. We had to make a decision, like, "Okay. We want to stay in business. Maybe we should just focus and make this more of a lounge bar community space, and maybe step away from the retail element."

MYRIAM: And one of the things that kind of was the motivation . . . everything was very stagnant financially for us. When we were open it was quiet. We were stressed out, a little depressed, anxious. But we knew—we pulled all of our financial resources from our retirement, we tapped all our savings, and no other partners. Not having that fallback was the driving force, and we were like, "We're not going to sink. We're going to swim. We're going to do this." So we were ready to do whatever we needed to do. We were afraid, but that fear was what was driving us forward.

MARVA: And from there on, the space began to organically build up. It definitely wasn't overnight. It was a slow and steady build, and a lot of times people say, "Well, you should do this if you want more people to come in. Put TVs, this, do that."

MYRIAM: And promoters. They would come and wanted a portion of this and a portion of that.

MARVA: Yeah. Promoters, all those kinds of things. But we were very firm about remaining true to who we are and keeping our space. One thing we wouldn't budge on is keeping the space the way we wanted. We felt like we were going to attract the people who are the same as us. We're going to attract the people who are energetic, positive, fun. You may come in, it might be poetry, and you're good with that. You'll come in, it could be a full-on dance party, and you're good with that. That's the beauty, for us, of New York—especially Brooklyn: You can walk into something that looks like a dilapidated building and it's a mansion. You just accept whatever you get and enjoy that. And that's what we wanted to embody.

MYRIAM: Or just leave in peace and come back another time—or don't come back if it's not for you. Marva and I were like, "We're always going to curate the crowd." Not in a way where we are being snobs or being elitist in any way.

Actually, we're so inclusive, and we're so open and receptive that we wanted to ensure that the people who came had that open-mindedness and that inclusivity energy. We knew the people who feel that will come and stay. That's how it organically grew into who we have in our energy.

MARVA: A very strong community—we attract wonderful, wonderful people in this space.

What advice would you offer to someone who wants to open and run a bar and lounge?

MARVA: I would say probably do every single thing in the beginning, all parts of the business part of it. Even bussing too, obviously, trying to make some drinks (even if you don't want to be behind the bar), answering emails, doing your social media, connecting with people. It's exhausting, but it's going to give you a realistic understanding when you are hiring what they are dealing with. When people are emailing you like crazy or upset or what their concerns are—you're the one doing it. You're the one understanding it, not getting it filtered through an assistant or someone.

MYRIAM: And eventually, you'll get to the point where you have a team that you trust, and they trust in your vision, and they pick up the baton that you pass.

One of the things I can probably say to someone if they're considering starting a bar—there's a different dynamic between a dive bar and a waterhole versus more of a lounge, more of an environment you're trying to evoke or create. Either way, you're going to have to be the kind of person who can stay levelheaded in every situation.

And I think that goes along in life. We're all trying to grapple with that, trying to stay centered and grounded. But you have to be able to know yourself. At three o'clock in the morning, you're kind of going to be with one eye and ear open because even if you're home, if your bar is still running that's a part of you that's still going on 100 percent.

What do you most enjoy about being the owners of Ode to Babel?

MYRIAM: Connecting with people.

MARVA: It's like a built-in friendship. You get just to meet people, and it feels like home.

What are some of your favorite things to drink and/or eat?

MYRIAM: I'm a huge coffee person. The coffee program [when we first opened Ode to Babel] was my baby. I love good espresso, good coffee. And my go-to alcoholic drink—anyone who knows me knows I'm a Negroni drinker.

MARVA: That's true. And for me, I'm a gin drinker. I love gin.

Ode to Summer Cocktail

BY MARVA AND MYRIAM BABEL / MAKES 1 SERVING

We love this cocktail because the lavender celebrates the floral and citrus notes of the gin without overpowering it, and it's beautiful to make and serve in social settings—at home get-togethers, picnics, al fresco dining, etc. It's an easy and approachable cocktail to make at home.

1½ ounces small-batch gin (preferably Ode to Babel)

½ lavender agave (see note)

½ ounce fresh lemon juice

Tonic (we prefer Fever-Tree)

Lavender sprig, gently crushed

In a 12-ounce cup, combine the gin, lavender agave, and lemon juice. Add ice, and top with tonic. Garnish with the lavender sprig.

NOTE: To make lavender agave, steep 1½ tablespoons lavender in 1 cup boiling hot water for about 30 minutes. Strain, discarding lavender, and stir in 1 cup agave syrup. Store the lavender agave in an airtight container in the refrigerator for up to 3 months.

Suzanne & Michelle Rousseau

RESTAURATEURS, AUTHORS,
TELEVISION PERSONALITIES
KINGSTON, JAMAICA

How would you describe your work?

MICHELLE: We are storytellers. Our purpose here is to document, trace, and retell lost stories of the past but also of people and individuals who are kind of unseen, unknown, unvoiced, undocumented, because that's a lot of the tradition of, the legacy of the Caribbean cuisine. It has come so much from oral traditions that were handed down and spoken and taught hand to hand. So for us, whether it's from a culinary perspective or whether it's from an experience in the restaurant or whether it's from television work we have done or when we write, what we perceive ourselves as doing is retracing and retelling a lot of those stories and converting them into a visceral experience so that you're not just talking about something from an academic perspective, but you're

almost embodying what those things are in a way that's modern and relevant to how we live today.

SUZANNE: Part of what we do very well is that we curate and—for lack of a better word—cultivate a lifestyle experience that we feel is "elevated Caribbean." I think for a lot of people and for many years, from an external perspective, the Caribbean is seen through a very limited lens, and that lens tends oftentimes to be brought down to Rasta, weed, beach cocktails—this very touristic sort of perspective and sometimes this very street culture, sort of reggae perspective. And really, there is so much more to the experience of being a Caribbean woman or a West Indian woman.

Part of what we have learned that we are able to do is translate or cultivate or create not only a narrative but the actual lifestyle that has for many, many generations been limited to a very one-dimensional school. And I think that is taking into account a feminine and female lens, but also experiencing and exploring the beauty and the softness and the other sides of what it is to be West Indian and Caribbean through the way we live, through the way we eat, through the way we entertain, through the way we speak— all these other things. All of the vehicles through which we work are just supporting that creation and that storytelling.

Can you tell me how you began in your field, and also, can you tell me about the vehicles through which you work?

MICHELLE: We are both arts majors. I have an undergrad in Spanish literature and history with a master's in Latin American studies from the University of Salamanca in

Spain, and Suzanne is an undergrad in English with a minor in art history. When we left school, we knew we wanted to come home.

Before I came home, Suzanne was working with my mother, who is an interior designer. She had a beautiful showroom, and Suzanne took over bridal registry and art exhibits and all sorts of stuff. And then my mother, in her decorating space—which was a lovely, old Caribbean home in the heart of Kingston that had big verandas—she wanted to do a café and our aunt was to run it—and at the last minute decided not to do it.

And she said, "Well, you girls are here every day. Why don't you do it?" So what began as a coffee shop, with just coffee . . . and then I said, "Well, when we travel, where we eat, the cafés and the salad and sandwich bars, that doesn't exist in Jamaica, so we want to do that." The store was called Ciao Bella, and the café was called Café Bella, and we still serve some of those dishes today, like our pumpkin soup, our marlin tartine.

The French embassy was next door. They came, and they ate every day in droves. It was just so immediately successful that we decided to evolve into a full restaurant with the nighttime fine dining. We went off to the Culinary Institute of America, we did some courses, and had Restaurant Ciao Bella and Café Bella, which over time became an off-premises catering company.

But we always wanted to do a book, and we had been for ten years planning the trajectory of writing our book— and I'll let Suzanne take over for the latter manifestations. But I was living in Montego Bay at the time, running an eighteenth-century sugar estate that was also on a cultural historical tour. I had an opportunity to come to New York to do a yoga teacher training, and I decided to take a leave of absence, and there we met Joy, our literary agent.

SUZANNE: It was always about "How do we do more than just cooking?" We had a desire to do more, contribute more, and really pursue our own natural inclinations, which was a book [*Caribbean Potluck: Modern Recipes from Our Family Kitchen*], and we had always been interested in television.

And at the same time as the book, we went ahead and filmed a series of pilots for television and decided, "Let's just try and do it ourselves." And similarly, through all of these people that Michelle met, and people we've met in TV in New York, they gave us the same advice: "You guys are the voice. You are who we want to hear—your perspective."

MICHELLE: It was in that period, that we then produced two seasons of our own television show in Jamaica called *Two Sisters and a Meal*, which was us exploring the island and telling stories about people, food, and culture, but through

our perspective, things that interest us being our very natural selves, which was incredibly joyful and educational.

That led into this very big chunk of time when we were writing for magazines, and then our second book, *Provisions: The Roots of Caribbean Cooking*, and then we did two episodes of a local TV show, and we did a web series for the tourist board. And then, lo and behold, a film company out of LA heard us on an NPR interview with *All Things Considered* for the first book, and they approached us about pitching us for an international or overseas program, and then we ended up getting signed with the Travel Channel and doing a pilot with them, which actually aired. It was called *Island Hopping*, and it was basically having us travel the islands of the world to tell these similar stories.

So we've had a lot of different iterations of our career, none of which really were planned. They all fed onto one another, and they all made us grow and learn so much because every time you go into a new field, the skills and talent of the other things sort of play out.

SUZANNE: Especially if you're women in business, people will always try to define you and put you in a box as to what you do. And that's just not the truth of the human experience. We're all multidimensional. We all have capacities to do many things, and why not explore everything if you can?

Everything doesn't need to be successful. That's not the purpose of it. The success is from the learning that you get, even if it never becomes anything bigger. That entire process—going through that vulnerability of learning something new and stretching yourself and growing into something—is actually a part of what defines us.

What are some of your favorite things to eat or drink?
SUZANNE: Well, to drink it's wine and Champagne.
MICHELLE: All day bubbles, yeah. We like the same kinds of food, that's the thing—which is why the food side of the business is always so easy because we actually like to eat and drink the same.
SUZANNE: Green olives, olive oil, tomato, good bread. An Italian thin-crust brick-oven pizza. A really, really good hamburger.
MICHELLE: Any fresh herbs—loads of fresh herbs on everything.
SUZANNE: And I love ackee. One of my favorite things would be a typical Jamaican breakfast: ackee and saltfish, plantain, a piece of avocado, roast breadfruit, and johnnycakes. That plate of traditional Jamaican breakfast to me is like heaven.

Passion Martini

BY SUZANNE AND MICHELLE ROUSSEAU / MAKES 4 SERVINGS

We prefer to use fresh passion fruit in this cocktail recipe, and you can likely find passion fruit in your local Caribbean grocery store and many specialty grocers, but if you can't find it you can use passion fruit juice (about 4 ounces) instead.

4 fresh passion fruit, halved and pulped

4 ounces coconut rum

2 ounces good-quality vodka

2 ounces simple syrup

1 ounce freshly squeezed lime juice

Rose petals, for garnish

Combine the passion fruit pulp, rum, vodka, simple syrup, and lime juice in a shaker. Add ice and shake vigorously. Strain into martini glasses and garnish with rose petals.

Island Greens

WITH AVOCADO, MINT, AND MANGO

BY SUZANNE AND MICHELLE ROUSSEAU / MAKES 8–10 SERVINGS

MANGO VINAIGRETTE

½ cup mango puree, preferably fresh

⅓ cup white cane vinegar or apple cider vinegar

1 teaspoon dijon mustard

1 garlic clove, minced

⅔ cup extra-virgin olive oil

Salt and white pepper

SALAD

1 pound mixed greens

Handful of mint and cilantro leaves

1 ripe mango, peeled and thinly sliced

¼ small red onion, thinly sliced

1 cucumber, peeled and julienned

1 red bell pepper, cored, seeded, and julienned

1 ripe avocado, peeled, pitted, and sliced

4 ounces feta cheese, crumbled

Freshly cracked black pepper

Salted plantain chips for garnish

For the vinaigrette, whisk together the mango puree, vinegar, mustard, and garlic. In a steady stream, gradually add the oil, whisking constantly until the mixture thickens and emulsifies. Season with salt and white pepper.

For the salad, arrange the greens on a chilled platter or individual plates. Top with cilantro, mint, mango, onion, cucumber, bell pepper, and avocado. Sprinkle with feta and black pepper. Just before serving, drizzle the salad with a liberal amount of mango vinaigrette and garnish with the plantain chips.

(Alternatively, combine all of the salad ingredients in a large bowl, toss with vinaigrette, and garnish with plantain chips.)

Korsha Wilson

WRITER AND HOST OF *A HUNGRY SOCIETY* PODCAST
NEW YORK, NEW YORK

How would you describe your work?

I would describe my work as part observation, part documentation. It's partially how I see the world as a Black woman in food, but also documenting the dope, amazing work that Black people are doing in food.

How did you begin in your field?

I decided I wanted to be a food writer at ten years old after finding a *Saveur* magazine in our Borders bookstore in Maryland. And I didn't know what that meant. I was just like, "I love this magazine that has pictures of food and people from all over the world."

I had no idea what that actually looked like or entailed, but I thought I'm going to both culinary school and then journalism school. (And obviously, you don't have to do that.)

So I started writing for free for an alternative newspaper in Boston when I was in journalism school, and I began working in restaurants, and I absolutely loved that. And basically I just built up enough clips until I could . . . Actually I made the jump to freelance before I fully had enough clients to sustain a freelance career.

But that pushed me to keep jobs on the side. I worked for a tech startup. I worked as a cheesemaker. I'll say that I didn't really see a path for what I was doing until I started to talk about my own experiences in the restaurant scene. Writing about the ways in which I was passed over for promotions or guests would say outlandish stuff to me. That's when I really started to find my place in food writing. It's been a long journey but I feel very lucky.

How do you take care of your mental health and deal with the stresses of your work?

Definitely by taking a break from social media. Which means that sometimes I don't post as much or someone will be like, "Hey, did you see this?" And I'm like, "No, I didn't." But that's just for keeping myself mentally okay. But also doing the specific kinds of stories that I do, where I talk to people about maybe something that happened to them or something that's totally heavy, that requires me to do the work and then go do something fun. So I'll go to the park or my husband and I will go out to dinner. Just having those firm boundaries in place with work has been incredibly important.

What advice would you offer to someone who wants to do what you do?

Something I always tell aspiring writers is, "If you don't see your particular take or point of view represented it doesn't mean that there's not space for it . . . That is a clue that you are on the right path, and you're seeing something that's missing and you should add it to the landscape."

How do you define success?

I was thinking about this recently, because I was talking to [Chef] Omar [Tate] actually about the word "freedom." What does freedom mean to me? To me freedom is the ability to do what you want when you want. I think that's what success is too. I want to take a week off and go to Senegal. If you're able to do that and make that decision for yourself, that's success. Not having other people make demands on your time, but getting to do what you want and what you love.

What are some of your favorite things to eat or drink?

It depends on the day, but I mean, I'm always a fan of french fries. They're one of my favorite all-time things to eat, and oysters.

Rasheeda Purdie

CHEF, FOUNDER OF RAMEN
BY RĀ *NEW YORK, NEW YORK*

How would you describe your work?

I would actually say it's innovative. It's really something that I have never put together on a regular basis. But as an African American woman, all I eat is either soul food or Asian food. And I merged them together. So I really think that my food speaks volumes about being innovative and stepping outside the box as much as I can tastefully and respectfully.

Tell me about Ramen by Rā, the business you birthed during the pandemic; what was your inspiration?

Well, I birthed Ramen by Rā very early on in the pandemic due to a lack of restaurants or ramen restaurants being open. So it was a bittersweet transition for me, where I just took the skills and the knowledge that I have as a chef and wanted to make ramen that can either be close to what I'm used to or better. And because I feel I put my own spin on it, it gives me some familiar ingredients, tastes, influences from the soul food, and I'm just mixing it with Asian food. And the inspiration comes from all over, whether it's from being here in New York, eating Chinese food, eating Thai food, eating so many different layers of Asian food as a woman and as a foodie. And then having this time off, I wanted to spend my time wisely.

So I geared myself toward more reading, more documentary watching. I sat there and literally read David Chang's books, got some inspiration from him, even when it came down to connecting to the mindset of a chef. And also, Ivan Ramen, and just all these different books that I would take in one layer after another. And you know how you buy one book and then there's plenty of recommendations that come with it. I would start to just guide myself toward the recommendation list. And then I would gear myself toward some documentaries.

Honestly, during the pandemic, it was very slow, quiet, and still . . . in a nutshell, it became an opportunity for me to slow down for things to taste better. And coming from such busy restaurants, where you have to move so fast—"I need this on the fly"—but I had to do the very opposite.

I grew myself into a chef that takes her time now. As an American, I had to readjust all that I've learned to create a stillness and experience that you will love. So, my favorite is collard greens, and no one wants to rush those. You really want to take your time with that, whether it's the meat, the ingredients, the collard greens themself. So I just had to really understand like, okay, it goes the same with certain ingredients and recipes in Asian cultures. And it just became such a phenomenal experience for me. There's inspiration everywhere, but I can definitely say during this time of stillness, being at home, those books and Amazon Prime really came in handy.

"My mission is for you to enjoy my journey one slurp at a time."

How did you begin in the food space?

I began as a student at the Institute of Culinary Education. I was a fashion stylist when I moved here to New York, twelve years ago. After eight or nine years of doing it, I went to culinary school because I love going out to eat so much. And whether it was a fashion show or just happy hour, I was centered around food all the time. So that's where the influence from food came from. And then when I was at Henri Bendel for that last two to three years, I was in culinary school while working full time.

Around 2015, 2016, I was a full-time stylist at Henri Bendel, a part-time student at ICE, and a part-time intern at the Cecil with Chef JJ [Johnson]. So I had absolutely no days off for a whole year and a half. And the transition from fashion to food, it was something that I said, okay, I'm going to dive into it full time. And that's what I did.

I made sure I paid down all of my debt through school, through the fashion industry, saved up all of my money. Then I knew that money wasn't coming in anymore. I knew that lifestyle was over, but I wanted to take the lump sum that I was making to put toward my future so that I could really focus on learning in the kitchen without that debt as a burden on me. And I'm very fortunate for that. I really didn't have that debt weighing on me. And whether it was through Chef JJ or Chef Marcus [Samuelsson], I was running around for like a whole two to three years, just taking up opportunities, saying yes to everything so that I could really get that culinary experience early on.

What advice would you offer to someone who wants to do what you do?

My advice would be do your homework, do your research initially, because you want to make sure you cross your t's and dot your i's. We are living in a sensitive world where you just want to make sure you are aware of what you're diving into. And ask questions. Like my best advice is the same advice that people have given me. Don't be afraid to ask questions. Don't be afraid to ask people of the culture that you're diving into, how do they feel about other people diving into their cuisines? What makes more sense for everyone to understand it respectfully? I definitely would say that's the initial step, because you want to make sure you represent not only something else great and top notch, but you want to come off like that too. And without that, you really can't say you've done it in a way that is appreciation. And you just want to make sure you come off as good as your food.

Do you have a mission or motto, and if so, what is it?

My mission is for you to enjoy my journey one slurp at a time. And that's my motto. And I don't know how I came up with that.

What are some of your favorite things to eat or drink? I know what one of them is.

Ramen and crabs. I still am a Maryland girl at heart.

Watermelon Poke

WITH TERIYAKI SAUCE TOPPED WITH SHICHIMI TOGARASHI

BY RĀSHEEDA PURDIE / MAKES 6 SERVINGS

TERIYAKI SAUCE

1 cup low-sodium soy sauce

1 teaspoon grated fresh ginger

2 garlic cloves, minced

6–8 tablespoons dark brown sugar

2–3 tablespoons honey

4 tablespoons cornstarch

SHICHIMI TOGARASHI

1 tablespoon dried orange peel

1 tablespoon red pepper flakes

1 tablespoon white sesame seeds

1 tablespoon black sesame seeds

1 teaspoon Sichuan peppercorns

1 teaspoon ground ginger

1 nori sheet, crumbled

WATERMELON POKE

1 small- to medium-size watermelon

Scallion greens, cut in very thin strips

NOTE: To make scallion curls, place the very thinly cut scallion strips in a small bowl of ice water for 5 to 8 minutes and remove them and drain on a paper towel once they have curled.

My inspiration for this recipe draws from my love for watermelon and the sea. As sweet and juicy as watermelon is, it's also the perfect fruit to absorb great flavor while marinating. To balance out the sweetness, one might add salt, but I prefer to use soy, and to add a little hint of spice I prefer using togarashi. Togarashi is a Japanese spice blend of chili flakes, sesame seeds, orange zest, and seaweed, and it's best known to add umami to any dish with just a sprinkle.

Adding both soy and togarashi to watermelon breaks the natural flavors down and makes it more savory. It also changes the texture, making it more "meaty-like" or "tuna-like," and that's how we get "poke." This recipe is not only good for summer, it's also a great way to create vegan sushi. You can pair this watermelon poke with steamed rice and nori, for an even more flavorful bite. And you can use leftover togarashi sprinkled on top of rice, fish, salads, eggs, udon noodles, and grilled meats.

For the teriyaki sauce, combine the soy sauce, ginger, garlic, brown sugar, and honey with 2 cups water in medium saucepan. Heat, stirring, over medium heat until simmering. Whisk the cornstarch into ½ cup water, and whisk the mixture into the simmering sauce. Cook, stirring, until thickened as desired. Set aside to cool. Makes 3 cups.

For the shichimi togarashi, combine the orange peel, pepper flakes, sesame seeds, and peppercorns in a spice grinder or mini food processor. Grind to a fine texture. Transfer to a small jar, add the ginger powder, cover tightly, and shake to mix.

For the poke, cut the watermelon flesh into ½- to ¾-inch cubes. Place the cubes in a bowl, pour 1 to 2 tablespoons of the teriyaki sauce over them, and gently mix well. Cover and marinate in the refrigerator for at least a few hours and as long as overnight.

To serve, spoon the watermelon poke onto individual plates, sprinkle with shichimi togarashi and crumbled nori, and garnish with scallion curls. (Refrigerate the leftover teriyaki sauce for another use—the teriyaki sauce will keep for up to a year in the refrigerator.)

Gabrielle E. W. Carter

CULTURAL PRESERVATIONIST,
CO-FOUNDER TALL GRASS
FOOD BOX CSA *FAIRFAX,
NORTH CAROLINA*

How would you describe your work?

I am a cultural preservationist and I feel like there's a lot of explanation in that title, but maybe not. The core of my work is to preserve and to honor the work that our foremothers and forefathers did in the way of agriculture, seed keeping, and our historic foodways, especially here in Eastern North Carolina. And so, it looks a lot of different ways because it involves textile, and print, and fabric.

Food is really the heart of it. So, of course, if we're cooking food we're growing food because it's about the relationship to the seed. It's about the relationship to the land. And so, my personal journey has been moving back home to Eastern North Carolina to preserve our little lot of land with our garden on it . . . My way of honoring that is naming it and fortifying it, so I just got a high tunnel on our property, being intentional about planting, about seed banking, and about preserving stories and oral

histories, so I've been archiving our oral history through video and audio since 2015.

I was having suppers also in the garden, and then our shop at the back of the house, which is my grandfather's mechanic shop, is to become a pickup for our CSA, and it's just a creative hub, so we've screened movies in there, and we're really just reimagining the space. My grandfather's still here. He's eighty-five. He's still building grills and working on parts, and welding stuff in the corner.

Cultural preservation can look a lot of different ways. I think right now I'm focusing on trying to build out a framework so that other people can apply it to their own mediums and their own art. But for me, it's always been fashion and food at their intersection, and so that's become textiles and growing the things that I'm going to make into fabric, or that I'm going to dye my fabric with, that might become a table linen for dinner where you learn about the stories on the land.

How did you begin in your field?

A couple of instances drew me home. I was working in New York with Chef JJ Johnson and I was coming back and forth as much as I could. I was super homesick, and I was also working on this grain project with him, which became his restaurant, Field Trip. But at that time, it was just something that was in development. Because rice is culture, and it was just a lot of crazy research and rabbit holes. So, I was learning about African grains and the things that travel down to South Carolina and even to North Carolina up the coast, but more of my own family's history was coming up.

So, my great-uncle Herbert, who is my grandfather's eldest brother, he remembers his grandfather John growing this red rice in the yard, and that to me was like an epiphany. I know it doesn't sound like much, but when you bring something

home that is the focus of your work and then an elder in your family has a connection to it and has a story for it—it was like, "Oh, this is why this is so important to me and I didn't even know this history." And so, every time I would come home I was learning more. I was learning how to make wine and how to ferment. I was learning all of these beautiful food traditions I never even knew were a part of my own food culture as a Black woman in the South.

And so, it was just so enriching, because I know you know French cuisine and Italian cuisine is so revered and so romanticized, and I love French food and I love Italian food, but I didn't know I had my own rich culture at home. So to come home and be like we are, saving seeds, and that's a part of our culture, especially for women, which I didn't know. And just the metaphorical value of seed saving is almost too much. It's just so beautiful. And then, to literally have this act of remembering this ritual that you have to be intentional about because it takes time, and so it's about intention, it's about patience, it's about the knowledge and the passing of the knowledge. And so, my first interaction with seed saving was my grandfather hanging collard seeds under our shed to dry, and I just wanted to take that, like these pods, to put on my table, because I was doing little dinner parties and things in Brooklyn.

I was really drawn to what it looked like, and so I was asking all these questions like, what is that? And Pop was just very casually telling me this thing that he's been doing and knew about because it's been passed for generations. You have to know when to harvest this thing, and how to dry it, and then this is how you mill it out of its hole. It was really eye-opening for me to even know that it was something that we've been doing for generations that would've been lost to my family had I not been asking questions because I found it visually interesting.

I was already keeping a journal about just my new interest in land and gardening. Summers prior I'd been picking okra and salad out in the garden with my grandfather and my uncles, and so I was journaling about this because I was finding myself more and more interested in my role in that, being something that my family doesn't stop doing, because my grandfather's eighty-five. And so, in the beginning it wasn't this big thing that was like I'll be the next one to carry it forward. It wasn't that.

It was just the genuine interest in learning about my own culture and our own foodways, and our own stories, like learning why I'm so interested in the things, and why I'm good at these things. It's like I'm really naturally good at fermenting things. I have a nose for fermentation. You

know? I have a love and a passion for sewing with a pattern and cutting things, and I always have since I was a child, and then I find out I had this rich lineage of women and men who knew how to sew and cut patterns.

And I was hearing all these names I never heard before, and learning about all this medicine that was in our yard that I never even knew existed, walking on top of things that actually were used at one point as medicine.

And so, it just opened my world up and it really pulls me away from seeking other folks' validation or what they felt was culture, or what was being lifted up by others. It was really like I want to lift this up because it's mine, and then finding community around that, right? And seeing other people's eyes light up when they learn about their own rich history because they have roots in the South, even if they aren't physically here.

What are you most proud of?

I think the relationships that I'm building with my family, and with my community. I think connecting people to their lineage, and their heritage, and their culture through food is always something that is super gratifying and just fun and makes you feel warm when people are like, "Oh my god, you made me want to talk to my grandma, and now I know that we have such and such land they were going to sell." It's things like that. It's just been really grounding for me.

I think I'm proud of myself and my ability to listen to myself, and to listen to my ancestors and the people who were calling me from the other side, who were telling me that it was time to come home, even when it didn't seem like it was time to come home. Everything that I was told growing up and believed was that you need to be in New York, or you need to be in San Francisco, or you need to be in one of these cities, not in no Apex, North Carolina.

"My personal journey has been moving back home to Eastern North Carolina to preserve our little lot of land with our garden on it."

Krystal Mack

INTERDISCIPLINARY
ARTIST, BAKER, WRITER
BALTIMORE, MARYLAND

How would you describe your work?

I would describe my work as interdisciplinary, but also . . . I would say new diasporic, which isn't really a term I've heard before but I'm making it up. It just means exploring food through the lens of my being a second-generation descendant of the Great Migration but also a Black American, also a woman, also a person who lives in the mid-Atlantic. I feel like all of those are influences, and I guess in a way that's what I mean when I say "new diasporic." I'm still a part of the diaspora, but my lens is from someone who's been out in the world, from the continent, and processing my experiences through that life of being outside of the continent and so far removed from it and not necessarily feeling comfortable enough to call it "home," but knowing that's where my roots are, in a sense. So it's a take on my history, I guess, but kind of reworking it into what it means to me personally today.

How did you begin in the food and hospitality space?

Well, with food, I guess I started as a consumer just like anyone else, just eating at restaurants and going to food festivals and stuff like that. And then over time, I was like, "This is expensive." I need to learn how to cook on my own, because there are things that I know I can make at home if I just dedicated time and practice to it, so I did that. But then also, in the process of going out and eating out, I developed type 2 diabetes. I still looked the same way I look now, but I was a type 2 diabetic, probably a little bit skinnier, and I also had high cholesterol. It was kind of just a combination of "Okay. Well, I want to cook better, and I also want to take care of my body, so let me explore food through that lens of healthy cooking—but food that is culturally appropriate for where I am and also being a city dweller and also being a Black person who loves good food."

The more I started cooking for myself and the more I started reading, the more I was like, "Damn. I would love to do this all the time—like, cook all the time." So I started applying to restaurants in the Baltimore area, and no one would hire me because I had no experience. And then finally, I applied to be a french-fry counter girl at this French bistro that was opening up here in Baltimore. It's now closed, unfortunately, but it was called Le Garage, and I wrote the cheesiest, most passionate cover letter you could write to be a french-fry counter girl. I was like, "I love fries, and da da da da da." I think even at the time my Instagram name was FriesB4Guys.

But I got the job, and actually they called me and were like, "Why don't you come in and be our garde manger?" and I was like, "Ooh, okay!" While I was there I learned a lot about the cold side and just desserts, but I also learned about the toxicity of the restaurant industry and hospitality.

"Being honest with yourself about what you need is a form of love and self-care."

It was really crazy. I had a chef who was a white woman. She was the head chef, and she was so awful to me. She was super disrespectful. I'll never forget one time, she even was yelling my name so loud during service that the owner of the restaurant had to come and say, "You can't yell Krystal's name this loud. We can hear it on the floor. It's really getting crazy."

Who were some of your mentors and role models within the food and hospitality space?

In the food space, I would say Miesha Taylor. She is a legendary agricultural phenom in the mid-Atlantic. I would also say Aliyah Fraser, who is no longer in

Baltimore. She's now in Lake Trinidad. But they are both really amazing organizers and community advocates, especially when it comes to urban farming in the Baltimore area—or just urban farming in Black communities.

Obviously, Ashtin Berry. I feel like there's no one person who is doing work in hospitality like Ashtin, and there is not one Black woman in food who can't say that Ashtin's work has not touched them, in a way, and made them question their role. I think she made me question myself and my intentions and the way that I show up in a space, and also to be very clear about who I am and what it is that I do.

How have you examined what you most love about food to create the work that you do now?

The end goal of my art practice is to discover who exactly it is that I am in this world, heal and recover from the trauma that I've experienced in the world as a Black woman just living—and that could be just from my experiences in hospitality, my experience as a survivor of sexual violence, my experience as a survivor of domestic violence as a child. All of these things, my experience as a disabled person. I think for people to think that you go to therapy once and then that's it, for me, my work is almost an extension of that. It is an art practice that is an art therapy practice.

It's everything that I do every day that allows me to express in a way that I can't really do otherwise, other than experiencing and living it every day. So a recipe that I create is probably something that I genuinely eat, like, every day. I really try to dive deeper into the *why* I'm eating this and how this seems to me and how does that ironically or coincidentally tie into the symbolism that I'm using it for. I don't try to pull things out of the air to make it socially relevant. I guess I just more so try to follow what's happening on the inside with me and let that be my guide, and I find that when I do that it does speak to, I will say, the community. But I feel like it does speak to the community in a way that feels genuine, because at the end of the day we are all traumatized people living in a supremacist, capitalist, patriarchal society.

I think that even if you are a white man looking at my work and you understand that you are a traumatized person, you can see some element of yourself in the work that I do. Even though you may not at first glance realize that it's for you, if you were to take a closer look and intentionally engage with what I'm creating, then you might see that it is for you.

How did you go about the process of transitioning from working full time in hospitality?

That transition was mostly just about listening to what it was that I need and then looking around to see if there was anyone available doing what it was that I needed, and I saw that no one was, and I was like, "Cool. I'm going to do it, and initially it's not going to be necessarily something for others." I don't do pop-ups like that. I don't do all those other things because that's not what this is about. This is not about getting money from folks. It's more about me living in my truth, living my example, and then showing other folks, like, "Hey. You can do this too." It doesn't necessarily have to serve the end goal of a pop-up or a dinner or something.

I think as food professionals we get really caught up in the idea that there has to be something that everyone can enjoy, and they have to enjoy it at a table, around the table, with you—and that's not true. That's not how food always has to be consumed. Sometimes it can be consumed in a poem. Sometimes it can be consumed in a recipe that doesn't require me to make it for them.

It's kind of like the idea that you can't pour from an empty cup, so we should be pouring into ourselves first, and if that doesn't look like being a chef on a line, that's okay. That's not what this relationship should always be about. That's no shade to chefs, but I think even with chefs there should be—you hear about chefs all the time who their favorite thing to cook at home is a one-pot meal because they get tired of cooking like that. They don't want to cook. They've been cooking all day, and I think that kind of makes me sad, because the joy that cooking brings you, you can't really fully save a space for yourself.

And that is not what is encouraged in this industry. In hospitality, you are supposed to be so giving, and if you're not then it's not good service. It's called hospitality, and that's like, if you're so giving beyond yourself, then you are very hospitable and you are the standard. I think that is so sad, because we should be reserving 10 percent for ourselves—even more than that.

So I think that transition, to me, just makes sense. I thank God I had the balls to do it, and I also thank God that I was in a place where for the most part people were open and accepting of it. I definitely got some eye rolls when I was like, "I'm an artist." People were like, "Ugh. Okay."

So it's just like, I'm going to take up space in this way. I'm going to call myself an artist. You can roll your eyes, but I'm actually doing it for us.

What is the biggest lesson you've learned about money, compensation, or finance so far in your working life?

Being honest with yourself about what you need is a form of love and self-care.

Love yourself enough to look into your own future and know that you'll be here in the future, hopefully, and be able to say, "Okay. I wasn't tripping when I asked for that amount," or "I'm glad I asked for that amount." I think I'm always proud of myself when I can look back and be like, "Damn. I definitely looked out for me in that moment. Shout out to past me for that."

What are some of your favorite things to eat or drink?

A tomato with sea salt and olive oil, and a side of aloe vera water.

Hibiscus Honey-Mustard Salmon

BY KRYSTAL MACK / MAKES 4 SERVINGS

HIBISCUS HONEY

8 ounces dried hibiscus flowers

8 ounces raw honey, preferably clover or wildflower

SALMON

2 pounds skinless salmon fillet

⅓ cup whole-grain mustard

¼ cup hibiscus honey

4 garlic cloves, minced

Grated zest of ½ lime

2 tablespoons freshly squeezed lime juice

¼ teaspoon smoked paprika

½ teaspoon kosher salt

¼ teaspoon freshly ground black pepper

1 or 2 scallions, trimmed and thinly sliced on the bias

2 tablespoons chopped fresh cilantro

This recipe pays homage to my family's Carolina roots with a mustard-based sauce that gets its sweetness from an herbal honey. Hibiscus, known as sorrel in the Caribbean, is used in plant medicine for its diuretic and antimicrobial properties. The hibiscus honey takes 6 to 8 hours to prepare, so make it a day in advance. You will have about ¾ cup left after making the salmon. Use the extra hibiscus honey to sweeten lemonade and iced tea. It will keep when stored in a cool, dark place. If you're crunched for time or can't find hibiscus, the recipe works fine with plain old honey.

For the honey, in a small pot, combine the hibiscus flowers and 1 cup water and simmer until the volume is reduced by more than half, about ¼ cup. Use a strainer to strain out the hibiscus. Pour the hibiscus liquid into a small bowl and stir in the honey to combine; stir continuously until the honey and hibiscus liquid are combined. Transfer to a covered storage container for up to 1 month in the refrigerator.

For the salmon, preheat the oven to 425°F.

In a bowl, whisk together the mustard, hibiscus honey, garlic, zest, juice, paprika, salt, and pepper.

Place the salmon on a parchment-lined sheet pan, and spread the honey mixture evenly over it. Roast until just flaky and still moist, 10 to 15 minutes. Sprinkle with scallions and cilantro, and serve.

Kaylah Thomas

CHEF *ANCHORAGE, ALASKA*

How would you describe your work?

I'm a person who was taught to cook and bake before I even hit twenty, before I even got into the real world of actually being in these kitchens and bakeries where they're intense. So I feel like I'm a very sustainable baker or sustainable chef. I guess I would say sustainable because I've lived a life growing up [in Alaska] where my parents will get a bang for their buck, where we would harvest in August to get prepared for the winter because my parents had six kids—just having to feed mouths and to get through the winter, and everything's expensive in Alaska when it comes to food.

We would pick and harvest for like a whole day in August. And we would preserve, and cook, and all this, and vacuum seal it all, and I still have that mindset to this day. "What can we do with this beet salad that's not selling anymore, and turn it into beet hummus?" And being a person that doesn't like to throw anything out if we can do something with it. That's how I've been with baking, and that's how I am in the kitchen. And I think that describes me best as a chef.

You were born and raised in Alaska. What were you harvesting?

We are known for having the best root vegetables because our soil is so cold, and that makes everything nice and sweet. So tons of carrots, tons of potatoes, rutabaga, and also collard greens and kale like no other. The berries— raspberries, strawberries, blueberries.

What did you want to do when you were a kid?

I want to say by eleven I knew I wanted to be a chef. I wanted to have my own place and to just create these dishes that I saw my grandma make. She was a chef herself in Alaska, and I'd see what she did with many different things in Southern and non-Southern cooking.

My mom created a neighborhood candy store at our garage, and people really enjoyed having homemade Rice Krispie Treats or brownies. She would have the other candy too, but she would try to make something with it and it brought happiness. And that's me being a Libra, I am all about happiness and love. So that is what I've always wanted to do, is contribute to the community as a chef.

What do you most enjoy about your career?

I enjoy getting to create so many different new things. I'm a science girl to the max. So when I get to make some pie dough that has garnet seeds [amaranth] in it, and make it to where it tastes almost like graham cracker crust dough, that makes me super excited. Stuff like that—and just putting happiness into somebody's belly.

What are some of your favorite things to eat or drink?

I'm not a picky person. But I do love casseroles or any- thing that's comforting . . . and my new thing is natural wine. Or sangrias.

Georgia Silvera Seamans

TEA SOMMELIER *NEW YORK, NEW YORK*

What made you want to start your blog, *Notes on Tea***?**

I started the blog when I was in graduate school, and that was one of the ways, one of my strategies for decompressing. I guess now you would call it a "self-care strategy." I treated it like a journal. It was just a way for me to make or keep notes about the teas that I was drinking, the tea places (as in tea shops) I was visiting, and then also the experiences I was having with friends around drinking tea.

Then, as I moved along on the tea path, the tea blog more and more became a way for me to systematically review teas I was drinking, and then that was a way for tea companies to get in touch with me, and they started sending me teas with the hopes that I would review them.

Tell me about your connection with tea.

I'm a daily tea drinker, and growing up in Jamaica (the island, not the borough, not Jamaica, Queens), my mom—like, we drank black tea, some sort of tea bag black tea, and I don't even remember the brand. Then my mom also made what I now know to be tisanes, and these were herbal teas made from plants that you'd grow in your yard or you'd get at the market. They were usually for if you were sick, and depending on how you were sick—whether it was a headache or a tummyache or a cold or a fever—you would drink different teas.

So I grew up drinking hot tea, and then when we moved to the United States, it was still tea bags, but it was definitely more of a black tea thing or maybe mint tea, and it wasn't the sort of herbs that you would pick from your yard. It was all a grocery store kind of tea situation.

Then when I moved to Berkeley, California, that was my first introduction to loose-leaf tea, primarily from China and Taiwan. And that was how I got into this whole idea that you put loose leaves in a vessel that had a name like Gaiwan or Yixing teapot. And then the fact that you had green tea, oolong, different kinds of oolong; that you would never put boiling water on top of a green tea.

And then I took a class, a tea sommelier class—I don't even like to say that because it sounds so pretentious. But I took it with a couple of friends, we started taking the class in 2015, and I think we finally wrapped it up in 2017 because it was a self-paced class, and so it really did take us that long to finish it.

"Tea . . . shows the good that people can do and the absolute worst and evil of humanity."

What are some of the more surprising things you learned in your tea sommelier course?

So I knew this before going into the tea somm course, but I think this is something that a surprisingly large number of people think, that the teas they are drinking are coming from different kinds of plants. But tea—not herbal teas or tisanes—but tea is just coming from one plant, *Camellia sinensis*. And it's really then about how the tea is produced that's then giving you that variety of white, green, oolong, black tea, pu-erh, hojicha. It's really just this one plant, and people have found a way to produce a diversity of flavor and leaf style just through production.

There are other things like terroir [which is] soil type, climate, where you are in the mountain—are you on the south side, or are you at the top with the mist and the clouds; there are cultivars that also play a large role in flavor too. But it's really this one plant, and then it fingers out from there. So that was really reinforced in the tea sommelier class.

I think people think of tea as being a very meditative practice, you know. You're drinking the tea and there's this swirl of the steam, but there's been so much political intrigue in tea. It's a very colonial crop, and there is a lot of theft and espionage that's part of the history of tea. If you think of Britain's role in India and Sri Lanka, you also think of Britain's role in China and how they went in and stole the tea plant and then created tea economies in their colonies.

Tea, I think, like so many other food crops, shows the good that people can do and the absolute worst and evil of humanity, and I think that came to light in the tea studies.

I think we can follow plants through their movement between countries and use that as a way to learn about how humans have treated one another over time.

So plants are benign, right? They don't have any kind of a moral center. But when you start to dive into the history of plants and how we come to, for example, consume them, the ways that we treat others come into full light.

I think maybe in the West you think about the traumatic history of rice production or cotton production under slavery, but there are similar histories with so many of our food crops and things that we consume daily and that we assume just come to us without any kind of baggage, without any trauma, without any death. Like chocolate. You eat it and feel so good, but then when you think about chocolate production you think to yourself, "How can I eat this and feel so good when it's come to me on a trail of human impoverishment, human slavery, and all the sorts of evil that people can do to one another?"

It's not that I want to stop drinking tea or eating chocolate, but I think we need to think more about the ethics of our food and what we're willing to ignore in order to enjoy ourselves and feel pleasure. And a big part of what's come out for me studying tea is an awareness of where these taken-for-granted foods come from—because I think there are the obvious ones, and then there are the ones that go under the radar.

Do you ever or have you ever experimented with using tea in any food preparations?

Oh, I have. I have baked quite a bit with matcha, and a lot of those were sweets—either a sweet drink or a sweet dessert. Matcha is pretty versatile. It's one of the easier teas to cook with. I have also eaten tea leaves—and particularly green tea. So once I have brewed a pot with leaves, then if I'm doing something that's rice based I will just add those tea leaves to the rice. Mostly if I was doing a rice dish that was savory, so anything that would involve mushrooms and soy sauce or savory greens, like maybe bok choy or something. Green tea leaves I find to be . . . they're either sort of nutty, or they have a sweetness to them, so I think it complements savory rice dishes. And it's not this big flavor, right? It's not. It's part of the mix.

Karis Jagger & Fabienne Toback

PRODUCERS OF *HIGH ON THE HOG* DOCUMENTARY SERIES *LOS ANGELES, CALIFORNIA*

How would you describe your work?

FABIENNE: The first thing that always comes to mind when Karis and I are working together is fun and joy. We have a lot of fun working together. I would also say engaged, inspired, challenged.

KARIS: I would say both our brains only make one.

FABIENNE: No. I would say we complement each other. We have similar strengths.

KARIS: We started working together in different ways, and because we were friends in the beginning we really knew who each other was. But I think we've really grown so much in our depth and digging deeper into our work and becoming better writers, becoming better speakers, becoming more equipped at facilitating each other. It's a really amazing partnership . . . We're very different personality wise, and so I think in the end it's really complemented how each round of edits we do we see different things. We challenge each other to go a little further.

How did this partnership begin?

KARIS: We met in pregnancy yoga. When we were pregnant with our first kids and our instructor said to us, "You have to find someone in the room to walk with, so you have to find someone who lives near you." We both live in the same area of Laurel Canyon in the hills. I guess, Fabi, you were probably seven months pregnant when we started walking.

FABIENNE: Yeah.

KARIS: We would start walking in the hills and we were both waddling around. That was the beginning of our crazy odyssey. We were cooking together after the kids were born. We would go on these crazy outings all over Los Angeles on the subway. We were exploring with a group of friends. It was a real early bonding experience.

FABIENNE: And we did a lot of volunteer work at school doing the class album, and we were room parents. I think it was when the kids were in fourth grade, we were just like, "Maybe we should try to do something that we really like and try to make some money at it." So we started just trying to put some film ideas together.

Can you tell me about your journey bringing *High on the Hog* to the screen? What were the steps?

FABIENNE: It's a culmination of things. We had been doing short lifestyle videos for the *New York Times*. I think once we got into the *New York Times*, at least for me because I grew up with the paper, you're like, "Okay, where do you go?" I mean it was really beautiful and we were pursuing that sort of aesthetic of like beautiful images and beautiful storytelling. It worked with our schedule. We would drop the kids off at school and then quickly go to set and then wrap it up. And it's like, "Okay, we have a hard out at two forty-five to go pick the kids up from school." But I think once the stuff was in the *Times*, we're just like, "Where do we go from here?"

There was a lot of racial unrest [at that time]. There were things that were happening at our kids' school, and we just took a little bit of a break. Because especially when you're doing short-form content, it's a hustle. We really felt like it was time, like we were ready to sink our teeth into something meaningful and real and resonant. Then around that time Jeff [Gordinier, friend and writer] sent this book [*High on the Hog* by Jessica B. Harris] to me and said, "Read this. It'll change your life." I read it in a sitting and I was just like, "Holy shit." And immediately gave it to Karis. She read the book, and thank God, she was just like, "Yeah, let's do this."

It was a little bit scary because it was bigger than anything that we've ever done together. It's one thing to drop the kids off and do a one-day shoot. But I think that we both saw the potential and really again held that space for us. With Jessica and her life's work, we really felt like, "Holy shit, we have this project. She's entrusted us with her baby." We just became the vessels, and we had to get over ourselves. We had to get over our fears, we had to get over our concerns and just be in service to this material.

KARIS: We really had a vision for what it looked like and how important it was in this time and place. And I think part of our get-up-and-go was that we were worried there were wolves at the door, like someone else was going to make it. Someone else was going to do it. You know what I mean? Which is crazy because that's in your own head, but at the same time there was this pressure . . . like we didn't have forever to sit on it.

We spent probably six months learning about some of the history and crafting it and finding out about more people and really digging deep, but then we were like, "Okay, now we've got to bring this to some outlets . . ." We were really focused on Netflix, because it seemed like the only place where the project could happily live, and that was nerve-racking.

What have you learned about creating a team to execute a vision or to make a vision come to life?

KARIS: I think the most important thing is being open

and sharing . . . knowing your strengths but also knowing your weaknesses and not being afraid of asking for help. It's not about trying to do everything yourself. It really is about bringing people that you love and respect to the table and listening and having their ear. Because everyone has a different opinion about how things look and are shaped or whatever, but I think what we're really good at is knowing what we want but also knowing how to get people to help us get there.

What is the biggest lesson you've learned about money, compensation, or negotiation so far in your career as filmmakers?

KARIS: There's never enough.

FABIENNE: I think as women, especially women of color, I think we've learned how to advocate for ourselves much better. I think it's a trial and error sort of thing, but I think we're getting better at asking for what we need.

What advice would you offer to someone who wants to do what you do?

KARIS: I think for me it's finding that first project that you're really passionate about, because it gives you the drive to keep going. I think once you have that one thing under your belt, you can bring on other things that you're not so passionate about, but they fill other slots. Maybe that's the thing that's going to make you money or that's a connection you want to make, but I think finding something that you absolutely love to work on, first and foremost, is really important. Because that book just resonated so much with us, and it held such a special place for us, I know that's why we fought so hard for it.

FABIENNE: Ask questions . . . And work with people you like. That's really important, because I think we both have worked for people that we don't like or who haven't been kind or generous or nice. I think the other thing is also really being kind to the people that you're working with. We definitely can go to sleep at night not feeling bad about how we treated people.

What are some of your favorite things to eat or drink?

KARIS: Vodka.

FABIENNE: I like tequila.

KARIS: I'm so crazy about shellfish. If I could have a baked oyster with butter and hot sauce every day, I would be in heaven. Fabi, you love a burger.

FABIENNE: I do love a burger.

Hey Sistah Cocktail

BY FABIENNE TOBACK AND KARIS JAGGER / MAKES 1 SERVING

2 teaspoons ginger syrup (see note)

2 ounces blanco tequila or vodka

1 ounce freshly squeezed lime juice

Sparkling water

We both love tequila, fresh ginger, and a spicy cocktail, so this was a natural recipe for us to come up with—and one we're happy to sip any day of the week. If you want to tone down the spiciness, just use a little less of the ginger syrup.

Combine the ginger syrup, tequila, and lime juice in a shaker with lots of ice. Shake vigorously. Pour into a tall glass and top with sparkling water.

NOTE: To make ginger syrup, completely peel and coarsely chop 8 ounces fresh ginger and combine it in a blender with ½ cup sugar. Process until the sugar is dissolved, adding a bit of water to help it along if needed. Strain into a container, and refrigerate tightly covered for up to 2 months.

147

Ardenia Brown

PERSONAL CHEF
BROOKLYN, NEW YORK

How would you describe your work?

It's really a passion. It's nurturing. It's a lot of prayer going through it. It's all about nurturing and finding the palate of my clients, who just love great food. It's really about understanding what their needs are and giving them that in a soulful way. And my main source of focus with cooking and healthy eating is Questlove, who has been an awesome brother, and I honor him dearly.

How did you begin in your field?

I began cooking with my mom, with the church, with my aunts and uncles in the South. My summer camp was going to North Carolina. I'm a baby of the 1950s, so it was about family pulling together on the farm to prime tobacco, to be a part of that whole culture of where our food comes from—making sure that we can get the tobacco done, making sure the hogs are fed, the cows are milked— that's really how I learned and where I believed it started.

Can you tell me about changing lanes from being a music executive to creating a path in food and becoming a chef?

I have no regrets, but I didn't realize that I didn't have any regrets until fifteen years ago, when I had to change lanes. I had to flip the script. I was no longer the vice president executive that they were looking at anymore. And it wasn't just me, it's how the music industry changed.

I didn't know where it was going, but from being a VP and working with a lot of major artists—so many, my god, Janet Jackson, Michael Jackson, Public Enemy— from concert promoting and doing shows to running the national environment of the record industry. But when your time is up at one thing, because you lose the passion, you have to move forward.

Based on always having events at home, cooking for friends, cooking for family, that was the passion of where I wanted to go. But then I had to deal with illness in the family. My mom needed more attention at home. I was diagnosed with lupus. My brother had prostate cancer, and I was in LA at this time. I had to make a conscious decision that it's time for me to go home, to heal myself, and to be there for family. And it was the best thing that could have happened.

But I had to leave "me" in LA. I couldn't really bring me home. And what do I mean by that? My lifestyle as a gay woman, coming from a very religious family, my father being a bishop, my mother being the first lady of the church they built. I had to leave that behind, because I was coming to live with my mom, and she needed my full attention.

So changing lanes took a lot of different steps. But then once I came home, living in Bedford-Stuyvesant, I was disturbed by the choices of food in the community. There were only bodegas. You had to go outside of the community if you wanted a carton of milk that wasn't spoiled. I thought about opening up a market, but I couldn't do that and take care of my mom.

There was a café in Bed-Stuy called Solomon's Porch, on Halsey Street and Stuyvesant Avenue. And one day I went in for lunch, just hanging out, learning the community, and I'm seeing this beautiful space with a limited menu, but it had such character. And I got into a conversation with the owner, and in a matter of three months I was working there. And working there as the manager, and getting the owner to understand we needed to bring live entertainment into the community. So I'm going back to my music thing, because it doesn't really leave you, you know?

We started having local musicians come through, ten dollars at the door and limited menu. It became a very positive place for a cafe in 2004, 2005, 2006. It had a buzz. Chaka Khan came to play there. So that lasted for about a good five years, until the owner left the business.

And at that same time, my mom began to get really sick. So my eye was off the ball, had to be, because it was time to just totally give into my mom. And I had to shut the door [on my business ideas], because I needed to spend time making sure I was caring for my mom.

My brother passed in 2008. Mom passed in 2011, and my sister passed in 2013. With all of that happening, it was like, okay, I need to sit down. I need to regroup. Two weeks later, I got a phone call from a trainer who lived in the community, and he said, "I have a client that's looking for a personal chef. Would you be interested?"

I said, "Well, it really depends on who the client is."

So he says, "Well, I can't tell you who it's for, but can you do an interview?" Went to the interview, door opens, it's Questlove. We both look at each other like, "Yeah, you look familiar." He was at Def Jam after I left, but he had seen me in the industry. I knew who the Roots were forever.

It took a while to learn his palate, for him to trust me and for me to even trust that I made the right decision to take on this task. And here I am today, twelve years later. It's been a blessing. He's a mentor. He's family. He's an awesome brother. His family is fabulous.

What are you most proud of in your career?

I would say, my being able to have the ability and the health at sixty—how old am I? sixty-six—to do this and have an assistant, a young brother who I think is going to be an incredible chef long after I'm gone.

How do you take care of your mental health and deal with the stresses of work and life?

One: getting an assistant. Two: massages—gotta have a great massage, and especially with an autoimmune disease. These muscles and joints can wear me out. And then: prayer; staying close to family; my dog, Jack.

I have done the therapy thing. Therapy is no joke. There was a lot that I had to come to in my walk from the music industry, from my journey, from growing up as a PK [preacher's kid], and how I felt about religion, how I felt about my lifestyle . . . So through that and the death of family members and friends, I really had to sit down and be truthful to myself that I needed some support to make it through. And therapy has helped me with that.

What is an important lesson you've learned about money, compensation, or negotiation over the course of your career?

Money—I've had this lesson in the music industry as well: know your worth. If you are not familiar with certain terminologies of finance, you really need an accountant. From the very beginning of whatever you're doing, you need to understand where your dollars are going, how you can save money with what you're making. And don't be afraid to charge. If you really believe in being compensated and giving your best and your all, then do that. You may lose some jobs, but every job is not for you.

What are some of your favorite things to eat or drink?

Bourbon. And I truly really like branzino. Wild branzino, whole whitefish with a head on, let me go up in that.

Hibiscus Elixir

BY ARDENIA BROWN
MAKES ABOUT 8 QUARTS

This is one of my favorite elixirs to make. Hibiscus flowers are so fragrant and beautiful, especially when coupled with the spices I use. Serve it as a hot tea, a blood-pressure–lowering elixir, a virgin drink, or a cocktail with bourbon and simple syrup, or just with seltzer. You can buy hibiscus flowers online.

4 cups hibiscus flowers

2 navel oranges, quartered

8 cardamom seeds, crushed

4 star anise

2 cinnamon sticks

1 finger-length piece fresh ginger, peeled

1 slice lime

Plenty of fresh herbs such as mint or lemon verbena

1 cup honey or monk fruit sweetener (optional)

Combine the hibiscus, oranges, cardamom, star anise, cinnamon, ginger, lime, and herbs in a large pot with 8 quarts water. Bring to a simmer and cook, covered, until oranges are very soft. Turn off the flame and let the mixture steep for 20 minutes.

Strain elixir into a large container, discarding solids. Stir in sweetener if desired. Refrigerate, covered, for up to 1 month.

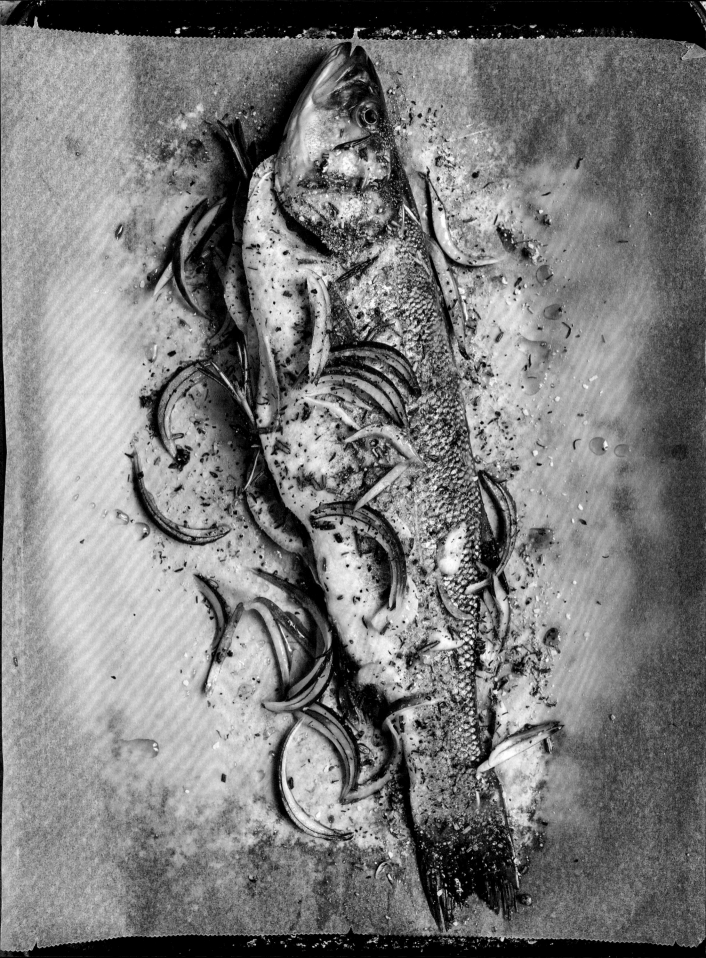

Whole Roasted Branzino

BY ARDENIA BROWN / MAKES 1–2 SERVINGS

1 whole branzino (about 2 pounds), gutted and scaled, with head on

2 sprigs rosemary

2 garlic cloves, thinly sliced

3 teaspoons coconut or olive oil

1 lemon, thinly sliced

½ red onion, chopped

2 teaspoons salt

1 tablespoon freshly ground black pepper

1 tablespoon onion powder

1 tablespoon garlic powder

1 tablespoon herbes de Provence

1 tablespoon paprika

4 or 5 multicolored mini sweet peppers

There is nothing better than a whole roasted fish for dinner, and I happen to love branzino. It's simple, buttery, and flavorful, even with a few bones to pick through. If you are having guests, plan on a whole fish per person. Trust me, you will not want to share. Have your fishmonger gut the branzino and leave the head on. There is so much meat in the head to enjoy!

Heat the oven to 425°F (use the convection setting if available). Line a roasting pan with parchment paper.

Rinse the fish to ensure there are no scales remaining. Using a chef's knife, score the skin 3 times at a 45-degree angle between the pectoral fin and tail.

Mince the leaves of half a rosemary sprig and mix it in a small bowl with the garlic and 1 teaspoon oil. Brush this mixture inside the fish. Place the remaining rosemary, the lemon slices, and chopped onion in the cavity.

Rub the remaining oil on both sides of the fish and sprinkle evenly with the salt, pepper, onion powder, garlic powder, herbes de Provence, and paprika. Spread a small amount of oil across the parchment paper to prevent sticking. Place the fish on the oiled paper and roast for 25 to 30 minutes, until it's cooked through and flakes easily.

Meanwhile, set an 8-inch cast-iron skillet on medium heat and cook the peppers until charred all around. Transfer the fish to a serving plate and garnish with the peppers.

Kelly Mitchell

WINE CONSULTANT AND
EDUCATOR *NEW YORK,
NEW YORK*

How would you describe your work?

I would say that my work is sharing wine with others. It took a while to figure out exactly what I wanted to do in wine. Sometimes I oversimplify it when I think about the industry, and I say you either make wine or you are selling or sharing wine with others. Being in the New York metro area, I found myself in wine sales, and then I've also branched out to do my consumer-facing work as well, which is also the sharing of wine and wine education.

I would describe my work as a steward and ambassador of great wine. I would also say that I feel like I promote wine culture.

How did you begin in your field?

It started with just a general interest in wine. First, of course, it was an interest in food. Even when I was in college in Atlanta, like when people were just eating pizza and wings, I would venture out to the suburbs to these unique restaurants and these neighborhood spots. Then as I became more of an adult, wine became more of an interest over time. I said, "Let me take a class and learn more about wine."

I took a course at the International Wine Center, which is one of two main curriculums in the New York area or in the world in wine. I was working a full-time job at the time in marketing and not loving it and having that "I'm thirty, I don't love my career. What am I doing?" kind of thing.

At the end of the class one day, the teacher pulled me aside and she was like, "I don't know if you're an enthusiast or if you're trying to become a professional, but I see natural talents and gifts within you related to wine. Your palate in particular is very strong and I just feel like you should lean into this."

At that point I was like, "Okay. What are the jobs? Because I don't want to work in a restaurant and I don't want to work in a store." I looked at other related fields like PR and marketing and corporatey wine jobs. I thought about it more and I thought, "What is the core business of wine in this area?" In my opinion, it's the selling of wine.

It's moving wine, whether you're selling it tableside as a sommelier, at a store, or distribution wholesale, which is my primary space. That's how I ended up in wine sales. I took a while to get in, but one of the teachers at the International Wine Center was actually a sales manager at a small distribution company and she hired me.

What are you most proud of so far in your career?

I would say I'm most proud of not going with the status quo, and taking risks early on. The biggest one I would say is the launch of Kelly Selects, which is my wine club. It's not subscription based, and it's periodic; when I feel inspired I put out a new set, so it's very rough, but it really resonated with the consumer audience during the pandemic.

People loved the wines. It became a social media community and generated a lot of organic content. It was very no-frills. It was just like a brown box of the wine coming to your house, but it's amazing wine. Because of all the overhead that other wine clubs have, and we didn't have, we were able to really just put the value in the wine itself.

How do you take care of your mental health and deal with the stresses of your work?

I have a therapist that I meet with.

I'm trying to find time for meditation. This is all still work in progress for me, because I am a naturally frantic energy person and it can be draining. I have been really trying to focus on energy management and saving my energy, reserving it for the things that are important and saying no to certain things.

I also do like that I have one of the day jobs in the industry. It's another thing that I gravitated toward. I knew I didn't want to work at night, and a lot of people who lead restaurants and all those kinds of fields, the biggest thing is the lifestyle, getting the late hours. I wanted a day job and so that's another thing that was mandatory for me.

What advice would you offer to someone who wants to do what you do?

I would say if you want to be in wine sales, I do think the formal education does help because it's empowering in a way. It's not a requirement or prerequisite for the job. It's just nice to have in your back pocket, but I find it does give you confidence and it gives you a leg to stand on.

What is an important lesson you've learned about money, negotiation, business, or compensation over the course of your career?

When it comes to sales in particular, which ultimately is a 100 percent commission job, you have to pay very close attention to your account quality and your portfolio quality, because essentially that is the makeup of your compensation. One of the biggest things I learned in the space as a salesperson is that your success is based on what you do and how many businesses you can open up. Account quality—when I say that, I'm talking about the level of restaurant, the level of wine stores that you are working with—is hugely important.

What is their potential? If you're working with just small neighborhood stores, there's a limit there. There, you can't grow in the way that maybe your skills could allow you to. Then portfolio quality. I think that's hugely important, and I think that the company I work for now, Skurnik—one of the biggest reasons I love working there is we have wines that I like to drink, like to share, and I'm proud to represent. I think that makes a huge difference.

I remind people when they're looking, or if they're negotiating an offer, that you have to be able to feed yourself, pay your rent, and not be kept up at night about bills because of your compensation.

If you're getting a crappy offer or that's below what you know you need to be able to sleep soundly every night without worrying about your bills, then don't take it. The ability to taste amazing wine is not worth that peace of mind. I feel like there's just a lot of unfortunately very low-paying jobs in our industry. I mean, hospitality has that problem across the board, but you're not exempt from it in the wine space.

What do you most enjoy about your career?

Working with an agricultural product, working with family-owned estates, having a connection to the earth and to land. We hear about all of these crazy climatic experiences that are taking place across the world. Unfortunately, wine regions have been impacted as well from things such as flooding, frost, hail, all kinds of abnormal occurrences that damage the grape-growing process. I just really love talking to winemakers and people who are connected to the agricultural aspect of our business. That's one of the things I love most, and telling their stories too, because they're busy making wine. I love adding the human element to the wine, to people's understanding of wine.

What's the most difficult aspect of your career?

Just figuring out how to get ahead because it's not a traditional career path.

What are some of your favorite things to eat or drink?

For drinking, it's definitely Champagne and white burgundy.

As far as eating, I'm a big foodie. I would say I love a lot of things that fall under the category of Asian—Szechuan Chinese is one of my favorites. Then my go-to whenever just to keep things simple is chicken and rice of any cuisine—from any part of the world. Give me your version of chicken and rice, and I'm almost always happy.

What is your favorite snack with either Champagne or white burgundy?

Freshly popped popcorn. I actually have a bowl sitting right next to me now. Usually I pop it in coconut oil, which is my secret trick that I think just makes it taste so good, that and putting on high-quality Diamond kosher salt. That is my favorite. If I were out, it would probably be french fries, because they're giving you the same salt and flavor that you're looking for.

"I would say if you want to be in wine sales, I do think the formal education does help because it's empowering."

Tiffani Rozier

CHEF, CULINARY INSTRUCTOR, HOST OF *AFROS AND KNIVES* PODCAST *PHOENIX, ARIZONA*

How would you describe your work?

"Transformative media." Because it's kind of never-ending. You don't necessarily have to transform just one thing. It can be transformative for a number of reasons. It can be transformative for the viewer and for the creator. The intention behind my work is for it to be transformative.

What do you say you do?

It took me forever to call myself a chef. What I say I do now is—up until last year, I said I was a food podcast producer. That was it. In the last few months, I started to really look at a different term for what I want to do.

So the name I've always wanted was "food media producer," and I thought that label was still probably a little too small because it didn't really encompass all the things I wanted to put my hands on . . . I want to produce the content I never got to see.

In 2019, I took a new job with a food start-up in Atlanta. I got moved into this apartment, got a car, started to just double down into basic adulthood, and this idea pops up again. I'm like, " I don't see any Black folks. Where are all the Black people in food media? What are we doing?" And so I was like, "Well, let me just do this podcast because I want to get this other idea off the ground," and podcasts seemed to be low-hanging fruit. If you're not interested in high-quality production, it's a cheap way to get into it, because if you have a microphone or a phone and an app that can get you to record things, and if you're not interested necessarily in editing, you're good.

I literally started there. So I just thought podcasting was probably—at the time, podcasting was—a simple way to do this.

What advice would you offer to someone who wants to do what you do?

I love the premise of "start where you are." Like, the idea behind that, the ideology behind that is wonderful. The energy is there for it. I find that it just lacks a certain amount of information. When you tell someone to "start where they are," that doesn't take into account a number of things. What most people are saying is don't be afraid of your own ideas. Don't be afraid of your own imagination. I think that's what that statement means, but the way it's delivered it can be—it kind of sets people up for failure because the "start where you are" is not about anything you're physically doing. The "start where you are" is really about a mindset, and it's not pitched to people that way.

A lot of folks try to start businesses and get into fields that they don't know anything about, and they end up falling flat on their faces, and they spend a lot of money and lose a lot of money and time trying to sort that out, whereas what people were trying to tell them was, "Well, if that's something you want to do, you should pursue it. Don't be afraid of that. It's okay that you want to pursue that goal. Do the things you need to do to do it successfully, or at least with minimal aches and pains."

What we should be saying instead is don't be afraid of your own ideas. Don't be afraid of your own imagination or your own ambition. It's okay to want to do that. Now the next step is figuring out what have other people done successfully, and what makes you different?

Cheryl Day

BAKER, OWNER OF BACK
IN THE DAY BAKERY,
COOKBOOK AUTHOR
SAVANNAH, GEORGIA

How would you describe your work?

I am a legacy baker specializing in Southern baking that was created by my ancestors. I write cookbooks that teach a very approachable style of baking. I am a serial optimist, entrepreneur, and creative thinker—always learning and growing. My latest passion projects are Janie Q Provisions, a jam and small-batch provisions company, and the Back in the Day Bakery retail shop. A treasure trove filled with all the things I love with products sourced from BIPOC, women-owned, and small-batch purveyors or vintage finds.

How did you begin in your field?

I am a self-taught scratch baker. After my mom passed away, I dropped out of college and took a job as a receptionist in an architect's office. I found it relaxing to spend my weekends baking. On Monday, I would bring it all into the office. Folks really enjoyed my treats and started asking if I would make my baked goods for parties and events and such. I spent many years dreaming about my "someday" special place, but it took me many years to have the courage to jump in and do it as a career. I give my husband, Griff, credit for helping me to realize this dream, and we created a dream business for the both of us. We decided that we wanted to create a business for the life we wanted to live. After 9/11, my husband and I took a leap of faith and created a neighborhood gathering spot to build a community place that Savannah needed.

Do you have a mission or motto, and if so, what is it?

My mother always used to say, "THIS or something better!" It has become my mantra too. For me, it is a constant reminder not to focus on something I think is best or something I think I have to have or need, rather I keep myself open to receiving what is truly meant for me. My favorite quote and words I do my best to live by: "I've learned that people will forget what you said, people will forget what you did, but people will never forget how you made them feel."—Maya Angelou

What is an important lesson you've learned about money, compensation, or finance over the course of your career?

My personal philosophy about money is to give it and accept it freely to keep with the ebb and flow in which it comes and goes. I can't say this has always served me well. But thankfully my husband taught me the value in saving at least 10 percent of our earnings for . . . life and all of its little surprises, both rainy and sunny days, which has saved us.

What advice would you offer to someone who wants to do what you do?

Be honest with yourself. Make lists of what you want to do and why. Find mentors. Work for others in the field to try it on (early mornings and long days included) for a year to see what it feels like and see if it still brings you joy.

What are some of your favorite things to eat or drink?

All sorts of tacos and margaritas. I also really love fruit. There is nothing better than a perfect plum, peach, watermelon . . . oh and fruit pies—the best!

Joy Spence

MASTER BLENDER,
APPLETON ESTATE RUM
ST. ELIZABETH, JAMAICA

How would you describe your work?

My role is mainly developing new products, so it is strictly innovation along with being the global ambassador for Appleton Estate. So I tour the world and spread the joy of rum—no pun intended.

How did you begin in your field?

It's a long story. I never thought in my wildest dreams that I'd ever become a master blender. In high school, I fell in love with chemistry because of my chemistry teacher. Then she died in Chatsworth, and it was very devastating for me, and so I made a vow that I would be the best chemist there is in her honor. I went to university and thought I'd become a medical doctor, but then I realized I couldn't handle trauma, so I continued along the straight path of chemistry. And when I graduated, I started to lecture in chemistry, and then I wanted to get some industry experience because I was teaching applied chemistry at the time. So I joined Tia Maria as the research chemist, and it was a one-product operation. I got very bored because I have to multitask a lot.

And so J. Wray & Nephew, which is

Appleton Estate, is right next door, and I'd look across the fence in my days of boredom, and I would say, "Oh, that's a happening place to work. People looking busy, everybody looking happy. Let me send my résumé over there." They called me for an interview, and they made it quite clear they had no openings; they were just totally impressed with my résumé. I left, and I said, "Okay. That's my destiny," and then a few weeks later I got a call from them to say they created the position of chief chemist for me.

My goal was actually to modernize the laboratory there at J. Wray & Nephew. So when I joined the company, I keep telling everyone that I never even drank a drop of rum, because in those days it was unheard of for a woman to be seen drinking rum—it just was not ladylike in that era. Look how things have now changed! I decided to work with the previous master blender, and that's when my whole life changed. That's when I discovered the amazing world of this complex, beautiful spirit that has so many inputs to it, so many different flavor profiles—and the fact that I could use my sensory skill along with my chemistry background to actually create a special craft and profession.

And he recognized that I had all these basic attributes to become an excellent master blender, and he said, "I'm going to take you under my wing and tutor you." So I spent seventeen years with him, and then when he retired I was appointed the master blender, and at that time I was the first female master blender not just in rum but in the entire spirit industry.

What are some of the responsibilities of being the chief chemist or master blender?

At the time, as the chief chemist I was responsible for analyzing all inputs into the process. So from distillation through aging, blending, bottling—all the quality aspects of the operation, I had to basically certify those processes and move the product from one step to the next until it was finalized and approved for bottling. As a master blender, on the other hand, I would develop new products and ensure the consistency of the existing products.

What are you most proud of in your career?

There are so many proud moments in my career, not just one. I can list them: being awarded a national honor by the government of Jamaica for my contribution not just to rum but the brand of Jamaica; being awarded the Most Influential Blender for the past ten years in the UK; being given honorary doctorates by the University of the West Indies and my university in the UK; being nominated as one of the Top 20 Women in Innovation by *Forbes*.

And I would say, last but not least, having our experience named in my honor. So the Appleton Estate experience [tour] is known as the Joy Spence Appleton Estate Rum Experience, and that was a very touching moment for me, because I keep telling people these things happen to you after you die—you know, they say, "Okay. Let's name a road in that person's honor," or "Let's name a building in that person's honor." But to be alive and be given this opportunity, I'm so grateful to Campari [owner of Appleton Estate] for this.

What is an important lesson you've learned about building a team or working with others over the course of your career?

I think my philosophy as a leader with my team is to have an open-door policy, and not only to instill the technical aspects of the operation. I was also like a mother figure. So I would discuss the problems that they're having in life, encourage them to own a home if they don't own a home and to own a motor vehicle if they don't, just to try to let them improve their lifestyle. So it was a balance, and I'll always be sitting down and just having a chitchat with everybody, not just about work but about life, and what is your next step in life. It's a holistic approach as a leader, which I think is very important—and being a good listener. It is so important to listen to people.

Do you have a mission or a motto, and if so, what is it?

My personal mission is to help as many less fortunate young ladies as I can to attain a good education. I have been supporting a lot of mentees, especially encouraging them to go into STEM. It's basically young ladies who have the potential, but their parents just are not financially capable to even buy books for high school, buy laptops for high school. And so at the beginning of the school year, I'll provide them with all the necessary equipment that will make them be successful.

> "My personal mission is to help as many less fortunate young ladies as I can to attain a good education."

What is it that you most enjoy about your work?

I think I enjoy touring the world, meeting people, and just watching them appreciate the complexity of Appleton Estate and recognizing how beautiful a spirit it is.

What's the most difficult aspect of your career?

I think the most difficult aspect of my career is to keep creating new expressions that would entice the consumer and that would keep the consumers aware and interested in Appleton Estate. because it's not easy to have that momentum continuing year after year after year.

What are some of your favorite things to eat or drink?

Jamaican curry goat, and I like jerk lobster topped with pineapple.

12-Year-Old Blue Mountain Serve

BY JOY SPENCE / MAKES 1 SERVING

2 ounces Appleton Estate 12-Year-Old Rare Casks Rum

12 coffee beans, plus 3 or 4 more for garnish

Lightly muddle the coffee beans in a shaker, cracking them only; do not grind them. Stir muddled beans with rum over ice. Strain into a double old-fashioned glass over one large ice cube. Garnish with 3 or 4 whole beans.

Mai Tai

BY JOY SPENCE
MAKES 1 SERVING

2 ounces Appleton Estate 8-Year-Old Reserve Rum

½ ounce freshly squeezed lime juice

½ ounce orange curaçao liqueur (or Grand Marnier)

½ ounce orgeat (almond) syrup

1 lime shell and fresh mint sprig for garnish

Combine the rum, lime juice, curaçao, and orgeat in a shaker filled with ice (crushed and cubes). Shake until chilled and pour into a double old-fashioned glass. Garnish with lime shell and mint sprig.

Shanika Hillocks

FOOD AND BEVERAGE
MULTI-HYPHENATE
HARLEM, NEW YORK

How would you describe your work?

A cocktail of digital strategy, storytelling, marketing, and content creation under the food and beverage umbrella.

How did you begin in your field?

I come from very humble hospitality industry beginnings. I started slinging beer and wings at sixteen at a bar in my hometown and kept the job throughout college because of the fast cash and flexible scheduling. Once I signed a lease for an apartment my senior year of college, I knew I had to rake in higher tips. One of my regulars put me in touch with the regional manager of Seasons 52, a fine dining restaurant under the Darden umbrella. It's there where I tasted wine more consciously and discovered the beauty of pairing wine with food. After graduating college, my interest in PR grew and led me to New York City, where I serendipitously answered a Craigslist ad for my first public relations job in the beverage alcohol space.

Who are some of your role models or mentors in the food and hospitality space?

Ashtin Berry and Andre Mack [sommelier and winemaker].

What are you most proud of?

Relationships—the real, authentically invested relationships—that I've built over the years. I am most fulfilled and successful when I'm able to plug or create with talented friends in my circle.

What is an important lesson you've learned about money, compensation, or finance over the course of your career?

Two things have helped me stay financially sharp as I've grown in my career. The first is to negotiate, especially that first offer, and to do it regularly. The second is to enlist the help of professionals who can keep your finances in check as you grow. Both my CPA and financial adviser are Black professionals who consider the unique aspects of our lives. Things like family care and support, building a nest egg, or making investments for the first time.

How have you approached using social media for the work you do?

Social media is a huge component of my work, both for my personal brand and professional responsibilities. To stay balanced, I take intentional breaks, and aim to take any connections I make online to another platform, ideally a phone call or in-person meeting.

What advice would you offer to someone who wants to do what you do?

Connect with as many people as possible with curiosity and interest instead of your end goal in mind.

Do you have a mission or motto, and if so, what is it?

Time is your greatest asset. Be frugal and spend it wisely.

Michelle Braxton

RECIPE DEVELOPER, AUTHOR OF *SUPPER WITH MICHELLE* BLOG *ATLANTA, GEORGIA*

How would you describe your work?

I am the creator, writer, recipe developer, and photographer behind the food blog *Supper with Michelle*.

How did you begin in your field?

I started *Supper with Michelle* back in 2014 after a lot of encouragement from friends and family. I would share pictures via social media platforms of dishes that I had created, and to my surprise, my friends and family started requesting the recipes. So, I started *Supper with Michelle* as a way to share not only the images of my latest creations, but the recipes as well.

What advice would you offer to someone who wants to do what you do?

The first thing is: Start. The hardest part is always starting. Stay true to your vision and what you love and know that it will evolve. Enjoy the journey and don't be so hard on yourself when you make mistakes because that's all a part of your growth. Be professional and understand the value of what you do and any services that you offer. And if you do work for brands/companies, always ask the brand what their budget is for expected deliverables prior to telling what your rates are. It's easier to start with a higher rate and negotiate from there. Also don't be afraid to reach out to other bloggers that you admire or respect to ask general questions and network with. I've learned so much from many of my foodie friends and gained some incredible bonds and friendships along the way.

Do you have a mission or motto, and if so, what is it?

My biggest goal or mission has been to show and inspire people how to work more delicious and flavorful veggie-filled meals into their everyday lifestyles.

How do you take care of your mental health and deal with the stresses of your work?

I've found that self-care is extremely important, and finding a good work-life balance is equally important. I take breaks away from my phone and social media anytime I start to feel overwhelmed or stressed. I also have made it a habit to do some type of physical activity every day like walking, running, and/or yoga. This is my form of meditation and how I release a lot of stress. And as crazy as it may sound, I also make time to do absolutely nothing. Lastly, I protect my peace.

What are some of your favorite things to eat or drink?

Oh goodness, that's hard because I love so many different things. First will always be soup. I love soup all year round. And after that, I'm always looking for a new favorite because I love trying and experimenting with new foods.

Kale & Fire-Roasted Tomato Acini di Pepe Soup

BY MICHELLE BRAXTON / MAKES 4–5 SERVINGS

3 tablespoons olive oil

1 medium onion, diced

1 or 2 ribs celery, sliced

2 medium carrots, peeled and sliced

3 garlic cloves, minced

½ teaspoon dry Italian seasoning blend

1 pinch red pepper flakes

14½-ounce can fire-roasted diced tomatoes, with their juices

8 cups vegetable broth

Salt and freshly ground black pepper

½ cup acini di pepe, orzo, or ditalini pasta

3–4 cups roughly chopped lacinato kale

The smokiness of the fire-roasted tomatoes makes this soup special. During the colder months, you can make it a bit heartier by stirring in a rinsed and drained can of navy or cannellini beans. Add a little freshly grated Parmesan cheese on top and some freshly baked bread alongside.

Heat the oil in a large pot over medium-low heat. Sauté the onions, celery, and carrots until the onions are translucent and the vegetables are soft, about 10 minutes. Stir in the garlic, Italian seasoning, and red pepper flakes, and sauté for a few minutes more, until the garlic is fragrant.

Add the tomatoes and vegetable broth. Taste and season with salt and pepper. Bring the mixture to a boil and stir in the pasta. Reduce the heat and simmer, uncovered, stirring occasionally, until the pasta is tender, 8 to 10 minutes. Stir in the kale and cook a few minutes, until wilted. Serve hot.

Mashama Bailey

CHEF, CO-OWNER OF
THE GREY RESTAURANT
SAVANNAH, GEORGIA

How would you describe your work?

Aside from it being hard, I would describe it as a journey. I think it's really a fortunate medium to be a part of, especially when you are Black in America and you get to peel back all these layers of how the food that you grew up with is significant and important, especially when you did not grow up thinking it was significant and important. So I think that the work that I'm doing is—I really just think of myself as a cook. But the longer that I'm on this journey the more I'm realizing that I am becoming a role model, I am a historian, I am a chef, and all those things give me a lot of creative license to really discuss and in a lot of ways demonstrate how food has progressed us as a people and how it is still so influential in how we live our lives and a lot of decisions that we make.

I bring up my grandmothers a lot because they're my anchors. I needed something to anchor me in this crazy world that was and is very white male dominated. I needed something to anchor me and they are, and they continue to do that. And one of my grandmothers just thought that what I was doing was insane and that all the different types of cuisines I would try were damaging to my stomach and my innards, and I need a good, old-fashioned this and that, and I think the older I get the more I crave those good, old-fashioned things. So I think my work is a journey, and I'm happy that I'm happy on this journey.

What did you want to do when you were a kid?

When I was a kid, I wanted to be a poet. That was the first thing I wanted to be. I had a little book—I think my mom still has it—where I drew pictures and wrote little poems about the sun and being kind and all this stuff. As I started to go through school I became really interested in science, and so I thought that I was going to be a physical therapist or a doctor, and I just couldn't sit still. I just can't do it. So I think ultimately I was going to work with my hands, and I knew that. Now that I look back on it, I knew that; maybe that's why I wanted to be a physical therapist, because I knew I needed to do physical work. So I really fell into cooking because I wanted to be a part of a community, and I wanted to be that person in the community who provided sustenance for people and that people low-key admired. But I never wanted to be the face of it or the front; I always wanted to be sort of in the background, just kind of feeding people and nourishing people and getting little high fives because of that.

What's something that you like to do that not many people know about?

During high school, I took a class in casting pottery, and I hadn't taken a class in pottery since then, and it was tragic—I had this beautiful black vase, and I went out and

"You have to understand that what I did did not happen overnight."

I showed my friends and I broke the vase. I literally hadn't taken pottery since that class, and so I'd been thinking about it since I moved to Savannah seven years ago. There's a pottery studio that I drive by, and finally a year ago I went in, and I signed up for classes because I had the space and time to do so. We were only open four days a week, so I picked one of those mornings and I went and did pottery, and I've been doing it for almost a year.

How did you begin in your field?

I was initially a social worker. I think because I couldn't sit still, I lacked a lot of discipline when it came to a lot of things, and so being a social worker was great, but I had to manage someone and that wasn't good for me because I wasn't really ready. And because I wasn't managing properly, it reflected on my work negatively, and I became fired from my position.

Right around that time—it was around the holidays, and

I was simultaneously talking to someone about catering because I had been cooking at home, and my friends were coming over and they were liking the food that I was making. So I think that there was this underlying thing of me being able to cook or being good at cooking, and so since I was recently unemployed, I decided to go into this work-study program at Peter Kump's, which is ICE (Institute of Culinary Education) right now, and that program taught me from the bottom up how to work in a kitchen, how to pull ingredients, what certain tools were when it came to professional cooking. It took a lot of the mystery out of cooking for a living, and I did my internship, and I just fell in love with it.

What is the biggest lesson you've learned so far about money or compensation or negotiation in your career?

When you work so hard and your motivation is not money—I don't think many of us should be doing what we're doing for money. I think some of us do, but I know that a lot of us who share this space creatively don't get into food because of money. It's just not realistic. It's not a realistic goal to think of yourself as being a rich cook or a rich chef. But I do think that there's a certain threshold that you can take because you start to really sacrifice a lot, and money or compensation are ways to validate that—I mean, the money is a way to validate all of the energy that you put into it, all those sacrifices that you put into it. You don't want to have to worry about being able to pay a bill or being able to afford to buy a home. You want those things to come from the fruits of your labor.

And so I think that it's very important that you express those needs that you have financially, because you won't be able to focus on the creative part of what you're doing if you're worried about the financial part. It's important that you understand how to be compensated. It's important to negotiate those things in your contracts, because they really can interfere with how you express yourself creatively, because you don't want to be resentful or you don't want to be regretful of the decisions you make when it comes to using your—now everyone's a brand, right? So you have to be paid for that because creativity has value.

And I think that growing up in the 1980s and seeing people like New Edition and Bobby Brown getting ripped off—that's one of the saddest stories. The New Edition story is one of the saddest stories known to mankind, because these young boys just got completely exploited, and you have to think about the things that are going to make you happy when you are doing what you love, because you've got to be able to afford the lifestyle that you want if you're pursuing a career that you really love.

What advice would you offer to someone who wants to do what you do?

I think the first thing you should do is really evaluate your motives—why you're doing it. I'm constantly reassessing what is motivating me because it's such a difficult field that I want to make sure that I'm not exploiting it. I want to make sure that I'm not overexaggerating or exploiting the reputations of my family members by constantly drawing from them. So I think that you've got to get really real with yourself, like, do you want to do it?

You have to understand that what I did did not happen overnight. I am forty-seven years old. I've been cooking professionally for twenty-one years, and you also have to be open to nontraditional ways of how to climb the ladder of success, because I think that my business partnership is very nontraditional. We were two people who had not owned a restaurant before. My business partner had not worked in the food industry at all, so for me to even consider being in a partnership with him I had to kind of take a leap of faith. So I think you have to trust yourself. I think there's a little bit of "fake it 'til you make it" and believe that you have learned and have the skills to be successful.

And if you want to do what I do, seek good counsel—financial counsel, mental health counsel. The first time I really saw a therapist was prepandemic, when I started to feel like a success—it was right after winning the James Beard. I was like, "I need to talk to someone who's not my mom, who's not my friend, who can give me an objective opinion about how I'm dealing with where I'm at, how I'm leading the team and what type of business partner I am because I'm starting to spiral out a little bit."

I've always discussed having a support system, and I think that's super important, and I think as you grow your support system changes. So first it can be your homegirls, then it could be your business partner, then maybe it needs to be something professional, like a lawyer or a financial adviser or a psychiatrist. Your support system has to grow with you as you grow into your career.

What do you most enjoy about being a chef and having your own restaurant?

I enjoy the food. I enjoy the camaraderie. I love cooks and restaurant people. I love people who work in restaurants who cook the food, who serve the food, who pour the drinks. I love farmers. I love people who work their ass off, and so being in that environment brings me complete joy. I love it, love it, love it.

What are some of your favorite things to eat or drink?

Well, it depends. One of my favorite things to drink is lemonade—just a nice, cold, icy, perfectly sweet, perfectly tart glass of lemonade. And if it's alcohol, it's probably a Negroni. I have a lot of favorite things to eat. A nice, crunchy—and I'm saying this because it's summer and I'm in Austin, Texas, and I've been sitting out in the sun—a nice, crunchy summer salad with tomatoes and green beans and cucumbers and a creamy sauce and lettuce and celery and all that crunchy goodness—or a nice fried chicken sandwich.

Shannon Mustipher

COCKTAIL CONSULTANT,
SPIRITS EDUCATOR,
AUTHOR OF *TIKI: MODERN
TROPICAL COCKTAILS*
BROOKLYN, NEW YORK

How would you describe your work?

I would say that the work is a celebration of the history and the culture of cocktails. So I tend to look at classic templates as inspiration for my points of departure for my original recipes, and I like to bring in the stories of the original cocktail, the original bar or bartender, when it was served and created, because I think that just adds a little bit of juice to the proceedings, so to speak.

It's definitely based in history and wanting to be aware of that and honor that. But then on a practical level, in terms of how [my cocktails] are executed—and take this with a grain of salt. I don't like the term "bar chef." I think that's a little much. But I do like to be really hands-on with my ingredients. I enjoy the prepping, the R&D. I cook as a hobby in my off time. I've been tending to spend my weekends in

what I call "domestic goddess mode," like making sauces and stocks and soups.

How did you begin in your field?

About twelve years ago, I was working as a wardrobe and styling assistant in the photo industry and took a part-time job at a wine shop and really fell in love with the service element of helping our clients in the store pick out bottles that they would love, and I subsequently went on to help that store open up a wine bar, and after that I did a little wine buying—and at this point, this is like, eight years ago. I was working as a server at a restaurant that added a bar program, and when I heard they were adding a bar I was really excited, so I wrote up this menu concept. Now, I'd been bartending at home for at least a decade prior, and at the time I was really obsessed with golden-age American classics, like the martini, the Martinez, the Manhattan. So basically, how I got started was working in wine and discovering I really enjoy helping the layperson navigate a category and feel comfortable picking out something that they would like; signing up to tend bar at a restaurant I was working at; I was already nerding out over vintage spirits and cocktails; and I was able to land a few shifts at a few friends' spots. I had a shift at Do or Dine; and about two years into working part time in various restaurants, I joined the crew at Gladys.

About nine months in, one of the partners at Gladys decided to move back to the West Coast to be closer to family, at which point the remaining partner decided to turn it into a Caribbean restaurant, and that's when he approached me to take that bar program and turn it into a rum concept. And mind you, I'd never worked with rum in cocktails before— maybe all of four or five rums in my life up until that point, and so I was there every day for a month. I tasted something like 250 rums. And I just dove right in.

What advice would you offer to somebody who wants to do what you do or follow in your footsteps?

It's very easy. It's summed up in a Rihanna song: "Work, work, work, honey." Because I really don't see how—what I've been able to do and the opportunities I've been exposed to just wouldn't have been possible without my putting in effort first. Let's just go back to my first bar shift: the only reason they put me in the bar is because they saw how motivated I was. I had no skill. Wherever I was working, when I saw a need, I offered to contribute to solving the problem. And then, of course, in my own personal time, because I have a tendency to just be extra nerdy about whatever it is, I just immerse myself. So I make myself available for the learning process, and I also am very proactive to try new things and offer my services to people.

How do you take care of your mental health and deal with the stresses of your work?

A long time ago I adopted what I would call the "drama-free diet," and what that essentially consists of is being really discerning about people that I allow in my personal space, deciding what kinds of relationships and dynamics I engage in or don't engage in, and getting really good at spotting potential issues within myself or with other people and finding a way to defuse or avoid them or just not get involved. I just avoid stress. Basically, it's like, how do I cope with stress? I'm like, let's not even get there in the first place.

One of my coworkers at Gladys had this tat, and it had this logo on it, and it's priceless. It just said "Don't trip," and I was like, "Yes. Don't trip." So I have what I call a "don't trip policy," you know what I'm saying? It's just realizing that everything is a choice, and I choose to save my energy for things that I want to get done and things that I enjoy, and things that I don't have control over or that are unpleasant— then, yes, I'll acknowledge them. I'm not a denier of reality, but I don't have to get wrapped up in temporary situations, which is 90 percent of everything going on anyway.

What are some of your favorite things to eat or drink?

I pretty much eat anything, but seafood is a catchall—like anything. I say if it has fins and scales, bring it to my plate. And I joke with myself about this because I kind of feel like a senior citizen because I love soup. At any given time I have like three soups in my freezer. I'm always making soup.

> "Everything is a choice, and I choose to save my energy for things that I want to get done and things that I enjoy."

North Star

BY SHANNON MUSTIPHER
MAKES 6–8 SERVINGS

Apple cider has held a special place in my heart since I attended college in New England. This cocktail is reminiscent of early-nineteenth-century punches that incorporated rum and baking spices.

10 ounces Barbados rum, such as Mount Gay Eclipse

100 milliliters cinnamon-clove syrup (see note)

25 milliliters allspice liqueur, such as St. Elizabeth or Hamilton

175 milliliters pink grapefruit or pomelo juice

300 milliliters freshly squeezed and strained lime juice

100 milliliters aromatic bitters

Chilled hard apple cider, for serving

Dried citrus peel, star anise pods, or freshly grated nutmeg, for garnish

Combine rum, syrup, liqueur, citrus juices, and bitters in a jar or other glass container with a cover; shake to mix. Refrigerate, covered, at least 4 hours and as long as overnight.

To serve, pour over ice cubes in rocks glasses and add a splash of hard cider to each glass. Garnish with dried citrus peel, star anise, or freshly grated nutmeg.

NOTE: For cinnamon-clove syrup, make 4 cups simple syrup, simmering it with 2 cinnamon sticks and ¼ teaspoon ground cloves.

Dr. Jessica B. Harris

AUTHOR, CULINARY HISTORIAN *BROOKLYN, NEW YORK*

How do you describe your work?

There's a lot of different stuff going on. I am called by many people a culinary historian or a culinary anthropologist. I guess I am that. I mean, I think the methodology is more participant-observer, but then there is a researcher element to it as well. So it's a lot of different things. I think if we're talking straight-up academic disciplines, I probably step on a lot of toes. I'm not a historian. I'm not an anthropologist. I'm none of those by training. I was trained in French and in theater, so it's all a little bit of this, a little bit of that. I basically follow my nose.

How did you begin in your field of work?

Well, totally by accident, I guess. In the 1970s, I was the travel editor for *Essence*, briefly. And as the travel editor, I ended up starting a column that was part of the travel column, but it was called "The Go Gourmet." I would go to a place and write about the food of the place, so that's kind of what started me thinking about food and culture, and certainly food and culture in the African-Atlantic world, because those were a lot of the places that I went.

What are you most proud of in your career so far?

I guess that I've had a career. The fact that it has happened at all, the fact that somehow I got a book published back in 1985 that then spawned a whole lot of things—that have spawned this moment. I guess I'm proud of the fact that I put my nose to the grindstone, got it done, and got a book written that in some ways still holds up. It doesn't necessarily and always, because there's much in it I probably would recant. You know, stuff has changed, and things have moved—the world evolves.

What's an important lesson that you've learned about compensation, money, or negotiation over the course of your career?

When I started, the thing that I probably should have known is you are worth more than you think you are. I think young people today kind of have another sense of their worth and don't mind asking—and demanding, in fact, in some cases—being paid appropriately. But I certainly didn't have a sense of my worth and didn't do that.

What do you most enjoy about your work?

The doing it. I really like the researching. I am a curious person, and so I can start to write and then look up and go, "Oh, my god. Three hours went by. Where'd they go?" So that I very much do enjoy. I enjoy the researching, and I enjoy the writing. The part that I don't enjoy and that I am going to try to do considerably less of is I'm not really a lover of writing recipes, because I don't really cook that way.

What have been some of your feelings seeing the resurgence or the rebirth of *High on the Hog*, to see it as a show that you are in and also to see it gain popularity years later?

Well, I mean, one of the things is I am immensely grateful to Karis and Fabienne—and Roger and Shoshana and everybody who was involved in it, in the creation of it, because they took a vision that was my vision, but then they moved it to a different medium and a different space. And I think all of those things created something that has now taken on a life of its own. Somebody was telling me that there are people posting recipes from this on the web and there are people who have started their whole conversations. It has spawned another kind of discussion, and I am immensely honored and proud of that.

What brings you joy, and what would you like to experience more of?

I am a sociable person, so I like being with people. I like entertaining. I'd like to definitely experience more of that because I really haven't been able to do it under the pandemic. And I love to travel. I'd like to do more of that. But I'd like to, I think—not think. I'd like to have a companion in life. It's not the rock of my soul. I will live on and die happily if it doesn't happen, but I will be, I think, a little bit more fulfilled and happier if it does, and so I'm just telling everybody out there, "If you've got an uncle, think about me." But I think I'm—I'm okay. I'm okay. There's a lot of stuff I like to think I have left to do. I know I've got— well, I've got two books to write that are under contract, so I know I've got to do those. But then there are a couple of other projects after that that I want to do as well. There's stuff that I'm just beginning to think about.

How do you take care of your mental health and deal with the stresses of your work?

Honestly, I don't know that I do, and I'm going to start trying to. I'm going to spend a bit more time pampering me. I've got to find a mani-pedi place in Brooklyn, so if you've got one let me know. I need to find a massage person and a place in Brooklyn. I've got one, ironically, in New Orleans, and I've got one, ironically, up here [on Martha's Vineyard]—but in the place where I spend much of my time (probably most of my time), I don't have one, and that's sort of telling about my connection to that space. So I need to find those people in that place.

I'm going to try to spend time with friends, and I'm going to allow myself to create, actually, a space where I have a lovely comfortable chair in which I can simply sit and read.

I don't have that. I have it up here. I don't have it in New Orleans, but I'm going to make sure that I have that in all places—and where I can also watch television. I think I'm getting ready to get a little bit back to television. I haven't been really a TV person. It is not something that got me through the pandemic.

What are some of your favorite things to eat or drink?

Wine. And I am trying—I have actually upped my wine game. I'm drinking more expensive wine, and that's good and bad at the same time, but it's—why not? And for food, clearly I love okra. It's everywhere, sort of, around me. I think it depends on time and place. There are some nights that I want a comforting soup, and then there are some nights that I may just require a steak. I am a carnivore. I was with a friend who is a vegan, and she said, "No. No meat," and it was like, "Oh, well." "And no cheese." It's like, "Wait a minute. No meat, no cheese—what?!" So I am an omnivore. I try to do everything in moderation, including the red wine.

"High on the Hog has spawned another kind of discussion, and I am immensely honored and proud of that."

Rahanna Bisseret Martinez

CHEF, COOKBOOK AUTHOR
OAKLAND, CALIFORNIA

How would you describe your work?

I would describe my work as just all-around food: food media, cooking in restaurants, food writing, culinary TV shows, and just anything that involves food, I really love to do.

How did you begin in your field?

I first started off on a competition show, *Top Chef Junior*, and that's where I first started, I guess, professionally cooking. And it was definitely a strange way to start in the culinary industry, but it was a really fun experience. And I'm glad that I got that as one of my first experiences in a professional kitchen.

How old were you at the time?

I was fourteen at the time.

Who are some of your role models or mentors in the food space?

I have a lot of mentors and role models.

My number one role model has been Leah Chase, because she just inspired me from such a young age, from being the inspiration for [Disney's] *The Princess and the Frog*, and then the Dooky Chase's [restaurant], and just her legacy all around, had the biggest impact on me growing up. Also people like Bryant Terry and Julia Turshen have been supportive and really great mentors to me.

What are you most proud of?

I am most proud of my book deal because I got it when I was sixteen years old. I didn't know much of anything about pitching a book, so it was really just tweaking things and looking at other examples. It was a fun experience.

What advice would you offer to somebody who wants to do what you do?

Just cook whenever they can and however they want. What I love about cooking is the creativity, and I think that's what inspires a lot of other people. And then also finding out what it is about food that you really love and continuing with that.

What do you most enjoy about your career?

What I most enjoy is being in community with other people who really love to cook and then also being free to express myself with my food. Because I love to cook food from my culture and being able to connect with my ancestors and relatives in that way, and then also show it to other people, is something I find super special.

Whole Roasted Sweet Potato

WITH CANELA GINGER CRUMBLE

BY RAHANNA BISSERET MARTINEZ / MAKES 4 SERVINGS

2 medium sweet potatoes, scrubbed

4 teaspoons butter, at room temperature

½ cup light brown sugar

1 teaspoon grated fresh ginger

¼ cup chopped pecans

½ teaspoon salt

1 teaspoon ground cinnamon

1 teaspoon ground nutmeg

1 teaspoon grated lemon zest

½ cup flour

In my family, we roast sweet potatoes whole, cut them in half, and sprinkle the cut surfaces with cinnamon, brown sugar, and butter, or for a more savory taste we use turmeric, cumin, and white pepper (inspired by the flavors of the Middle Eastern squash dish Borani Kadoo). Finally, we pop them under the broiler for a minute or so. My adaptation has a streusel-like topping that adds a zesty, warmly spiced accent. It would even be good served with ice cream for dessert.

Preheat the oven to 425°F.

Place the sweet potatoes on a foil- or parchment-lined baking sheet and roast until tender, about 1 hour.

Meanwhile, in a small bowl, mix the butter, sugar, ginger, pecans, salt, cinnamon, nutmeg, lemon zest, and flour. The mixture should look sandy. Set aside.

The sweet potatoes are done when they can be pierced easily with a fork. Remove them from the oven (leave it on) and, protecting your hands with potholders or oven mitts, cut each one in half lengthwise.

Place the halves cut side up on the pan and sprinkle each with a quarter of the topping mixture. Return the pan to the oven, placing it on the top rack, and roast the sweet potatoes for about 20 minutes more, until lightly browned. Serve warm or at room temperature.

Ashtin Berry

HOSPITALITY ACTIVIST,
SOMMELIER, MIXOLOGIST,
FOUNDER OF
RADICALXCHANGE *NEW
ORLEANS, LOUISIANA*

How would you describe your work?

I would say my work is three-pronged, is the best way to put it. There is work as @thecollectress, which is my social media presence. There's the equity work that I do with clients short term and long term, and then there is the work that we do as RadicalxChange. So I would describe my work as a multi-hyphenate, and I would say that it kind of ranges from structural organizational work all the way to social influencing–type work.

How did you begin in these various fields?

It's been a long journey. I have a long history of doing community work and having training around equity. I started off with bystander work surrounding sexual assault and domestic violence in my early adulthood, and that was informed by the work in community practices that I had been groomed in

as a child, and then eventually I started integrating those into the industry.

What are you most proud of?

I would say my personal growth. It's probably the thing that I'm most proud of. I would also say I'm pretty proud of the commitment to the process rather than perfection. I think that it's really easy in this industry to get caught up in a performance of what things should look like, rather than for the process and whether you're actually doing . . . if you actually are having the conversation that needs to be had and doing the work that is necessary.

What are some of the things you would most like to see change in the hospitality and beverage industry?

I'd like to see more of a discussion about how our systems within hospitality of food and beverage are a reflection of political policy. I'd like to see more of a discussion of, literally, what that means on a local, state, and national level. I'd like to see a more overall language or lexicon of language, in terms of being able to have discussions around equity and antiracism or whatever social disposition. I think the hospitality industry tends to work in very niche and siloed sectors, with people in fine dining, or nicer dining spaces, operating and pulling together, while people who are in backroom areas, kind of being siloed separately, with people who are laborers being separate, with people in beverage who are being separate, even the breakdown of beverages, beer and wine, all operate independently, there is no overall language for the industry and therefore there's not an overall language for consumers. And I think that's really prohibitive to forming or even regulating or restructuring many of the issues that people are saying we have. There's a lack of collaboration in terms of resources because of that.

How do you take care of your mental health and deal with the stresses of your work?

I am definitely in therapy, that is critical, I think, and ongoing. I do not think that therapy is a crisis-only kind of support system. I think therapy is one of those things that I do and keep to, in order to keep my mind where it needs to be. The other thing that I do is reading, making time for dead silence throughout the day, with no phone, no nothing, just making time. Meditation is really important, but also I think, understanding and establishing boundaries and keeping those boundaries. American culture, but specifically the hospitality industry, is not used to people having established boundaries and keeping them, and therefore people can respond to a boundary being set in very ungracious ways, because we told people that they should always have access to us. I think setting boundaries is one of the ways that . . . I'm okay with even like, "no." I think "no" is a complete sentence.

What advice would you offer to someone who wants to do what you do?

Go and actually do the training and do the work. I think one of the ways that misogyny and white-supremacy culture work specifically against Black women, is people see Black women do something and they assume that they don't have the expertise or skill set, and that's just simply not true. I have people who email me regularly saying, "I want to do what you do." And then when I tell them what I've done, suddenly they want a shortcut, right? Yeah, I am significantly young for the things that I've done, but I started this work, not intentionally, but because of proxy of the work that my mother did, I started this work at a young age. You don't get to skip those steps just because you're older, right? I think it's more wanting to be interested in dismantling white supremacy, it's more than academicizing, I'm making up a word, or intellectualizing what antiracism is, it's an internalization of understanding how those systems operate in real time. So you can disrupt them, and that takes a lot of practice over a lot of time.

It's a muscle memory, right? I would say to anybody who wants to do that, ask yourself, "What is it you exactly want to do?" Because when I ask, people tell me, "I want to do what you do." And I say, "Well, what is it that you think I do?" Most of the time, 90 percent of the time, they point to the work that I'd call social media. Right? But I don't get paid for that work. That's 15 percent of my work. And I say, "Okay, well, if you want to do that, I think starting with probably taking some courses," right? So that you can have

a deeper-level understanding, not just reading the books, would be a great start.

What are some of your favorite things to eat or drink?

Eating really depends on the season, I'll be perfectly honest. I'm definitely a seasonal eater. I eat a lot more of fish and seafood in the summertime and fresh greens and things of that nature, but I will say overall, Chinese and Korean food tend to be two of my favorite cuisines. Right after that, I would probably have to say like Central American, Mexican kind of food, or Caribbean flavors. I love the uniqueness of the Caribbean from island to island to island. There's all these variations, you can see them linked together, but there's all these different variations. To drink: If I'm drinking neat, which I tend to do often in the summertime, it's going to be agave. I love to have some type of mezcal or tequila.

Or I love Paranubes rum, which is a Mexican rum. It is my favorite rum in the world, and it is so good, it has notes that remind me of Agricole. Those would be my two go-to. I live in New Orleans now, so we don't have a real winter, but back in the day when I lived in Chicago and we had a real winter, I was a huge scotch drinker and loved scotch. I tend to prefer things neat. I also drink wine. I keep Champagne in my fridge—that's the only thing you can count on me having in my fridge. That and mayo.

Amanda Yee

CHEF, CREATIVE DIRECTOR AT 4 COLOR BOOKS
BERLIN, GERMANY

How would you describe your work?

My overall general work has always been about community building through food, whether that's cooking or cookbooks or community events. General storytelling, I think, has been my overall life's work basis.

How did you begin in your field?

I actually went to university for English and sociology, and I noticed very early on that as a sociologist, I noticed this way that food connected people.

What I admired about the American—Black American—church was how, at one point, the church was the place for connection. And then I noticed that could be done with food, right?

So I graduated with my degree in sociology and I was like, "Okay, I'm going to build community and I think we do this using food." So then I went to culinary school and always had that intention in mind.

How I want to use food is not a restaurant, or if it is a restaurant, it's a restaurant that's community minded. Whatever I'm doing with food is just the conduit for community.

What advice would you offer to someone who wants to do what you do?

That's a great question. I think that I would say to get dirty. To not be scared to fail and fail again. I think that's important. My restaurant was not a success. It was in some ways positive, but in a lot of ways I deemed it a failure, but I didn't let that set me back, and I let it kind of mold and shape me and help me to identify what it is I really wanted. *Oh, I like these parts of it, but I don't like these parts of it.* And *This is true to me, but this isn't true to me.*

I think that the best thing that you can do is take a risk. And I think a lot of people are really scared to do that. I have an ex, this guy I used to date, who would always say, "You got to pay to play." And I think that's important. Rarely can you get something for nothing. You have to pay to play and you have to be willing to show up in life, I think, to speak what's on your mind and be okay if people reject you. To do the bold thing. I think that's really important.

Do you have a mission or motto, and if so, what is it?

My motto has always been: Good storytelling is good art. And then my mission, I just want to be me. I want to be free to be me. So I'm constantly looking for the best way to do that.

What do you most enjoy about your career?

I mean, obviously eating. Eating is up there. Getting to travel, getting to meet new people has been part of it. But I think what I love most is just that I get paid to think and be creative, which is just such a blessing. I get paid for my ideas, which I think is just really cool and I love that.

What's the most difficult aspect of your career?

Overall, what's the most difficult? I'm still a baby in some ways, and I haven't been able to really find stability, the stability that I want. I think that's the flip side of always being a risk-taker—sometimes you don't find stability because you're always taking risks. And so I think that has been a hard thing for me; I just have not felt settled or stable because I'm always flying by the seat of my pants.

What are some of your favorite things to eat or drink?

I love dim sum. I love Cantonese, Californian Cantonese cooking. And then I think to drink, I've always been a kombucha fiend. The Better Booch cherry kombucha, I'd date. I go to sleep thinking about that sometimes.

Octopus in Rougail Saucisse
WITH SQUID INK HUSH PUPPIES

BY AMANDA YEE / MAKES 8 SERVINGS

OCTOPUS

8 octopus legs, about 1 pound total

2 medium oranges, halved

1½ cups white wine

4–6 bay leaves

4 scallions

1 teaspoon pink peppercorns

Salt and pepper

Chopped parsley, for garnish

This recipe is my spin on Rougail Saucisse, which is a rich tomato stew made with sausages and aromatic spices and simmered on low heat. The word "rugail" means a mix of spices and condiments, and the dish Rougail Saucisse is a staple in Mauritius, Reunion Island, and Madagascar. It's often served with rice, but I've added octopus and squid ink hush puppies instead as a twist. The sauce is hearty and delicious and begs to be scooped and sopped up by the hush puppies. I highly recommend this dish for a casual dinner party among good friends.

You can buy squid ink on Amazon, and your local fishmonger or Fresh Direct will have octopus.

HUSH PUPPIES

1¼ cups coarse cornmeal

¾ cup all-purpose flour

2 tablespoons brown sugar

1 teaspoon baking powder

¼ teaspoon baking soda

Pinch of salt

2 eggs

1 cup buttermilk

2 tablespoons squid ink

Canola or sunflower oil, for frying

Salt

ROUGAIL SAUCISSE SAUCE

6 large andouille sausages,
cut into chunks

2 large onions, peeled and diced

4 cups canned fire-roasted tomatoes

2 garlic cloves, peeled and crushed

2 ounces salt-cured capers

Salt, freshly ground black pepper,
and Aleppo pepper flakes

For the octopus, in a large pot combine the octopus legs, oranges, wine, bay leaves, scallions, pink peppercorns, and salt and pepper to taste. Bring to a boil over high heat, reduce heat, and simmer, covered, for 1 hour. Octopus legs should shrink by half and be fork tender. Set the pot off the heat and let the octopus rest in the cooking water for about an hour.

Meanwhile, mix the hush puppy batter. In a large bowl, whisk together the cornmeal, flour, brown sugar, baking powder, baking soda, and salt. In a medium bowl, beat the eggs and buttermilk. Stir the egg mixture into the cornmeal mixture. Once mostly stirred, add the squid ink and mix until the batter turns black. Cover the batter and allow it to firm up in the refrigerator for 30 minutes to 1 hour.

For the sauce, brown the sausage in a large, heavy-bottomed pot over high heat. Remove it from the pot and set it aside. Reduce the heat to medium, add the onions and cook, stirring occasionally, until caramelized, about 5 to 8 minutes. Stir in tomatoes and garlic, and simmer for about 5 minutes. Using an immersion blender (or working in batches in a countertop blender or food processor), process the sauce until smooth. Stir in the capers, reserved sausage, and salt, pepper, and Aleppo pepper flakes to taste. Adjust the heat and simmer the sauce, partially covered, for 20 to 30 minutes.

Preheat the grill to 375°F or set to hot, or heat a grill pan on the stovetop over medium-high heat for the octopus.

Heat several inches of oil in a Dutch oven to 375° F and fry the hush puppies: Scoop small balls of batter into the hot oil and fry, turning once, for 2 to 3 minutes per side. (Because the batter is black it will be harder to tell when they are done, so fry a test hush puppy first to get the hang of it.) Drain the hush puppies on paper towels.

Once the hush puppies are finished and waiting, drain the octopus legs and grill them for 2 to 3 minutes per side to give them some color and a little char.

To serve, divide the Rougail Saucisse sauce among eight shallow bowls, top each portion with an octopus leg, and surround it with hush puppies. Garnish with parsley.

Zella Palmer

CHAIR AND DIRECTOR,
DILLARD UNIVERSITY
RAY CHARLES PROGRAM
IN AFRICAN AMERICAN
MATERIAL CULTURE *NEW
ORLEANS, LOUISIANA*

How would you describe your work?

I would consider myself a cultural anthropologist, a storyteller. I am really focused on telling untold stories about Black chefs, particularly in the eighteenth and nineteenth centuries, and through that it's also me digging and just correlating it back to New Orleans, the South—I am really rooted in the South and the Great Migration. And it's really me, also, trying to learn more about my parents and grandparents and their ancestors. I'm the third generation to work at an HBCU.

That means a lot to me when I look at the trajectory of what they've done. My great-grandfather was Madam C. J. Walker's doctor, and my grandfather—he taught at Lincoln, Howard, and Tuskegee. So that means a lot to me. I'm just trying to tell stories and curate stories, but also really focused on this academic program because we're the first food studies program at an HBCU.

I'm a material culturalist and I try to expose our students to our rich culture and history. Because if we don't pass it down to them and get them to have real hands-on experience, then it's lost, or it's become somebody else's, and then somebody else is telling our stories—which happens all the time.

We received a grant to look at the legacies of American slavery from Yale University and the Council of Independent Colleges, so this whole summer we've been working on filming. We wrote the culture creativity portion of the grant, which is going to focus on looking at the legacies of American slavery with food, music, and tourism. My students get to interview Dr. Howard Conyers and look at Black farming and the legacy of slavery with Black farming. With music, we interviewed the director of the New Orleans Jazz Museum: How was Congo Square and jazz pivotal to spreading this American music genre?

And then with tourism, we get to interview Dr. Erin Greenwald, who was curator of "Purchased Lives," an exhibition at the Historic New Orleans Collection, and looked at the domestic slave trade: How Southern towns like New Orleans and Charleston, were hubs for tourism during slavery that brought all the world to them, but also had slave pens everywhere? There's a hotel in the French Quarter that still has the word "exchange" on the side of the building, and that was where enslaved people were sold, and right across the street is Pierre Maspero's restaurant. It's been there since 1786. That was where people—after they bought a slave, then they sent them across the street with whatever outfit, and they go eat. That was really common.

I am honored to come behind Dr. Jessica Harris, who was the first endowed chair, and I just pray that I continue to make this program just totally epic.

Can you tell me more about the food program—the full name and how it was conceived of and when it began?

So it's the Dillard University Ray Charles Program in African American Material Culture. Ray Charles has always loved New Orleans. He was very good friends with Leah Chase and Dooky Chase, Jr. There's a lot of focus on Ms. Leah, but Dooky Chase, Jr., he was the man in

New Orleans. He brought all the best Black musicians in the 1940s and '50s to New Orleans. He was a music promoter, so he was bringing Ella Fitzgerald, Ray Charles, and all these headliners, and it was Mr. Dooky who told Ray Charles, when he was at his lowest point and he was living in New Orleans—he was on drugs—and he told him, "Listen. I want you to do a country album," and he did it, and that took his music to a whole other plateau and opened up so many different doors for him. He even has a song called "Early in the Morning," and he talks about eating at Dooky Chase.

So in 2003, Dillard wanted to give an honorary degree to Ray Charles, and he was so honored that he sat down with then president Dr. Michael Lomax, and he said he wanted to do something with the food. He wanted to make sure that we preserve our foodways, but then it started a larger conversation. It was like, "No. We need to do more than that. We need to also have a material culture program because it's the entire culture, the entire Black culture."

So I became the second chair, and immediately I wanted to have a food studies academic accredited program because I was looking at New York University, I was looking at Boston University, and I know that we needed that in this city. We are not in executive positions when it comes to journalism, when it comes to food media, when it comes to restaurant management. Whatever it is, we have got to be in those positions in food photography or whatever, and if we can create the theory and practicum behind it, then we can create opportunities for our students.

I also wanted to do continuing education, because there was such a need for Black chefs and caterers in the city to get the skills they needed to be successful, and we launched a restaurant and catering management program, and it was amazing because we even had a distance learner who was a food studies student at NYU. So that was super exciting.

And then, finally, right before the pandemic, we launched the food studies minor, and I tried to follow in the same path that the film majors. We have an incredible film program, and a lot of those students are also food studies students and Ray Charles Scholarship recipients, so we get to visually tell these stories.

And the greenhouse on campus—it's a huge greenhouse, and it's sitting in the middle of the oaks, and it's been lying dormant for years. A kind donor fixed the glass, and so now the part of the money that was raised from the foundation is going to go toward actually growing things. We want to grow food on campus. We're in a food apartheid area, and when you think about college students and the access to food . . . And just being able to work in that greenhouse too, it floods back to food studies, it floods back to botany, biology, so it supports all of our programs. And just the joy of alumni coming on campus and seeing, "Oh, those are Creole tomatoes growing. That's okra growing. Like, what?!" I want them to get excited about that, so that's the ultimate goal.

How did you begin in your field?

Actually, like a lot of people, in women's kitchens: in auntie's kitchen and my mom's kitchen, my grandmother, just listening to their stories—even extended family because I have such an extended family. I grew up in Chicago. My mother and my dad were activists. They were part of the Free South Africa movement in Chicago. My mom was a senator, and my dad, he worked closely with Kofi Annan and the United Nations, so we lived all over the world. We lived in Mexico. We were in Germany. It was always these political exiles who were in my house, you know what I mean, and they were always cooking. So I had aunties from Cuba, uncles from Kenya, all of these different people that just made all this tremendous food, and the dining room was always this place where people would bring their dishes, and there was conversation. There was a hotel called the Palmer House, and we used to call our house the Palmer House South. That's really what got me started.

What are some of your favorite things to eat or drink?

A good gumbo, and grilled cheese. One of my favorites is from Heard Dat Kitchen. Their gumbo is really good. Ms. Leah's gumbo is really good. Ms. Linda—oh, my god. Ms. Linda Green, the Ya-Ka-Mein Lady. She's definitely one of my mentors, and she's like a mom to me.

New Orleans Barbecue Shrimp

BY ZELLA PALMER / MAKES 20 SERVINGS

6 pounds jumbo shrimp (preferably Louisiana)

1 cup (2 sticks) butter

1 sprig fresh rosemary, chopped

2 tablespoons brown sugar

1 tablespoon smoked paprika

1 teaspoon Creole seasoning

1 teaspoon crab boil

2 lemons, cut into wedges

⅓ cup chopped fresh parsley

French bread, for serving

New Orleans Barbecue Shrimp are not actually barbecued or doused in barbecue sauce—they're simply sautéed in a generous amount of butter and spices. Apparently, long ago a Chicago businessman raved about the "barbecue" shrimp he had eaten in New Orleans. But it was more likely that he was referring to shrimp at Pascal's Manale, which was and is famous for its BBQ shrimp (though many restaurants in New Orleans prepare the same dish).

Preheat oven to 325°F.

Rinse any grit off the shrimp, leaving heads and tails on.

In a large cast-iron skillet, melt the butter over medium heat. Stir in the rosemary, brown sugar, paprika, Creole seasoning, and crab boil.

Add the shrimp and cook it, basting constantly with the seasoned butter, just until it turns completely pink, 3 to 5 minutes. Transfer to the oven for 8 minutes.

Remove the pan from the oven. Squeeze a little lemon over the cooked shrimp and garnish it with the parsley. Serve immediately with french bread and the remaining lemon wedges.

Gumbo Z'Herbes

BY MRS. ERNEST CHERRIE / MAKES 6–8 SERVINGS

Salt and freshly ground black pepper

1 bunch spinach

1 bunch watercress

1 bunch turnip greens

1 bunch beet greens

1 bunch collard greens

1 bunch mustard greens

1 head green cabbage

½ pound ham, chopped

½ pound pickled pork or salt meat or ham hock, chopped

1 pound hot sausage (such as andouille), chopped

1 onion, chopped

1 garlic clove, chopped

When I think of Gumbo Z'Herbes I think of Miss Leah Chase. On Holy Thursday, it's tradition in New Orleans to have Gumbo Z'Herbes. Leah Chase was the gatekeeper of Creole cuisine in New Orleans. Every time she served a dish, she had a story behind it. And Holy Thursday, you're lucky if you can get a seat at Dooky Chase's Restaurant. In the Gumbo Z'Herbes you have an uneven number of greens, because that's supposedly good luck. You never want to put even greens in your gumbos. Also, she would talk about how the old Creoles used to collect peppergrass and that would give the food a kick, and then you'd have all types of assorted meat in the gumbo. Everyone in New Orleans has their own style of making Gumbo Z'Herbes. This recipe is a version of Gumbo Z'Herbes by Mrs. Ernest Cherrie, who contributed the recipe to the Dillard Cookbook many years ago. This version has seven different kinds of greens plus ham and sausage.

Bring a large pot of water to a boil and add a pinch of salt and pepper. Coarsely chop the spinach, watercress, greens, and cabbage. Add the greens to the boiling water and cook for 2 to 4 minutes, until vibrant green. Reserve 4 cups of the cooking liquid, drain the rest, and chop the greens.

Heat a large Dutch oven over medium-high heat. Add the chopped meats with the onions and garlic and cook until browned, 8 to 10 minutes. Add the greens and reserved cooking water and simmer for about 60 minutes.

Sarah Thompson

BUTCHER, BAKER, BREWER, FOUNDER OF TALL POPPY POP-UP *PHILADELPHIA, PENNSYLVANIA*

How would you describe your work?

I do a little bit of everything. My work is an amalgamation of the many skills I've picked up over the past ten-plus years of working in the service industry. I bake, I make charcuterie, I forage. I currently have a pop-up called Tall Poppy, where I make buttermilk biscuits and I use those as a blank canvas for anything and everything. I've layered on lardo (from Pennsylvania pork, which I'd had in cure for a year), stacked pork roll (the fermentation of which was a fun learning experience), and slathered on foraged herb spread, which I gathered with friends on a day off from work. People always ask about the name Tall Poppy as well so I figure I'll clear that up now: Tall Poppy syndrome is a New Zealand–Australian concept of "jealous people holding back or directly attacking those who are perceived to be better than the norm, 'cutting down the tall poppy.'" In

other words, you're not supposed to be seen as having any pride in yourself, otherwise it could be interpreted as boastful and pretentious. This cultural phenomenon I had to work around coincided perfectly with a time when I was just learning to be proud of myself and recognize my achievements. I *obviously* had to be a Tall Poppy.

How did you begin in your field?

When I was a teenager I spent summers scooping ice cream at a local shop in my very touristy hometown. Simple as all hell, but being able to have a hand in someone's "dining experience" was so gratifying, plus I got to eat all the ice cream I wanted. Later it was working in a salad shop on University Avenue in Palo Alto while I struggled to figure out my place in higher education. I dropped out of community college and decided to move to the Pacific Northwest and go to culinary school. That nine-month program ended up being kind of a bust, but it got my foot in the door for a baking job at a restaurant, which subsequently landed me in the world of craft beer (baking and brewing are not all that different!). I ended up brewing for a couple of years, and then after a bout of depression and a feeling of stagnancy, I decided on a whim to move to New Zealand and apprenticed with an Auckland-based butcher/charcutier I'd found on Instagram. (A Lady Butcher in Auckland! Cheers, Hannah!) I mention all of these jobs because each one was its own "new beginning," challenging me to start from square one and build up the necessary skills from basically nothing.

What are you most proud of?

I really admire community builders. And while I'm not sure I would call myself that, I can say that I am very good at maintaining connections with people, even if I've only

met them once or twice. Two of my previous colleagues are people I met on Instagram, so I think that speaks for itself. My Tall Poppy pop-up has allowed me to work with folks who I otherwise might never have met, people who also want room to play with their skills or show off their talent. Through the pop-up, my friend and co-runner, Andy, has been able to revisit some of the things she learned as a kid, like jamming, pickling, and canning. I'm just happy to have helped create a space that invites people to do what they love, and then have strangers enjoy it! I guess I'm also pretty proud of the Tall Poppy fan club.

Do you have a mission or motto, and if so, what is it?

I want Tall Poppy to be a pop-up for industry workers. I've mostly hosted them on Mondays (i.e., the industry weekend) because that's when I had use of the kitchen, but it worked out perfectly because my industry friends would actually be able to come through. I also want to continue to work with service workers who might not always have a place to show off their personal skills. Oftentimes you might be working for a few years making someone else's product with little individual input other than staff meal (No shade! Bless all ye who make staff meal.). I want to collaborate with workers who want to put their food out in the world. As I've said, I love community. I think it's a special way to gather people and make them feel a part of something. Whether it's providing food or skills for a community event, trading biscuits for homemade pizza, collaborating with a local beekeeper (all things that have happened!), it's all a part of being in community with one another and I want to continue to hold that space.

What do you most enjoy about your work?

My work is really one of the few spaces where I get to express myself creatively. I'm someone who finds comfort in structure. Charcuterie, beer, biscuits, all have a specific series of steps you must take to get the completed product. Once you know those steps, and feel comfortable with the process, you can play around within those confines. With beer and charcuterie specifically, you can introduce different spices, herbs, fermentation processes, etc., and get a wonderful array of outcomes. Biscuits are a little different, but as I said earlier, they're just another canvas. I get to make jams, sausages, spreads, cultured butters, whatever I want to put on the sandwiches. It's such a perfect jumping-off point for me. I also love to forage, so it gives me an excuse to get outside and find ramps or flowers or mushrooms. I love that my work

allows me to combine all of my interests in a way that feels fulfilling to me.

How do you take care of your mental health and deal with the stresses of your work?

I come from a long line of nappers. For better or for worse, I'm really good at taking naps, whether it's a twenty-minute catnap or a three-hour mini sleep. This doesn't help as much when you're working on your feet all day, but it's certainly a great way to help recover from rough work weeks. I also am a huge advocate for therapy. I found my first therapist at a center in Philly. She billed on a sliding scale and she truly turned my life around. Group therapy is also an amazing experience. I was fortunate enough to go to weekly group therapy sessions for "Womxn of African Ancestry," and that was incredibly powerful in healing my issues around self-worth and identity. Lastly, I've found that nurturing strong relationships with my coworkers is hugely beneficial—specifically those who bring positivity to my life. The industry is rough, and it's so easy to get caught in cycles of negativity. My industry coworkers have become some of my best friends in life. For instance, I had one friend who would pull me aside and make me sit in the stairway to cry for ten minutes while they watched my tables. Or sometimes between services we would make up dumb games or imaginary scenarios to entertain each other and keep our spirits up. So yeah, naps, therapy, and cracking jokes during service is how I survive.

What are some of your favorite things to eat or drink?

I'm a big gin gal. Love it over ice or with soda water. I love its herbaceousness, and it's cool to see what botanicals different distillers add, whether to change it for the season or to otherwise make it their own. It also helps that it's one of the very few liquors I can drink without suffering an immense hangover.

It's almost too hard to choose a favorite food. Lately I've been craving meat less and seafood more. For those who don't know, there's a ton of pescatarian Jamaicans, and my dad is one of them. I've heard him describe it as just losing a taste for things like goat, chicken, and pork. I wonder if the same is happening to me. With that in mind, seafood boils are absolutely one of my favorites. I grew up on the Eastern Shore of Maryland, so I can pick a crab with the best of them, and crab feasts were practically a mandated summer event.

Rice & Peas

BY SARAH THOMPSON / MAKES 5–6 SERVINGS

Medium-grain rice (Grandma Gloria didn't specify the type, but I always saw Uncle Ben's parboiled rice in her kitchen)

Dried pigeon peas, soaked overnight

Onion, peeled and chopped or diced

Garlic, whole cloves smashed ("never too much")

Thyme, preferably fresh, stem and all

Whole black peppercorns

Lawry's Seasoned Salt

Canned coconut milk (Parrot or Grace brand if you can find either)

This my late grandmother's "recipe" for rice and peas. She was the first of her family to immigrate to the United States from Jamaica, bringing my twelve-year-old father with her. Eventually the rest of her family joined her in New York City, and being that she was one of twelve siblings, each of whom had their own families, it was quite the exodus. Fast-forward to my childhood, nearly thirty years later, and my dad moved our immediate family from Staten Island to the rural Eastern Shore of Maryland, where Old Bay was the spiciest seasoning going. Every summer we drove the five hours to New York, and for two weeks my siblings and I would stay at my grandma's house. Those were the only times I'd get to eat Jamaican food, and I fell in love with curried goat, brown-stew chicken, and callaloo cooked down with onions and peppers. But it was the rice and peas that carried the whole plate for me. Fragrant rice with full stems of thyme and whole peppercorns, all dotted with little round brown peas that gave way perfectly as you bit into them.

Rinse your rice with cold water until the water runs clear. The amount doesn't quite matter, as you'll find out shortly.

Set your peas in a heavy-bottomed pot and cover them with about 2 inches of water. Add your onion, garlic, thyme, and peppercorns, and shake in some Lawry's—you're really giving these peas some love.

Let this come to a boil so that your peas are getting soft and they are infused with the aromatics. If they're still hard and you need to add more water, that's fine. You'll want much of the water to steam off the peas.

Stir in the rice, let's say a cup and a half or so. Try to level off the contents of the pot, making the surface as even as possible.

Pour in a can of coconut milk and add water to cover the rice and peas—enough to reach just below the first knuckle of your fingertip. In other words, dip your pointer finger in the pot, and the liquid should come just to the crease in your fingertip, right above your nail.

Bring everything to a boil and then lower to medium heat, cooking off liquid until you can just see the top of the rice. Cover the pot with a lid and cook for another 10 minutes or so.

Turn off the heat, uncover the pot, and fluff the rice to your liking. You can pick the thyme sprigs out or eat around them as I did as a kid.

Jillian Knox

FOOD STYLIST *SAN FRANCISCO, CALIFORNIA*

How would you describe your work?

That is a loaded question. I wear many hats. I do food, wardrobe, and prop styling. But I think most of the time I do food and props, usually in tandem or one or the other. Not so much wardrobe these days, just because of the pandemic and being in people's personal space. And that kind of feels weird to be shoving your hands down someone's pants to fix their shirt. It's kind of weird, so I don't really do it that much. But yeah, mostly food and props these days, which is really great.

How did you begin in your field, and specifically, how did you begin as a food stylist and prop stylist?

Well, I went to school for photography, I went to the Savannah College of Art and Design. I have a BFA in photography. My final year was supposed to end in 2008, but I had a quarter left over, but everyone knows 2008 was the worst year to graduate. So I had to pivot pretty hard. And I started doing wardrobe styling and shooting my own stuff for my vintage store. So I basically started a vintage store. And it's so interesting how everything pieced itself together, over many years of going full time as a stylist and photographer in-house for a fashion company and then starting a food blog with my friend. And then when I left styling as a full-time employee, I went freelance and just used my repertoire and all of my food photos and recipes as a jumping-off point to start food styling.

Who are some of your role models or mentors in the food space?

I would say one of my mentors and kind of encouraging, cheerleading people would be George McCalman. Bryant Terry is definitely one of my food heroes. Dr. Jessica B. Harris is amazing. Really just such a smart woman. I also look up to you . . . There's so many—like Michael Twitty and Stephen Satterfield—just really smart people who are in the food industry. And every year I get to meet more of them, and people who I hadn't heard of before. And I still feel like a baby bird in this situation. My dad was a caterer for over twenty years. And so I grew up around food, just learning from him—how to hold a knife, how to cut a carrot, how to peel potatoes, and different techniques of cooking. And even growing food, I learned a lot from him. So my dad has had a huge impact on my life with food and how to love yourself through food, how to love other people through food and sharing.

What advice would you give to someone who wants to do what you do?

My advice is to find people who do it well and to ask them questions. And to just open yourself up to the possibilities of perhaps needing them because it might happen. I didn't think it would be possible for me and it did, it actually happened. And I was doing it just because I loved it. And I think if you really love something you should just try. So, I think put your big-girl britches on and do it. Just start asking questions, write things down, journal all the time. Take notes when you're in the kitchen. If something's really working, take notes. If you have a question about a technique or a type of food or a cuisine, either find someone who does it really well and ask them the question or really do your research and dive into it.

What are some of the attributes you think make a really good food stylist?

It's interesting for me because I have a photography background and I also have a wardrobe styling background, so I was already like hyperfocused and detail oriented. One of the biggest things about styling and food styling is that you have to pay attention to even the smallest thing. But also because I speak the language of a photographer, I know what they're looking for. I think it gives me kind of an upper hand, because I can communicate with them in a way that other stylists can't. And also I can read them and understand their needs. And I kind of anticipate that. And even with prop styling, I see the photographer, I see what they need. I look at the food and I'm like, what is this food saying?

What is the story of this food? And then the props also feed into that. What do the props say about this food, what do the props say about the story? What are we saying here? What is the whole picture? So I think really picking things apart and looking at the different levels of the story is really kind of . . . it's what makes the food so special because all food has story. All food has history, has emotion, has sentiment. And so I think if you are just like, I'm going to make this sandwich, it's not the same as, where did the sandwich come from? Who made this sandwich? How many hours does it take to make the meat or the sauce or the bread that makes this sandwich? You know what I'm saying? I think just really looking at it on kind of a molecular level is really important.

What is the most difficult part of your work as a food stylist and prop stylist?

I think the most difficult thing is when someone doesn't understand food, and they want you to make it look like something that's not possible. So, an egg, right? Maybe like a ramen egg, that's six to eight minutes. But what you're describing is a hard-boiled egg. I have to show you what that looks like. So I have to say, okay, this is what I think

you want. You want this jelly egg. Runny, yummy, gooey egg. But what you're describing is a hard-boiled egg, which is 12 minutes. So for me to explain it, I sometimes just have to do it and just be like, this is what it looks like. You want a full fish on a platter, but you don't want the head on the fish and you want it to . . . but the picture that you're showing me has the head on the fish.

What do you most enjoy about your work?

I just love the whole process of being able to create something with a team, to create something that looks delicious. To create something that tastes the way it looks. That's really cool to me. I work with [photographer] Oriana [Koren] a lot, and I remember I had to make this ham and liver pâté. And I'm straight up vegan, for real. And I'm like, I don't know. I'm just going to make it up. I'm going to see how it comes out. And there was a really old recipe that I was following that was from 1950-something. And so I was making it kind of old school in that way. And after we shot, it looked great. I was totally shocked that it worked. And Oriana tried it and was like, "This tastes just like it's supposed to." Stuff like that really makes me happy. When a recipe works, it's a real achievement.

What are some of your favorite things to eat and or drink?

My absolute favorite thing to drink is Earl Grey with almond milk. It's just cozy for me. And then, my other favorite thing . . . I mean, I love wine and mezcal, and Negronis. My favorite things to eat: My dad's food is just so good. He makes really killer cornbread. His chili is amazing. My mother-in-law makes delicious nopales.

"My advice is to find people who do it well and to ask them questions. And to just open yourself up to the possibilities of perhaps needing them because it might happen."

Savory Oatmeal

BY JILLIAN KNOX / MAKES 4 SERVINGS

2 cups rolled oats

Coconut oil

Herb salt (fine sea salt blended with dried herbs such as thyme, oregano, fennel, rosemary, and/or lavender)

10 sliced mushrooms, such as cremini or shiitake

1 small diced onion

2 garlic cloves, minced

2 fresh sage leaves, cut in chiffonade

1 tablespoon tamari

1 cup chopped delicate greens such as baby spinach, swiss chard, radish tops, or beet tops

1 teaspoon grated fresh ginger

2 teaspoons toasted sesame oil

½ teaspoon red chili flakes

Maldon or other sea salt

1 teaspoon sesame seeds

3 radishes, sliced

2 English or Persian cucumbers, sliced into half moons

This is a hearty bowl that has a stick-to-your-ribs feeling, great for cold fall mornings or just straight-up comfort food. It features a blend of mushrooms, herbs, greens, and alliums that will make you go back for seconds.

Toast the oats in a Dutch oven or other large, heavy pot over medium-high heat, stirring often, until fragrant and lightly browned, 2 to 3 minutes.

With a wooden spoon, stir in enough oil to coat the grains and add a dash of herb salt. Let the oats sit for a few seconds until fragrant. Stir again and let sit. Repeat this process until the oats are toasted to a golden brown on the edges.

Add 3 cups water and cook over medium-low heat, uncovered, stirring often and scraping the bottom of the pot, until the oats look fluffy, 8 to 12 minutes. Turn off the heat, cover the pot, and set it aside.

Add enough coconut oil to a large, heavy skillet to coat the bottom. Add the mushrooms, spread them so they don't crowd the pan, and cook for 2 to 4 minutes until browned. Turn them over and brown the other side. Transfer to a bowl.

Add a little more oil to the pan, and cook the onions, garlic, and sage until the onions are translucent, about 5 minutes. Stir the mushrooms into the mixture. Add the tamari and stir vigorously, scraping the pan bottom to deglaze it. Transfer the mixture to a bowl.

Add coconut oil and your choice of greens to the pan. On low-medium heat, stir or toss the greens to coat in oil. Add a few tablespoons of cold water, and fresh grated ginger. Stir, cover and cook until greens are bright green and wilted, about 2 to 3 minutes.

Remove lid and add a dash of toasted sesame oil. Stir quickly and remove from heat. Sprinkle it with chili flakes and flaky sea salt (I like Maldon) and sesame seeds. In a bowl, add your oats and layer on your mushrooms and greens. Garnish with slices of fresh radish, and cucumber, and a drizzle of toasted sesame oil. Serve immediately.

Cha McCoy

SOMMELIER, OWNER OF
THE COMMUNION WINE +
SPIRITS *HARLEM, NEW YORK*

How would you describe your work?

I am a Beverage to Human Experiential Producer. I prefer this title to describe my role in the industry, as sommelier captures only a portion of the work that I do. I curate and lead beverage-focused events for both business-to-business and business-to-consumer clients. Mainly, I am in wine sales, tourism, and currently running my own destination-themed wine subscription, Flight Cru, which also doubles as a tour operating company. In addition, I lead a nonprofit program, Lip Service, which raises awareness of language barriers in hospitality, internally among our team and for guests. The idea is to make more Black, Brown, and people of color hospitality professionals more marketable globally and expand their opportunities beyond the United States.

As a sommelier, my job revolves mostly around storytelling—selecting wines and winemakers that resonate with me and pair well not only with food but also with my mission and how it is being experienced.

How did you begin in your field?

After returning to Harlem after living in Italy, I was looking for a way to still connect to Italy. Nothing said "la dolce vita" to me than drinking white wine before noon and then getting paid to do it. I accepted a position at a boutique wine shop in Harlem. I learned about the wine industry here, I started to understand and define my own palate. It was here that I was granted access into the world of wine.

Who are some of your role models or mentors in the food and hospitality space?

Eric White, GM of the Winery, was my first wine boss and exposed me to the different avenues of the industry. Monique Greenwood, founder and owner of Akwaaba Inns, also a previous boss, hired me as an innkeeper and events manager at the Akwaaba Brooklyn property when I told her my goals of building a hospitality company.

Christy Frank, owner of Copake Wine Works. As a new entrepreneur, having someone in your court who knows how to navigate the wine industry, knowing all the rules and regulations regarding wine and spirits—it has been important to have her in my back pocket.

What is an important lesson you've learned about money, compensation, or finance over the course of your career?

After a decade working engineering as a project manager, I recognize that money is not my motivator in this industry, but finding purpose is. Living more intentionally and purposefully is what will truly get you to show up for yourself and others.

Moving to Italy exposed me to a certain joy in my everyday life and in the mundane tasks like going to the market,

"Self-awareness is the cheat code."

meeting friends for aperitivo, and exploring the region. I am relearning now how to balance the two worlds of caring more about money in a way that I am able to use it as a tool to complete the mission I am called for.

What advice would you offer to someone who wants to do what you do?

Don't! Do what *you* do! Seriously. It takes time to learn your strengths, weaknesses, hobbies, and passions. I am fortunate that early in my life I started to question the path I was on and decided to start shaking things up. Traveling often on my own dime, exploring different industries, and also remaining a student has played a major role in my development. After completing my bachelor's and my MBA, I still enrolled in cheese classes at the Institute of Culinary Education, interior design courses and product styling classes at Fashion Institute of Technology, the executive wine business program at university in Portugal, and this is separate from classes related to becoming a sommelier.

Do you have a mission or motto, and if so, what is it?

Self-awareness is the cheat code.

What do you most enjoy about your work?

I simply love working with creative people—in my case it may be farmers, winemakers, distillers—and being able to share their product with the world. Connecting people to a place, culture, or one another has been very fulfilling, and I am happy to use wine as my vessel or oil to do so. I recognize my assignment is centered on the word "unity." I feel very connected to my ancestors, like a wine griot telling the stories about traditions, culture, and terroir of what is in the glass. Oral tradition is in my DNA. It is how my ancestors passed on history and connected us not only to our past but also to this sense of places where we are from. My role as sommelier allows me to take control of the narrative.

What are two of your favorite pairings?

Chablis and crustaceans. Caviar and cava.

Elle Simone Scott

CHEF, FOOD STYLIST,
AUTHOR, HOST OF *THE
WALK-IN* PODCAST,
FOUNDER OF SHECHEF
BOSTON, MASSACHUSETTS

How would you describe your work?

I think I would describe my work as eclectic, because I do a lot of different things in addition to my nine-to-five job, which is essentially food styling, being a personality on a TV show, and podcasting. I think the art world calls that like multi-disciplinary.

I do everything from recipe testing to developing. I do consulting for people who are in the media industry. And while they all to the core probably are similar, or have the same core principle, it varies on any given day. I could be invited to cook at, like, a Hog Farmer Appreciation Dinner by Niman Ranch, and then I can be doing a video for the Jacques Pépin Foundation. And then everything in between.

How did you begin in your field?

It's kind of tragic. I was just kind of fresh out of college, not too fresh, maybe . . . I was just getting my feet wet in my field of social work, which is what my degree is in (one of them). And I was working in social services in Michigan when the recession hit in the early 2000s. And a lot of the nonprofits closed during that time, and I was working in the nonprofit sector.

I love food, I love eating. Let me just be real. I love food, but I love eating more than that. And I always had a restaurant job, like a hospitality job, like being a hostess.

But I love people and so I pursued social work. I love helping people. I love building resources, teaching people how to find resources for themselves, teaching independence. It was something I still love to do. But while I was doing that social work, I would still kind of keep hospitality jobs. Hostessing, being a server if the opportunity was there. So when I lost my job at the agency, I had to lean into the hospitality full time.

And I asked if I could get more hours as front of the house and they were basically like "no." I was working for Darden Restaurants. And they were like, "Well, no, but we just lost a prep cook. Do you know how to do . . ." I was like, "I mean, I've chopped some vegetables in my day, I guess." So basically I would work, sometimes another eight-hour shift back of the house. And I was taught everything about prep by three sisters who were from Guatemala.

And they taught me everything. I mean, there was a huge language barrier between us. Because I don't speak Spanish. Not proud to say that, but I don't. But they helped me a lot and they taught me so much and I never went back. So I was like, I'm going to lose my house, this is not enough money to live on. And I lost everything. I lost my place, I lost my car. I literally hit rock bottom. And just when I was at my very, very end, I saw that Norwegian Cruise Lines was hiring for one position.

So I thought, "Okay, well, this is a great way for me to see if I'm really passionate about this work. Let me just try it out." And I got hired. And I think like three months later, I shipped out to Hawaii.

It was five months on five weeks off. So we only got about five weeks' vacation in the middle of the year, depending on how your contract worked out. And I did that for a few years. I loved it. Not only that, I realized I love cooking. But I loved traveling.

What was it like working on a cruise ship?

So at one time, I think Bravo was trying to do like a reality show. They were auditioning our ship, the *Pride of Hawaii*, for a reality show about living on the ship, because it's its own universe. We're our own community floating in the ocean.

We're a crew of fifteen hundred. And then there are fifteen hundred passengers that revolve every week on the ship. So it's basically like living with the people you work with. It becomes your whole community. We date one another. We become friends. We have fights. People get married and jump ship together. People who have never dated on the ship end up dating off the ship. We have our crew bar where we go and hang out after work.

We have a crew mess, which is like our mess hall, our cafeteria where we eat, and it's the place where you can find a budding couple sitting at a table when the cafeteria is closed, no food being served, they're talking and holding hands. We have our own hours for the spa, we have our own hours for shopping in the gift shop. So it's their own world and you work with these people, all of us are on different work schedules.

You could be in month three, and someone new could come on board and be your new roommate. Because your other roommate left because they were already on month five. So there's always rotating people. So you're always meeting new people, you're always meeting people from all over the world, because they're the international employees. And then there are the American employees. We were the only American flagship for a long time. I don't even know if there are more now. But it was the best job I've ever had. It was amazing.

What are you most proud of?

I am most proud of *The Walk-In*, my podcast, because in a very Eurocentric media space, like *America's Test Kitchen*, I have a chunk of that space that is completely, authentically me. No one tells me how to interview, I am the machine. I do have the production team behind me. But I talk about what I want to talk about, I select the people whose voices

I want the world to hear. And not for nothing, from season one of *The Walk-In* podcast almost everyone . . . if there are sixteen guests in season one, eight of them have reached higher heights since *The Walk-In*. I'm not saying that *The Walk-In* is the reason for it. But I think I have an eye for game changers before the world can see it. And I don't think that *The Walk-In* has quite reached the point of platform where it's the catapulting thing. But it is the place where you can meet the people who are about to change the world. And I am proud of that.

What's an important lesson you've learned about money, compensation, or finance over the course of your career?

I've learned that how I feel about money is the way that I project my feelings about money to people who dole out the money. When I had a scarcity mindset I was always taking what was being offered to me. Because I felt like I needed it so bad that I couldn't run the risk of bargaining or even actually really evaluating my work in that particular space. Once I was able to get myself out of that scarcity mindset, it was easier for me to really examine an opportunity and see how much energy it required of me, and to make sure that the dollars matched the energy. I'm not here to pocket gouge.

I just want to make sure that my energy is a match and compensated appropriately. And that is the advice that I give women in SheChef. You don't have to say yes to the first thing, you can always negotiate, because the worst that can happen is you come back to your original numbers, the best that can happen is you get more than what they offer, which is usually the case most of the time.

And you know when the money's not there. And that's the flip side of this money conversation. I do a lot of shit for free. I do it to help businesses grow. I do it to help our people get our brands off the ground. I'm not going to charge a new solopreneur, a woman of color, the same price I'm charging Pepsi, not doing it.

What is it? You want to go fast, go alone, but if you want to go far, go together. To me, that's a proverb about money.

So I encourage people, don't live in a scarcity mindset. Because a lot of people just, their upbringing was really centered in poverty and things like that. So I don't have the same conversation about money with all people. We're not a monolith. But like, know your worth. Do your research and find out what other people in your field are making. What are the top people making? What are the new people making? And figure out where you are on that line. Don't be afraid to not get a job because you're charging your worth.

Special Loaf

BY ELLE SIMONE SCOTT / MAKES 6–9 SERVINGS

1 tablespoon dried onion flakes

1 tablespoon poultry seasoning

1 teaspoon onion powder

1 teaspoon garlic powder

1 teaspoon dried parsley

1 teaspoon paprika

1 teaspoon salt

1 teaspoon black pepper

¼ teaspoon celery seed

2 large eggs

2 cups ricotta cheese

1 medium onion, chopped fine

¼ cup chopped walnuts

1 cup shredded white cheddar cheese

1 cup roughly chopped portobello mushrooms

2 tablespoons soy sauce

4 cups Special K cereal, crushed in a zip-top bag with a rolling pin

3 tablespoons salted butter, melted

This is my adaptation of Special K Loaf, a Seventh-Day Adventist legacy recipe. I attended SDA schools, where vegetarianism was a pillar, and although my family were meat eaters, my upbringing was informed by the church's strict "health and temperance" laws. Cooking and nourishing were our family's most treasured values. My grandmother Marjorie Price was head deaconess and hospitality chairwoman, organizing community meals for holidays, visiting pastors, and Detroit's political leaders. This Special Loaf is one of the most comforting dishes you will find at an SDA potluck. When I miss the days of old, it's my go-to. The bread may also be baked in two 9-inch loaf pans; reduce the baking time to about 35 to 40 minutes. Either way, it's best served with gravy as part of a hearty dinner, but ketchup is also appropriate.

Preheat the oven to 400°F with a rack in the middle position. Coat a 9 x 13-inch baking dish with cooking spray.

In a small bowl, mix the onion flakes, poultry seasoning, onion powder, garlic powder, parsley, paprika, salt, pepper, and celery seeds. Set aside.

In a large bowl, whip the eggs until foamy. Add the ricotta and beat until fully incorporated. With a rubber spatula, fold in the reserved seasoning mix, the onions, walnuts, cheese, mushrooms, and soy sauce. Finally, fold in the cereal and butter. Press the batter evenly into the prepared pan.

Bake for 45 to 55 minutes, until the top is an even, deep brown and the bread pulls away from the sides of the pan. Set the pan on a rack to cool and firm up for at least 20 minutes; it's too fragile to cut when hot. Cut the bread into 6 large pieces or 9 small ones.

Carla Hall

CHEF, TELEVISION
PERSONALITY, COOKBOOK
AUTHOR, ACTRESS
WASHINGTON, DC

How would you describe your work?

Ever changing. I tell people that I do food television. But I'm also involved in creating products, food products. I have one company that does food television, which is an appearance and I am the product. I have another company that is about everything that I create in terms of food. So that would mean anything that I do with Goldbelly. That would be anything that I want to create in terms of fabrics and products and all of those things. I also want to be an actor. That is new on the list. It's not really new to me—it's new for me going after it because that's what I wanted to be when I was a teenager.

How did you begin in these multiple fields?

I got into food because, in hindsight, I wasn't afraid to say, "I don't want to do that." And so I was constantly looking at bridges going away from the thing that I didn't want to do, and that was accounting. And I didn't know what it was. I just knew that it was a bridge to . . . not a bridge to nowhere, a bridge to somewhere and I didn't know where that was. That's

how I ended up modeling in France and England. That's how I sort of found food. I always loved to eat. I mean, I just love to eat always. I would be thinking about the next meal during the meal I was eating.

Sunday suppers were really big growing up and going to my grandmother's house. And the Sunday brunches became a big thing when I was in Paris with a bunch of models, and I didn't realize how that connection to having people around me that I care for, but also the importance of food and sharing food and stories about food. So that became a big part of my life.

And when I wasn't gone to my grandmother's house and she was cooking, my mother doesn't like to cook, then that became something that I did out of gratitude for people allowing me to couch surf, basically. And then when I think back to *Top Chef* again, I wasn't at home and I was stressed. So that's why people saw me making comfort food. I didn't really have a name for it at the time. I was just making things to make me feel better.

And it was only in hindsight that I realized the importance of the dishes that I made and how connected I was, because I didn't want to do that food after I went to culinary school because I didn't value it. And it was really coming back to the food that made me feel grounded. And so food has played a really big part in me as a person and helping me to feel grounded.

What are you most proud of in your career and body of work so far?

I'm really proud that I went through *Top Chef* twice. It was a very public journey of finding myself, of validating that I could do this thing with food. When I did *Top Chef*, I was catering in a very small world. I mean, I had my clients. And I think what *Top Chef* allowed me to do was, one, to be comfortable with the uncomfortable, but two, realize that I am emotionally tough. It wasn't just about food. I mean, I'm really good when there is an emergency or something, and when it's going down, you may want me on your team.

What has it been like becoming a television personality?

I was approached about the job [ABC's *The Chew*], but even though I'd gone through the casting and the chemistry test and everything, when they came back to me, it still wasn't a done deal. I had to ask my husband because we live in DC, and I was going to be working in New York, and I'm like, "What do you think? Are you okay with this?" Because I needed his support. A lot of times people think, oh, the opportunity is for the individual, but the opportunity still had to work in my life and a life that I had built. Matthew was always so supportive of me during *Top Chef*. So then when I got it, he was like, "Yeah, I want you to go and do this thing."

I said to a friend of mine, "Why me? Why did I get it?" And she said, "It's about you being authentic and finding your authentic voice."

That didn't happen automatically. I didn't know how to be a host. I didn't know how to do a television show and cook in six-minute segments and learn how to balance conversations with four other people.

And to be myself in the midst of all that was another learning curve. I could very easily say that was one of my proudest moments. But it took three years, and I don't think a lot of people knew what I was going through in terms of learning how to be on the show.

It was a lot and it was stressful, and I remember going home crying sometimes.

I felt incredibly inept. I just . . . I'm so hard on myself. When I get stressed, I go into perfection mode. And so if I feel like I don't know something, I become very analytical, and it's not pretty.

The thing that I learned, looking at three of my cohosts, Michael [Symon], Mario [Batali], and Clinton [Kelly], they make it look easy. And I don't care what discipline you do, what you do for a living. If you make it look easy, you're good.

We got a lot of pushback, that the recipes are easy and everybody can do that. It's easy for somebody to criticize if they're not doing it. There are a lot of Monday morning quarterbacks. I had to learn how to shut out the noise of all of the critics. There are people who just aren't going to like you.

How do you take care of your mental health and deal with the stresses of your work?

I have good people around me who I trust. My husband is incredibly supportive. So, talking to him all the time, and prayer, meditation. [During filming] I did a lot of yoga and I did hot yoga. I was working out. I was eating well. Because I'm in a city where everybody . . . I mean, even when you're a

chef people are like, "Oh, where do you eat out?" And eating the kind of food that everybody thinks is sexy and awesome is not good for you to have every single day. Or even once a week. So, it's understanding that just because you could get the reservation doesn't mean that you should take the reservation all the time. So, it's that and taking responsibility for my body, which is my greatest asset.

What advice would you offer to someone who wants to do what you do?

The most important thing is to understand who you are. Who you are, what you look like, what you care about, because that is going to be tested. It will be tested time and time again. When I decided to have my hair go gray, ABC execs were like, "Oh, you want your hair to go gray? We'll see." I'm like, "Wait, what?"

So I had to be willing. Understand what you care about, because it will be tested and you may feel like you may lose your job over it. You have to know what your boundaries are. You have to stick to them.

I went to a media trainer. And she said, "When you're looking in the camera, you're talking to your next boss."

Something about that triggered for me, because I was really nervous about getting fired. But the scariest thing for me was when I realized I was not being myself. It wasn't getting fired. So I almost look at my job like social media. You find your own people.

So you shouldn't be taking something that you don't think is right for you. If they don't like what you're doing, that's not your right thing. And you have to be willing to give up that thing that's not right for you in order to find the thing that's right for you.

Do you have a mission or motto, and if so, what is it?

My motto is say yes: adventure follows, then growth.

What are some of your favorite things to eat or drink?

Favorite thing to eat? Anything with lemon. I just love lemon. I love lemon meringue pie, I love lemon curd. I love lemon curd because I can put lemon curd in anything.

When I was homesick in New York, the thing that I always wanted, and it goes back to, I guess, my grandmother—collard greens, a big pot of beans, could be mixed beans, pinto beans, white beans, and cornbread. That would be my go-to.

"You have to be willing to give up that thing that's not right for you in order to find the thing that's right."

Adjoa Kittoe

CHEF, WRITER, FOUNDER
OF SEULFUL PANTRY
BROOKLYN, NEW YORK

How would you describe your work?

As a chef and as a brand, Seulful Pantry is what I call "refined" and nutritional. A lot of the times, when we think about being a cook we're more about service first and having really flavorful foods and just bringing excitement. But I like to take it a step further and try to bring back our ancient techniques in regard to holistic medicine, in regard to the herbs that we use, the preparations. So my work is very intentional and, I think, also very spiritual. It's not just, "Okay. How can I just give you good food?" but, "How can I give you food that's also good for your spirit, that's also good for your mind and your body overall?" It's the really holistic way of how I prepare my food and how I make my brand stand out.

How did you begin in your field?

My background is in forensic psychology. I studied forensic psychology and criminal justice, and I got rejected from my desired master's program twice. (Just got accepted into a graduate program, though!)

So I started working with people with intellectual disabilities, and through that work I created a plant-based nutrition course, because I was also going more onto the vegan route, and people were like, "Oh. Your food looks really good. You need to make this into a business."

So I did a free pop-up at first, then I turned it into a meal kit service, and then one day somebody was like, "Can I just hire you as a personal chef?"

I did that for about a year, and people really enjoyed my pop-ups, they enjoyed my meal prep, and I said, "Okay. So how can I make this into something bigger?" I made it into an actual brand and not just a hobby, and that's when I left my career in the educational field and focused more on the culinary world. From there, I eventually went to culinary school, and I started working in restaurants here and there, but it was all mostly self-taught.

How would you describe your business and how you use psychology with food?

Colors are very important; word choices and how you describe your menu are very important; and there are times—when I'm doing more private, intimate settings—the music choices that I use are important to open up the dining experience.

Seulful Pantry is very spiritually based, so regardless of your religious background (and even if you're not religious at all), I think one thing as human beings that we do agree on is that this is our planet, and this is the only planet that we have. So how do we show thanks to that? So I kind of like to open up with libation, where we drink wine, we drink water, and I try to step more into the Ghanaian realm with palm wine. So I open up with that kind of experience, like, "Oh, this is a technique we use in Ghana. It's not your rosé, but it's still a different type of wine."

And the atmosphere—like the textures of the cloth, the plates that I use. I really love pottery, so I'm learning how to make my own plates. I've made a couple of things, and I've served on it, and people are like, "Oh, this feels really nice," and I'm like, "I made it!" So that kind of sensory detail and the visuals and the audio, all of that. And just the food itself, you look at it and it looks so simple, and then you taste it, and your brain goes, "What? What is that? Hey, that's different. I've never tasted that before."

Adrienne Cheatham

CHEF, AUTHOR, FOUNDER OF SUNDAYBEST POP-UP SERIES *NEW YORK, NEW YORK*

How would you describe your work?

I would really describe it as being a grown-up child. You get to play with food. You essentially get paid to play with food, and it's a creative outlet. It's a cathartic outlet. It's everything that I ever hoped it would be in terms of working in food as a professional career. It's like when you're at a buffet as a kid and you just start putting stuff together on your plate and trying different things and you're like, oh, that's gross. Why did I do that? But then you find something that's delicious. That's what it's like.

How did you begin in your field?

I began because my mom was in the food industry and it was where I felt most comfortable, within a kitchen setting and environment. I was really sick as a kid.

I was really socially awkward. I didn't feel comfortable around people. I had eczema that ate off 40 percent of my skin. I looked like I'd just been in a fire, and kids are assholes. I was teased and picked on and I just never really felt comfortable outside, socializing with classmates and kids my age. But in the restaurant, nobody stared at me or looked at me like there was something wrong with my skin or asked questions or pointed. It's where I felt most comfortable. They knew I was sick and they gave zero fucks as long as my mom could have somebody help wash dishes or bus tables or mop a bathroom. I always gravitated back to that.

How do you take care of your mental health and deal with the stresses of your work?

I used to smoke weed. But I stopped. I actually stopped smoking weed probably seven years ago. It was just one day, I was like, I don't feel like smoking, stuck my weed away and never pulled it back out. You choose a vice that helps you forget at the end of the day, especially when you work in kitchens. At that point I was like, I can't be tired and lethargic in the morning. I can't have brain fog in the morning because I have to be in the kitchen at seven a.m. I was just like, I'm going to stop smoking.

That was difficult. But I started working out, which was great. Nothing crazy. I'm not one of these hard-core people, but just elliptical for thirty minutes or core or something that just takes your mind off the constant rotation of the daily tasks that you've either accomplished or need to accomplish. It just literally makes you forget, without having to be hungover or have brain fog in the morning. There was a twenty-four-hour Planet Fitness in Harlem, right off the train. And I would just stop there, work out for thirty, forty-five minutes, walk home, have a glass of wine when I got home or a little bourbon, and then just be knocked out.

Especially as women and as minorities, you're always told you just put your head down and you get through this shit.

Don't let anybody see weakness. Don't let anybody see you crack or anything like that. You're almost feeling guilty if you do feel like something's wrong. Finding something to help you clear your mind, which for me was exercise, is a huge, huge, huge help.

What have been some of your favorite jobs along your path?

I worked in pastry at a resort on the Gulf of Mexico, a banquet kitchen. And it was not a glamorous job. It was literally the banquet kitchen on this massive resort that has four Starbucks, six beach shacks, twelve restaurants, casual restaurants on different levels, and then one fine-dining restaurant. And the banquet kitchen supplied the baked goods and pastries for all of those. I did the overnight shift. And then I also would stay after the overnight shift, which ended at seven or eight a.m., I would stay when the pastry chef and sous-chefs got there, to work with them all day. And it was the most amazing . . . I learned so much. I learned that some recipes are done a certain way, and even if it's counterintuitive to what you think you know about something else, this recipe works in this way for a reason. Respect the technique and don't try to deviate and change. But that was one of my absolute favorite jobs. I had never gone to culinary school when I worked there. I had worked in restaurants before, but I hadn't moved to New York yet. I was still in Florida and yeah, I loved it. I would volunteer on the savory side whenever they had banquets for plate-ups for five hundred people. And it was just the coolest thing I'd ever seen. I was awestruck.

What do you most enjoy about your career?

I think that would be all the amazing people in the industry. 'Cause honestly it's an industry full of, in a weird way, weirdos and misfits and people who don't fit into conventional environments. We put on a good face. We can pretend like we fit in or feel comfortable, but there are more like-minded people in this industry than sometimes I even have in my own family. I don't know. It's just this weird camaraderie that you have among the people in it. And it's such a beautiful thing. That's probably my absolute favorite part—that no matter where you go in the world, you're among family, as long as there's a restaurant nearby.

What's the most difficult aspect of your career?

Honestly, it's the physicality of it. You can be physically exhausted but still have to perform. You can be physically exhausted and still have to create a menu. The hardest part is just the physical nature of it, when you need to be creative or have mental space to think instead. If you're exhausted and you need to be creative, it's like trying to write a chapter while you're falling asleep before bed. Your mind, it doesn't have the space that it needs because it's starting to fricking shut down because you're exhausted. It's like your body is literally diverting energy to what needs to get done. That's the hardest part: knowing how to balance that when you have creative stuff to do, knowing when to pull back and take a break and sit down.

What are some of your favorite things to eat or drink?

For drinking, it would be Champagne and bourbon. Eating would be eggs in almost any form just because they are so versatile and can do so many things.

"Especially as women and as minorities, you're always told you just put your head down and you get through this shit."

Red Cabbage & Beet Salad

BY ADRIENNE CHEATHAM / MAKES 4 SERVINGS

¼ cup extra-virgin olive oil

1 teaspoon poppy seeds

½ teaspoon celery seed

½ small head red cabbage

1 large beet, trimmed and peeled

1 large shallot or ½ small red onion, peeled

Salt and freshly ground black pepper

2 tablespoons dijon mustard

¼ cup sherry vinegar

Greek yogurt or sour cream for serving (optional)

Torn fresh dill, parsley, and/or tarragon

The Red Cabbage and Beet Salad came about during my research of regional Southern cuisine and finding its intersections with the cuisine of other cultures. I grew up in Chicago, where there is a very large Polish population (the largest concentration outside of Warsaw, or so I've been told), so I saw dishes using beets and cabbages in many forms as a kid. My father is from Mississippi, so I was also familiar with Southern preparations of beets and cabbages. But somehow they were compartmentalized in my mind. When I started my pop-up series, SundayBest, I wanted to use Southern cuisine as a way to show how much Black culture has shaped American cuisine, and that once we get to the fundamentals of how and what we cook, there is so much that spans continents and culture. For this salad, a typical Southern dish of coleslaw (which has roots in Dutch and German cuisine) can swap green cabbage for red, use beets instead of carrots for sweetness, and incorporate the flavorings typically associated with Polish borscht (beet and cabbage soup). I find so much beauty and joy when I see these intersections.

Combine the olive oil, poppy seeds, and celery seeds in a small sauté pan. Warm over medium heat until the seeds are fragrant, about 4 minutes. Set aside to cool.

Cut the cabbage into two pieces and slice each piece into ribbons about ¼-inch thick. Transfer to a large mixing bowl. Grate the beet on the large-holed side of a box grater or with the grating plate of a food processor. (Alternatively, cut it on a mandoline with the julienne attachment.) Add it to the cabbage. Cut the shallot in half, thinly slice each piece, and add it to the bowl. Season the vegetables to taste with salt and pepper.

In a small bowl, whisk together the mustard and vinegar. Whisk in the cooled oil and seeds. Pour this dressing over the vegetables and toss with your hands or a couple of forks to thoroughly combine. Taste and adjust seasoning if needed. (If the acidity of the mustard and vinegar seems too strong, add a pinch of sugar.)

Transfer the salad to a serving bowl and top, if desired, with a spoonful of yogurt or sour cream. Sprinkle with herbs and serve.

Mango Champagne Gazpacho

BY ADRIENNE CHEATHAM / MAKES 4 SERVINGS

1 ripe but firm mango, peeled, seeded, and roughly chopped

¼ cup white balsamic vinegar

½-inch piece scallion (white part)

1 small jalapeño pepper, ribbed, seeded, and sliced

2-inch piece cucumber, peeled and chopped

¼ red bell pepper, cored, seeded, and sliced

½ teaspoon salt

1 cup good quality extra-virgin olive oil

Granulated sugar (optional)

Grated zest of 1 lime

1½ to 2 cups Champagne or sparkling wine, preferably dry

1 teaspoon tajin seasoning

This Mango Gazpacho is special to me because it is a variation on the sauce that was part of my first full dish on the menu at Le Bernardin. It went with a striped bass tartare with mango, jicama, cilantro, and scallion. I started off trying out a mango vinaigrette, with the other ingredients added to make it a little more savory than sweet. The vinaigrette was still too thick and didn't pour like I wanted; it also needed something dry and effervescent to not only lighten but brighten it up. My mind immediately went to Champagne! I asked the somm for a glass of a dry, tart Champagne, stirred it in until the sauce reached the perfect consistency, and it was a huge hit! When I brought the dish to Eric Ripert to taste and tweak before going on the menu, he tried it and said, "No changes, this is exactly how it should be." I was so proud!

It's fun to serve this rich, elegant cold soup with a bowl of Takis or hot Cheetos on the side. The mango emulsification can be made up to 2 days ahead and refrigerated, covered.

In a blender or food processor, combine the mango, vinegar, scallion, jalapeño, cucumber, bell pepper, and salt. Process on low speed until the mango is broken up (add up to 2 tablespoons water if needed).

With the motor running, slowly pour the olive oil through the feed tube. Gradually increase the speed until the mixture is smooth and emulsified. Stop the machine and taste for seasoning, adding a little sugar, vinegar, or salt if needed. Add the lime zest and process until incorporated.

Pour the mango mixture into a pitcher and gradually whisk in 1½ cups Champagne. If the soup is too thick, add another ½ cup. Pour the gazpacho into individual cups and garnish each with a pinch of tajin.

Ayesha Curry

COOKBOOK AUTHOR,
TELEVISION PERSONALITY,
FOUNDER OF SWEET JULY
SAN FRANCISCO, CALIFORNIA

How would you describe your work?

I would describe it as ever evolving, which I think is fine. Some people are like, "Just do one thing. Do one thing great, stick to that." But as human beings, as women in general, I feel like our views, thoughts, and opinions shift and change often. So for me to be my best self, it's always important for me to lean into the evolution. It's funny because when I started out, I would have described my cooking style as fun, effortless, approachable comfort. But now I feel like I'm shifting into a space of wanting to eat more intuitively, if that makes any sense to you, and cook intuitively, with purpose and intent. I think that happened because of the pandemic. I started realizing, "Gosh, what am I putting into my body?" So I'm shifting right now into this space of purposeful eating, and it's been fun to explore.

How did you begin in food?

I've been cooking since I was a little girl. It's all I wanted to do. I came from a home with two full-time working parents and there were five of us kids. So my way of giving back to the family was helping out in the kitchen and preparing meals whenever I could, whenever they'd give me the chance to, and I fell in love with it. But in the same vein as the reason why you're writing this book, there was no representation at the time for me to realize that it was something I could turn into a career. So I fell into it pretty late. I mean, late for me, but I was in my early twenties when I realized I could take this on as a career. It wasn't until after I had my first child, my daughter, and I had to start preparing food for her, and I was like, "Well, where does this come from? It doesn't all just come from the grocery store. So what farm did it come from? How was it produced?"

I started to do a really deep dive into the nitty-gritty of food and fell in love with it, started a blog, and the rest is kind of history.

What are you most proud of in your career?

That's a great question. I think I'm most proud of my resilience and ability to push through the naysayers who said I couldn't do what I'm doing, and sort of just the ability to block out the noise and push forward based fully off my passion. But I think it's important for people to do that, because when you're passionate about something, even in the midst of all the nos, that yes is going to pop up because somebody's going to see that passion exuding from you. So I think that's what it would be, my resilience.

Do you have a mission or motto, and if so, what is it?

My motto would be the past is the past, the future is not promised, so always live in the present moment. I try to live by that. Because when we're always thinking about what's next, we deflect the present. I've really been trying to meet myself where I am now, and let the future hold whatever it holds, but not to focus on it.

What are some of your favorite things to eat or drink?

My favorite thing to drink is a margarita. I love margaritas. Then my favorite thing to eat is Jamaican food. It's how I grew up. It's how I feel connected to my ancestors, my extended family. I just love it. It feels like a hug every time I eat it. So anything Jamaican.

Fatmata Binta

EXECUTIVE CHEF OF FULANI KITCHEN *NAIROBI, KENYA*

How would you describe your work?

I would say I'm an ambassador for a cuisine that's old but new to people. So basically I am trying to promote food and culture. I'm a chef and a storyteller.

How did you begin in your field?

I've always loved cooking. It started up as a hobby and then became a happy hobby. When I was in university studying international relations, in my dorm my roommates loved my cooking so much that everyone put money together and begged me until I cooked. When I lost my job, I had to provide another way to make a living, and I decided to start selling sandwiches. I would go and deliver these sandwiches to the MBA students and then also cook African food for the African students. And I realized that people were really, really enjoying the food.

I took a leap of faith and went to Ghana (I couldn't go to Sierra Leone because of Ebola).

What year was it and what was one major motivating factor when you created Fulani Kitchen?

In 2018 we hosted our first group of students, from Harvard. The students pointed out that even though they'd been traveling together for a week in a bus across cities in Africa, they only got to truly connect and have meaningful conversations when they were on my mat. That was when I realized that food is powerful, and there's something about the mat that grounds people and creates a real space for vulnerability. For me, it was inspiring just for myself.

How do you weave in the storytelling with Fulani Kitchen?

I try to reflect on my childhood, because for me, most of the stories I tell, and the creation behind Fulani Kitchen and Dine on a Mat, all stem from me growing up in the villages and vacationing in Guinea, spending time with my grandmother, having to go there [to Guinea] during the civil war in Sierra Leone to seek refuge . . . Those are the fondest memories for me, just having all my cousins together, just seeing all the aunties—because I come from a large family and most of them have passed away. I know it will be difficult to relive those moments, so I always go back to the lessons I learned in food culture. Everything I enjoyed, I like to go back and tell those stories. I worry because they're fading away. I try to keep them alive by telling the stories on the mat.

Do you have a mission or motto, and if so, what is it?

I want to change the way people see food and Fulani style and people. That's what drives me. African food is amazing, and lots of amazing chefs out there are telling their stories, but for me my main goal is to really change the narrative around the world

"Have faith in yourself and be authentic. It's a lonely road and sometimes people will think you're crazy—even your family members. Just have faith in yourself."

What are you most proud of?

My most fulfilling moments are when someone walks into my space, or sits on my mat, and then they walk away saying things like "It's powerful." The culture is beautiful.

What advice would you offer to someone who wants to do what you do?

Have faith in yourself and be authentic. It's a lonely road and sometimes people will think you're crazy—even your family members. Just have faith in yourself.

What do you most enjoy about your career?

Meeting people.

What is the most difficult aspect of your career?

It can be demanding. We all have days when you need to take a break and sometimes those moments hit you when you're in the middle of standing in the kitchen and really pushing yourself. So I think that's the tough part.

There are days you have to give so much of yourself even when you're exhausted.

What are some of your favorite things to eat or drink?

I love ginger beer. It's a local specialty. Baobab also. Love baobab juice. And then okra. I never get tired of that. Outside of African food, I'm obsessed with sushi.

Palm Oil Fonio Jollof

BY FATMATA BINTA / MAKES 6 SERVINGS

⅓ cup palm oil

3–4 medium yellow onions, sliced

4–5 fresh plum tomatoes

1 habanero or other very hot pepper

1 head garlic, cloves peeled

2 teaspoons curry powder

1 cup tomato paste

1 cup flaked smoked-fish meat
(preferably herring)

3 bay leaves

Salt

2¾ cups fonio

2 cups chicken or vegetable stock

1 small handful fresh thyme leaves

1 cup finely chopped carrots, scallions,
and bell pepper

Jollof is a popular dish throughout West Africa. It's traditionally made with rice, but these days that usually means imported rice from Vietnam. That's why we, in my family, cook it with fonio, an ancient grain indigenous to West Africa. To my family it's a super grain because it played an essential part in keeping us alive during the civil war in Sierra Leone. Fonio is highly nutritious and gluten-free. It gives more nutrients back to the soil than staple crops like rice and corn, and it is better equipped than they are to resist disease and drought. This tiny grain might very well be an answer to climate and food-security challenges and a lifesaver once again! You can buy fonio and palm oil on Amazon. You can also buy fonio on Yolele.com.

Heat oil in a large skillet over medium heat, and add the onions. Reduce the heat to low and cook, stirring occasionally, until the onions caramelize.

Meanwhile, combine the tomatoes, habanero, and garlic in a blender and process to a pulp. Set aside.

Sprinkle the curry powder on the caramelized onions and cook, stirring, for 2 minutes. Stir in the tomato mixture. Bring to a simmer and cook over medium-low heat, stirring occasionally, until thickened, about 10 minutes. Stir in the tomato paste, smoked fish, bay leaves, and salt to taste. (You could add some allspice here if you like.) Simmer for 10 minutes on medium-low heat.

Remove half the sauce from the pan and reserve it. Add the fonio to the pan, bring the mixture to a simmer and cook, stirring, for 3 minutes. And 1 cup of the stock and the thyme leaves and simmer for 10 more minutes, until tender, adding the remaining stock if the mixture is too dry.

Stir in the finely chopped vegetables and simmer until they are cooked but still have a little bite.

Remove the bay leaf and serve the fonio with the reserved sauce.

Anya Peters

CHEF, AUTHOR, AND
FOUNDER OF KIT
AN' KIN POP-UP
BROOKLYN, NEW YORK

How would you describe your work?

I am a chef, storyteller, and children's book author and illustrator. I describe my work as inquisitive, playful, and very personal. It is ever inspired by my upbringing in a Caribbean home and all of the experiences, flavors, and memories that go with it. My work weaves together storytelling and knowledge keeping with new, exciting flavors and techniques.

How did you begin in your field?

I always knew I wanted to write and cook. I applied to one place out of high school— the Culinary Institute of America—with hopes of becoming a chef. After earning my associate's [degree], I wanted to experience the industry and found an amazing catering company in Brooklyn run by two badass women, Sara Elise and Ora Wise, of Harvest & Revel. There, I learned all about catering and event work and became their co-chef. During that time I also started my pop-up, now business, Kit an' Kin—with the desire to learn from my family how to cook the Trini and Jamaican meals I grew up with and share with the world.

Who are some of your role models or mentors in the food and hospitality space?

There is such a beautiful network of folks I have met along the way and I feel incredibly grateful to have collaborated and communed with some greats! Really, people often speak about how harsh and toxic the food industry is, but I have never experienced it, because of the values I set out for myself in the beginning and folks I've worked with I now consider family. It is hard to pinpoint exactly one but I love my FIG (Food Issues Group) crew and all the amazing work they do. An incredible chef and friend I am always inspired by and often share paths with is Chinchakriya Un of Kreung Cambodia.

What are you most proud of?

I am most proud of positioning myself to literally do what I love. It's not easy, not always financially rewarding, but I would not do anything else. I feel privileged, humbled, proud, and sometimes in awe that I am living out my dreams.

How do you take care of your mental health and deal with the stresses of your work?

This pertains to both mental and physical. I try my best to stay hydrated and find the foods that work for me while working. I often don't like eating while I am working/cooking, but recently found that plant-based meals and lots of fruits work for me while I am in the kitchen. I will also prioritize my capacity—mentally and physically—so if it's time for me to stop, I will stop; I no longer grind into the wee hours of the morning. Lastly, I do not hesitate to treat myself and my team. The day after a long work week, we go out to eat; I may get a massage and nails done.

Do you have a mission or motto, and if so, what is it?

I have a vision. We are a living, breathing, record of the Caribbean diaspora through food and storytelling. Starting out with my Jamaican Trini family and reaching out to the greater Cariglobal. Weaving together nuances of our experiences and strengthening intergenerational bonds, we are a home, 'round the kitchen table, sharing, loving, and learning. This is my mission. This is what keeps me grounded and focused.

Shrimp Cassava Balls

BY ANYA PETERS / MAKES 4

Salt

2 large cassavas (yuca root), or frozen yuca

2 tomatoes, diced, divided

8 garlic cloves, minced, divided

8 sprigs thyme, stripped, divided

2 scallions, trimmed and sliced, divided

Neutral oil for frying (such as canola or grapeseed)

½ scotch bonnet pepper, seeded and minced

1 cup white wine

1 pound shrimp, cleaned and cut into pieces

1 tablespoon butter

Juice of 1 lime

Freshly ground black pepper

¼ cup cassava flour

Pickled red onions and your favorite hot sauce for serving

Throughout the Caribbean, rum shops are everywhere, and many serve finger foods known as cutters or cuttas. This rum shop cuttas is inspired by the classic Guyanese egg ball with seasoned cassava and Creole stew shrimp. The cassava ball mixture can be prepared two days in advance and refrigerated. Let it come to room temperature for 30 minutes before coating and frying.

Bring a large pot of water to boil. Add 1 tablespoon salt. Peel and cut yuca into 3-inch pieces if using fresh, and add to the boiling water. Cook for 15 to 20 minutes, until the cassava is easy to pierce with a knife. Drain and set aside to cool slightly.

Cut each cassava piece in half and discard the tough, starchy vein in the middle. Return it to the pot and add half of the tomato, garlic, thyme, and scallion, along with 2 tablespoons water. Cover and cook on medium-low heat, stirring occasionally, until the cassava is completely tender, about 10 minutes. Set aside.

Heat a little oil in a saucepan on medium heat and sauté the remaining tomato, garlic, thyme, and scallion, and the scotch bonnet pepper a few minutes, until fragrant. Add the wine and let the mixture reduce by half. Add the shrimp and sauté for 3 to 5 minutes, until cooked and pink. Add the butter to the pan and take it off the heat, sprinkle with fresh lime juice.

Coarsely mash the cooked cassava mixture. Stir in the cooked shrimp and sauce. Taste for salt and pepper, adjust the seasoning to taste, and let cool for 10 minutes.

In the meantime, heat 2 inches of oil in a Dutch oven or deep, heavy skillet over medium heat. Set up a breading station with cassava flour in a plate, oil for replenishing the pan, a sheet pan lined with parchment paper, and another one lined with paper towels.

Oil your hands to prevent sticking. Using a tablespoon, scoop out the cassava shrimp mixture and it roll into balls. Coat the balls in cassava flour and place them on the parchment-lined pan.

Working in batches, fry the cassava balls until golden brown on all sides, 2 to 3 minutes per side, and drain on paper towels. Serve warm with pickled red onions and hot sauce.

Vallery Lomas

COOKBOOK AUTHOR, BAKER, TELEVISION PERSONALITY *NEW YORK, NEW YORK*

How would you describe your work?

My work is satisfying, and I use that word broadly because I feel very honored to work in food and not just in food, but from like a historian-type perspective of food, because when I create recipes, when I share recipes with people, I feel a responsibility to do justice to my people, my heritage, my culture, and I find that work very satisfying. And of course, I want the food to be satisfying, so I feel like that question can be answered so many ways, but my work is also this whole amalgamation of all of these different things.

How did you begin in your field?

I began blogging as an outlet to express myself. It was my last year of law school, and to put it lightly, I was over it. (I was also naive, and I was like, "Oh, it's the recession. People aren't handing out job offers, so screw them. I'll show them—I'll not apply for any jobs." Do not do that, kids.)

So, I just wanted to think about something else. That was the beginning of my last year of law school; I started a food blog and I was like, "I'm just going to cook or bake something every day and blog about it." And that's how it started.

Who are some of your role models or mentors in the food space?

I think it's such an important question, because I was an attorney for eight years, and I really felt like I never had that support of a mentor, and I feel like it's so critical. We all know how important it is, so to have that in this sphere. I would say: Jamila [Robinson].

She's a friend of mine, and I need friends, but she has such insight about this industry and strategy, and she is someone I can bounce those big-picture ideas off, and she helps guide me. And before I got connected with her, there were several other people at the beginning of my path in this space who were like, "I'm going to help."

Dana Cowin, she's one of those people. I remember I was just stumped when I was writing my book proposal, and I imagine she's probably a busy woman, and she, I think like the next day, made time for me. I met her early in the morning somewhere in the East Village to have coffee, and she talked me through the major blockage I had, and she was just like, "You are capable. You are a smart woman. You can write this book proposal." She was like, "Go finish it this weekend and then send it to me." That was such a pivotal point with my book project, which is hugely important to me.

I'll also say Nancy Wall Hopkins. She has been someone I could confide in, and she gives me motherly advice, but she's also a seasoned woman in the food media space.

What are you most proud of?

I'm proud of myself for betting on myself.

"I'm proud of myself for betting on myself."

How do you take care of your mental health and deal with the stresses of your work?

Therapy.

It's been a journey. I would say where I am now is very different from where I was late summer last year. I've always been a believer in therapy, but right now I have a therapist who is working for me, in the sense that the path that we are on is working for me. Being okay with doing my best, whatever that looks like that day, is huge. For me self-care is therapy, it's meditation, it's acupuncture, it's getting up in the morning and cleaning my house and not giving 100 percent of myself to my work.

What advice would you offer to someone who wants to do what you do?

I would say do it to see if you really want to do it. I think people often think they have to have the infrastructure in place, and they have to go out at the beginning and buy the fancy camera and buy the courses and spend all this money when really it's like, is this something you want to do? When you wake up in the morning is this what you want to do? Are you willing to make sacrifices sometimes? Because this industry, it's not a nine-to-five industry.

If someone wants to be in this space, doing something similar to what I'm doing or what you're doing, I would say find someone who you admire and take one part of what they're doing, something that you feel called to, and do it and see how you feel. See if you enjoy it, see if it's something that you really want to spend a lot of hours doing, because maybe you like to cook or bake or to be talking to the camera for Instagram, but maybe you don't necessarily want to do that in a more disciplined way. I don't think everyone's passion or hobby has to be the way they make money. You can have that hobby and passion and do it and it's not necessarily how you're keeping the lights on, cause it changes the dynamics.

What are some of your favorite things to eat or drink?

Let's start with drinking. Right now I'm on a total kombucha kick, but also Champagne because I am that girl. Can I say I like to eat what other people cook? It's amazing to have people cook for me. It makes me feel special. I get to eat without having cooked, and it's like a home-cooked meal made with all the love. Honestly, my favorite thing to eat is something I didn't cook, something someone cooked for me.

Single-Layer Carrot Cake

BY VALLERY LOMAS / MAKES 8–10 SERVINGS

CAKE

Baking spray with flour

1 cup all-purpose flour

1 teaspoon baking soda

1 teaspoon baking powder

1 teaspoon ground cinnamon

2 large eggs

½ cup vegetable oil

¼ cup milk

1 cup granulated sugar

1 teaspoon vanilla extract

¼ teaspoon salt

1½ cups grated carrots

½ cup roughly chopped pecans (optional)

½ cup raisins (optional)

FROSTING

4 ounces full-fat cream cheese (½ package), softened

1½ cups powdered sugar, plus more if needed

2–3 teaspoons milk

½ teaspoon vanilla extract

Dash of salt

This is one of the most popular recipes on my blog, **Foodie in New York.** *It's adapted from my dad's favorite three-layer carrot cake with all of its deliciousness and none of the fuss. Be sure to use freshly grated carrots (not the store-bought pre-shredded ones); they add moisture to the cake.*

Preheat the oven to 350°F. Coat an 8- or 9-inch-square cake pan with baking spray and, if desired, line the bottom with parchment paper.

In a medium bowl, whisk the flour with the baking soda, baking powder, and cinnamon until combined. In a large bowl, whisk the eggs and oil, mixing well. Whisk in the milk, sugar, vanilla, and salt until combined.

Stir the dry ingredients into the egg mixture until combined. Fold in the carrots and, if using, the pecans and raisins.

Scrape the batter into the prepared pan and bake until your kitchen smells like carrot cake and a toothpick inserted into the center comes out clean, 40 to 55 minutes. Set the cake aside on a rack to cool to room temperature.

While the cake cools, make the frosting: In a large bowl, whisk the softened cream cheese to loosen it. (If you forgot to take it out of the fridge in time, zap it in the microwave for 10 or 20 seconds.) Add the powdered sugar, 2 teaspoons milk, vanilla, and salt, and whisk until smooth. If it's too thick, add another teaspoon of milk. If it's too thin, whisk in a little more powdered sugar.

Spread the frosting on the cooled cake in an even layer. Cut the cake into squares just before serving. It will keep in a cake dome at room temperature for a few hours or in the refrigerator, covered, for up to four days.

Sicily Johnson

CHEF, RESTAURATEUR, ENTREPRENEUR *NEW YORK, NEW YORK*

How would you describe your work?

I would describe my work as rooted in Black American nostalgia. I love how we were raised, our culture, hanging out until the streetlights come on, from cleaning on Saturdays to church on Sundays. And how food is woven into all of that.

How did you begin in your field?

This was a second career for me, but being a part of a lineage of cooks and seeing how my Mum would open her home and feed people, just like her mother before, and her mother before. . . there was a point where I felt like it was pulling me and I couldn't shake it.

Who are some of your role models or mentors in the food and hospitality space?

Mentors and role models for me tend to be seasonal. Right now, I am grateful for Thérèse Nelson and Korsha Wilson. That they are making a huge impact on me personally and professionally with this new season that I am in in my career. I want to be able to figure out how to tell my version of food, fight, and culture the way that Vertamae Smart-Grosvenor did!

What are you most proud of?

Never folding, though it's hella hard to stay true to your desires, identity, and heart's intentions—never folding.

What is an important lesson you've learned about money, compensation, or finance over the course of your career?

Not to give a fuck what people think, even those closest to you that you have personal relationships with. It's business and you have to have a vision and play the long, solo game of your vision. Be grateful for people, but they are an added benefit. And know your costing, everything going out and coming in.

What advice would you offer to someone who wants to do what you do?

Don't despise small beginnings, run your own race, know your costing, have a solid team of counsel, shut up (we all don't need to know), and trust your instincts, because it will be hard sometimes but it's always worth it.

Do you have a mission or motto, and if so, what is it?

It would be don't despise small beginnings.

What brings you joy and what would you like to experience more of?

Teaching cooking—bringing together my two careers—making sandwiches, adventures with my kids and friends.

What are some of your favorite things to eat or drink?

Sandwiches and Kool-Aid with gin.

Catfish & Spaghetti

BY SICILY JOHNSON / MAKES 4–6 SERVINGS

SPAGHETTI

2 tablespoons grapeseed oil

1 medium yellow onion, diced

1 green bell pepper, cored, seeded, and diced

1 carrot, peeled and diced

1 tablespoon kosher salt

1 tablespoon freshly ground black pepper

1 tablespoon ground cumin

1 tablespoon crushed red pepper flakes

4 garlic cloves, minced

28-ounce can crushed San Marzano tomatoes

1 pound spaghetti

CATFISH

Grapeseed oil for frying (other oil options are canola or peanut oil)

2 cups all-purpose flour

1½ cups yellow cornmeal

4 tablespoons kosher salt

2 tablespoons freshly ground black pepper

3 tablespoons paprika

1 cup prepared yellow mustard

4 to 6 catfish fillets

Fresh parsley, for garnish

This recipe brings me so much joy. Raising four kids on her own, my mother made sure to fortify our lives with joy and tradition, no matter what, and Catfish and Spaghetti represents that for me. It is a celebration of the resilience of my people.

For the sauce, heat the oil in a large sauce pot over medium-high heat. Cook the onion, bell pepper, and carrot, stirring often, until caramelized, 5 to 8 minutes. Stir in the salt, black pepper, cumin, and pepper flakes. Stir in the garlic and cook, stirring, until aromatic, 1 to 2 minutes. Stir in the tomatoes, adjust the heat, and simmer until the sauce thickens, 15 to 20 minutes.

Meanwhile, cook the spaghetti al dente in a big pot of salted water, according to the package directions. Drain, reserving a little cooking water. Stir the pasta into the sauce, thinning if needed with a little pasta water. Cover to keep warm and set aside.

For the catfish, in a cast-iron skillet, pour enough oil to come ½ inch up the side of the skillet. Heat the skillet on medium-high heat. The oil should come to a temperature of 330–335°F.

Meanwhile, mix the flour, cornmeal, salt, pepper, and paprika in a shallow dish. In another shallow dish, spread the mustard.

Dip the catfish in the mustard, shaking off the excess. Dredge it in the flour mixture, coating it well. Fry the fish (two fillets at a time) in the hot oil, turning once, until golden brown, 2 to 4 minutes, then use a spatula to flip the fish and cook the other side for 2 to 4 minutes. Drain on paper towels.

To serve, divide the reserved spaghetti among 4 to 6 plates and top each portion with a catfish fillet. Garnish with parsley.

Mennlay Golokeh Aggrey

AUTHOR, INTERDISCIPLINARY
CANNABIS ENTREPRENEUR
MEXICO CITY, MEXICO

How would you describe your work?

My work uniquely connects cannabis, foodways, and the African diaspora in Latin America—specifically Mexico.

How did you begin in your field?

Mostly out of curiosity and survival. I entered the cannabis industry in Humboldt County, California, fresh out of journalism school in 2005. Although I did a brief yearlong stint at a radio station, I quickly decided to go on the cannabis cultivation path. At the time I felt like I was going toward a career path (albeit rare and unsafe) that would allow me to better support myself and my family back home. Cannabis provided that; it still does.

Who are some of your role models or mentors in the food and hospitality space?

DeVonn Francis, founder of Yardy, video host and chef at *Bon Appétit*, and someone who intentionally makes food in a nourishing and incredibly artistic way.

Ashtin Berry, a hospitality activist, sommelier, mixologist, and beverage consultant. She is a beacon in the community when connecting the dots between racism and the hospitality industry.

Michael W. Twitty, the culinary historian and educator, has turned me out, so to speak, and completely changed the way I conceptualized the historical value of food. He was quoted too many times in my previous cookbook, and I look forward to learning from his future work.

Yewande Komolafe, the professional chef, recipe developer, food stylist, and photographer is absolutely one of my biggest role models (after Klancy Miller). When I first saw her jollof recipe in the *New York Times* after many years of never seeing it on the internet, I knew she was a real one!

Too there's Dr. Marco Polo Hernández Cuevas, not necessarily directly within the food and hospitality space, but he is a tenured full professor of Spanish language and literature, Afro-Mexican, Afro-Hispanic, and Afro-Latino Studies culture at North Carolina Central University. For about a decade he has been able to connect the dots between the culinary ties between West African and Mexican cuisine.

What are you most proud of?

Carving out a legitimate profession and life in the cannabis industry. Having a clean police record. Lord knows the reality for so many Black people in the cannabis industry all

too often finds them in the carceral system. I am proud and frankly grateful I've avoided that.

What is an important lesson you've learned about money, compensation, or finance over the course of your career?

I've learned that generational wealth is everything—even in underground, underregulated economies like cannabis. I've learned that being financially literate is one of the most important skills. That and knowing how to cook for yourself.

How do you take care of your mental health and deal with the stresses of your work?

The past several years have brought me closer to a type of spiritual devotion that brings me great joy and internal balance. This 100 percent translates into my health both physically and mentally. Sometimes that looks like taking a twenty-minute break from working to meditate, nap, or even just stare off into the distance in peace and gratitude. Sometimes that's all I need to care for myself.

What advice would you offer to someone who wants to do what you do?

I give and take the advice as follows: be patient, be resilient, and be ready for a lot of setbacks. Cannabis is still such a new industry (in the legal realm) that there will always be moments of confusion and frustration. Cannabis legislation is murky, with a residue of stigma, prohibition, sexism, and racism. But if you are compelled to work in this industry and you know this is your life's work, do it.

Do you have a mission or motto, and if so, what is it?

I think my main mission is to live life and be true, useful, and joyful to others, but more important, myself.

What do you most enjoy about your work?

My "work" feels so much like survival that at times my relationship to working with weed can be so stressful and difficult to navigate because there are very real repercussions. But when I'm out of my head, not analyzing what would be better, or what is legal, I recognize that *I get to do this work*. I get to live out a life that my teenage self would've never imagined—a life that a young Black person can now imagine as a career. Despite the destruction of Black, Brown, and Indigenous communities because of the misguided war on drugs, one can go to university and study the cultivation of cannabis, or even cannabis culinary art. I enjoy seeing this evolution. I've enjoyed being able to live and work through this shift. It

somehow makes it all worth it. Makes it feel enjoyable and worth a damn.

What's the most difficult aspect of your career?

The fact that cannabis is federally illegal. Federal law still classifies marijuana as a Schedule I substance, meaning that, in the eyes of the US government, cannabis has no accepted medical use and has the highest potential for abuse. Crazy, right?

What brings you joy and what would you like to experience more of?

Silence and solitude have become a great privilege and the greatest opportunity for me to find inner joy and calm.

What are some of your favorite things to eat or drink?

The past couple of years have given me the patience and deep appreciation for juicing, and green juices have been solid in my life. My favorite thing to do is sneak in different types of microgreens and herbs that may not seem like they go well together but work perfectly and give me hidden benefits. Lately my favorite combination has been a blend of celery, ginger, garlic, kale, cilantro, pineapple, cucumber, mint, parsley, nopal, and lime.

My favorite thing to eat is my mother's fufu and soup. She makes it in both Liberian and Ghanaian style, and it's possibly the reason I live. Kidding. I've asked her for years to freeze it and send it over to me, but the US and Mexican customs aren't into that.

Infused Plantains

BY MENNLAY GOLOKEH AGGREY / MAKES 6 SERVINGS

4 black-ripe plantains

2 teaspoons cannabis-infused (optional) coconut, canola, olive, or vegetable oil

½ cup coconut oil or vegetable oil

Salt

Mexican crema, for serving (optional)

In our Liberian/Ghanaian household growing up, fried plantains were a special treat. My sisters and I loved to snatch them from the paper towel where our mother set them to drain, hot from the pan. Once I was grown I realized that plantains are an international treat, loved in the Caribbean, Latin America, Africa, Southeast Asia, and Mexico, where I now make my home. They are called platano macho in Mexican Spanish and are often steamed until soft and served with crema (Mexican sour cream). My mother's frying method remains my favorite, and I have created a sort of remix that combines the two.

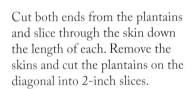

This recipe uses cannabis-infused oil, but you can omit it. Cannabis oil can be homemade or purchased online; a Google search will provide many recipes and purveyors.

Cut both ends from the plantains and slice through the skin down the length of each. Remove the skins and cut the plantains on the diagonal into 2-inch slices.

In a large frying pan, mix the cannabis-infused oil with the coconut oil and heat over medium-high heat for about 1 minute.

Working in batches to avoid crowding the pan, fry the plantain slices, turning them once, until golden, 5 to 7 minutes on each side. Drain on paper towels and sprinkle with salt. Serve at room temperature, drizzled with crema if desired.

Lisa Binns

CHEF, CO-OWNER OF STUSH IN THE BUSH
FREEHILL, JAMAICA

How would you describe your work and how did you begin cooking and farming in Jamaica?

The work is from a place of passion because I was in a past life an educator. I used to teach high school English, ultimately running a school in Brooklyn. Then I decided that I wanted to have this shift in my life, and so before I even knew what the shift was going to be, I had sort of decided I was going to close one chapter and move into another.

When I was doing that, I met Chris, and in meeting Chris I decided that "Okay. Well, maybe this is time to shift to a totally different career." I kind of just kicked into one of my passions, which was food—the thing that as an educator you generally don't have the time for until summer.

It was nice to collect all of the things that I love to do in summer and say, "Oh. Hey, here we can open this bed-and-breakfast and we can do all these other things," and I taught myself how to make bread because my bed-and-

breakfast experiences—the ones that I treasure—were always the ones that had food that was lovingly prepared.

In meeting Chris, it became about farming. It became about seed selection. It became about what to do with that produce. It became about how to change what you're doing and have it be applicable to a Jamaican environment—everybody thinks it's a 365-day-per-year growing season, but Jamaica has lots of little microclimates, so there are certain things that we can't grow. It just comes from wanting to share that love of Mother Earth and what you're actually doing and how people used to cook so long ago, in terms of your ancestors and working with seasons and not having everything available to you at all times of the year.

That is how it began, and then it also began with just our product line—making products, making jams, making things that were in season, and then when the season is over on the farm we don't have it anymore. So it kind of gives this whole aesthetic of looking forward to something, because we're so accustomed to having everything all the time. It's kind of like a harkening back to the past to pull us to the future, I would say.

What was the hardest part about changing lanes?

New York moves at a crackerjack pace, and Jamaica does not move like that at all. So that was part of it. The other things also were kind of, like, breaking yourself in and becoming known for something.

I just started working, as I said, from a place of passion. We had peppers. We had tomatoes. We started to make things, and I started to marry up a lot of the flavors that I loved and just use up excess produce. I put all those things out to market, attending festivals here and doing those kinds of things, and that's how we became known for product.

Stush in the Bush really started as a tasting tour. People

began asking about whether they could come up and experience what was happening on the farm, and could I put on a little soup or make some bread or something along those lines, then that became the way to creating some dishes for people. And I felt like the best application of trying a product is the way that it's intended to be used, so then we kind of married up the farm and the products to the table, so it sort of just evolved that way.

What advice would you offer to someone who wants to do what you do?

I would say so easily, "Be your true self. Be your authentic self." I feel like a lot of what we do and why people appreciate it so much is because it is who we are. It's how we live. It's how we do things day-to-day, day in and day out. You're just getting a little slice of our life. People have created farm-to-table experiences all around the world, and I think that each one is special. Each one is bespoke. Each one is curated to fit that design of who you are and what you want to value, and I think we do that really well. We can get people to understand that less is more, and to be in a place where we can slow down just a little bit.

We've been really fortunate because quite a lot of people who come and visit us are not necessarily just visitors. They are locals, people who are wanting to just get away from Kingston for the day, who really value a good experience. So I think that has been really great, and I think you can only get there if you are who you are.

The vibration that you give out is what draws people to you, and if you exist on this lower vibration all the time it never can be fulfilling to you or to anybody else. So it's really a wonderful thing if you can vibrate joyfully, because if you can, what comes to you and what you give off to people is invaluable, and it brings them that level of joy as well.

Do you have a mission or motto, and if so, what is it?

Fall in love with your food. At Stush in the Bush, what we encourage you to do is to fall in love with your food. So whether you're dining with us or you're using our products, the point is that you can make everything sexy. And so to do that, you can have a little bottle of chimichurri sauce that you take home, or a little bottle of our cherry tomato marmalade when you go home, or some hot pepper sauce. You can take Blow Fyah home with you. To me, any of those things allows you to fall in love with your food. So whether it's here or at your own home, you can still be with Stush.

What are some of your favorite things to eat or drink?

One of my very favorite things to drink is coconut water. Also, Barbados is always called Little England, and my mother had a tradition every evening of having a cup of tea and crackers and cheese, and I have not given that up yet, much to the chagrin of my whole system at times. But I have to say, it's still a favorite, and it will forever be a favorite.

"The vibration that you give out is what draws people to you."

Plantain Ceviche

BY LISA BINNS / MAKES 8 SERVINGS

5 firm, ripe plantains, peeled and cut in medium dice

1 red bell pepper, cored, seeded, and cut in small dice

1 yellow bell pepper, cored, seeded, and cut in small dice

1 large red onion, peeled and cut in small dice

½ teaspoon minced scotch bonnet pepper

4 scallions, finely chopped

½ cup cilantro leaves, chopped

Juice of 6–8 limes (about ¾ cup)

4 teaspoons pink Himalayan salt, or to taste

Freshly cracked black pepper

This raw vegetarian play on fish ceviche is bright, packed with flavor, and easy to make. It makes a fragrant appetizer on its own, pairs well with crispy plantain chips, grilled fish, or veggie burgers, and is delicious on top of avocado toast. If you prefer less heat, substitute jalapeño pepper or another chili for the scotch bonnet.

In a nonreactive bowl, combine the plantains, bell peppers, onion, and scotch bonnet. Reserve 2 tablespoons of the scallion for garnish and add the rest to the bowl along with the cilantro, and toss gently. Add the fresh lime juice and salt and pepper to taste. Refrigerate, covered, for about 3 hours. Just before serving, sprinkle with the reserved scallion.

Rosemary Red Stripe Beer Bread

BY LISA BINNS / MAKES 8–10 SLICES

2 cups all-purpose flour

1 cup whole wheat flour

¼ cup brown sugar

1 tablespoon baking powder

1 teaspoon salt

2 tablespoons fresh rosemary leaves, chopped, plus sprigs for garnish

2 tablespoons olive oil, plus more for drizzling

12-ounce bottle Red Stripe Beer

I came up with this quick bread to complement our potato and leek soup at Stush in the Bush. Typically Jamaican, the Red Stripe Beer adds a subtle yeasty flavor. I go overboard with the rosemary because it is just so fragrant and fresh, but that's farm life! The top will crack open when baking. The bread is so moist and delicious you might consume it all in one sitting.

Preheat the oven to 350°F. Coat an 8-inch loaf pan with cooking spray.

In a mixing bowl, stir together the flours, sugar, baking powder, salt, and rosemary. Stir in the oil and beer until combined.

Scrape the batter into the prepared pan and press rosemary sprigs into the top for decoration.

Drizzle the top lightly with olive oil and run a table knife along the edges of the pan.

Bake the bread for 45 to 50 minutes, until it pulls away from the sides of the pan and is golden brown on top. Cool on a rack before slicing.

Jessica Craig

EXECUTIVE PASTRY CHEF
NEW YORK, NEW YORK

How would you describe your work?

I'm a restaurant pastry chef. I have worked in mostly Italian restaurants. I consider my style of work rustic and revolving around seasonality. I try to take nostalgic flavor combinations and add a twist. Usually, once you hit the nostalgia button, most people will be willing to try a new addition to that flavor profile.

How did you begin in your field?

I went to culinary school right out of high school. I went to college while working simultaneously (I wouldn't recommend it). I would learn in class and then be able to have a better understanding of techniques at work.

It was the two baking/pastry courses I had at school, as well as a garde manger cook job, that made me realize that pastry is what I wanted to focus on. I realized how much I enjoyed plated desserts. I wanted to learn more about pastry and all that it entailed but knew I couldn't afford another round of school, so I pursued my first pastry cook job.

Who are some of your role models or mentors in the food and hospitality space?

One role model I am constantly in awe of is Paola Velez. My sous-chef when I was working at L'Artusi brought her to my attention in 2018. I actually met her at StarChefs' Congress in 2019. We spoke briefly as my very outgoing pastry chef friend made an introduction.

Paola has a very sweet and humble spirit about her. She cares so much about her craft, mentoring others, speaking out on issues within the industry or the world at large, and she's an all-around amazing human being. For me she is #goals. I push myself to get more involved and be more publicly open about my views. Especially being a first-generation Jamaican American.

Another role model I have is Jessica B. Harris (it's not just because we share the same name). I shamefully admit that I didn't know much about Dr. Harris or her work until I was tasked to create the dessert for the MOFAD 2019 Spring Gala for their African/American exhibit. Her name was listed as being involved, and I went down a rabbit hole as I researched her. I learned about her knowledge and work in cultivating the history of the African diaspora. It totally blew my mind. When I presented my dessert and got to meet her, shake her hand, and bask in her amazing aura, you could've tipped me over with a light poke on my shoulder. I was fangirling so hard. I hope to acquire just a fraction of her depth of knowledge.

What are you most proud of?

I'm most proud of being able to have an executive pastry chef title in New York City. That's something that I've aspired to for my whole career but didn't necessarily think would happen.

What is an important lesson you've learned about money, compensation, or finance over the course of your career?

The biggest lesson I've learned is to counteroffer. Women as a whole don't ask for our worth. I've settled on salaries that I know no man would ever accept for the amount of work that's required. I've gotten better and more confident concerning my salary requirements and asking for a raise.

How do you take care of your mental health and deal with the stresses of your work?

Therapy is very important. Talking things out really helps to keep my head space clear. Meditation helps so much. It balances my energy, helps my anxiety, and just simply brightens my mood. Sometimes some music with a dance and/or singing moment is great too.

How have you approached building a team?

I look for personality traits more than I look for a specific set of skills. I look for a positive attitude, willingness to take direction, and enthusiasm about cooking and food. If those traits are there you could always work on the technical cooking stuff over time. Those positive personality traits can't be taught.

What advice would you offer to someone who wants to do what you do?

The advice I would give is to work at a variety of establishments. This isn't to say to hop around from place to place over the course of months if you can help it. However, moving around a bit exposes you to more types of places, different recipes, different techniques, different cuisines, and so on. Also, it helps you to figure out what niche or part of the industry you want to focus on.

Do you have a mission or motto, and if so, what is it?

My motto is "It's okay not to be okay." There's a level of perfectionism that women put on ourselves and sometimes we need to allow ourselves the space to be perfectly not perfect.

What do you most enjoy about your work?

I most enjoy the fact that I have a positive impact on someone's day. It's hard to be upset while eating dessert or a pastry. It may be just a moment, but every moment counts.

What's the most difficult aspect of your career?

The most difficult aspect of my career is having to maneuver handling and dealing with harassment. Pastry is usually the most female-centric part of most hospitality and restaurant establishments. Especially once I got higher up in management, it was pretty depressing how hard I had to fight to make sure my department was respected and treated like a viable part of the team.

What brings you joy and what would you like to experience more of?

Spending quality time with family and friends are the moments of pure joy for me. Simply enjoying your time and sharing positive energy with someone you care about is truly one of life's treasures.

And I'd like to experience more dance parties! I miss dancing so much.

What are some of your favorite things to eat or drink?

It honestly depends on the season. During the summer I want cherries! I can eat them by the pound. I also love vanilla ice cream with chocolate sprinkles and a pinch of salt. During the winter and holiday season I crave my mom's Jamaican carrot juice.

"Sometimes we need to allow ourselves the space to be perfectly not perfect."

Strawberry-Pear–Black Pepper Jam

BY JESSICA CRAIG / MAKES 5 OUNCES

8 ounces strawberries (about ⅔ pint or 8 large berries), washed, hulled, and quartered

1 large Bartlett pear, cored and diced (peeling isn't necessary)

¾ cup granulated sugar

2 tablespoons fresh lemon juice

½ teaspoon freshly cracked black pepper

There is no cooking project more satisfying to me than creating a jam. As with most jams, this one is particularly lovely on toast. You can also use it for so many other things: as a filling for a tart or cake, over ice cream, or as an accompaniment to cheese.

Place the strawberries and pears in a medium bowl, add the sugar, and toss to coat. Cover tightly and refrigerate overnight.

With a rubber spatula, scrape the fruit mixture into a medium-size, heavy-bottomed pot. Stir in the lemon juice and pepper. Place a small plate in the freezer.

Place the pot over medium heat and bring the mixture just to a simmer. Reduce the heat to maintain a bare simmer and cook the jam, stirring occasionally, until it thickens, coats the back of a spoon, and is reduced almost by half, about 18 to 25 minutes. Remove the plate from the freezer and spoon a little jam onto it. When you tilt the plate the jam should move slowly. If that doesn't happen, cook a little longer until it thickens. Keep watch over the pot so it doesn't burn.

Allow the jam to cool completely before transferring it to a jar or other container with a tight-fitting lid. It will keep in the refrigerator for up to 4 weeks.

Zoe Adjonyoh

CHEF, COOKBOOK AUTHOR,
FOUNDER OF ZOE'S GHANA
KITCHEN *LONDON, ENGLAND
& NEW YORK, NEW YORK*

How would you describe your work?

I'd probably describe it as cooking up consciousness with a great load of collaborators.

How did you begin in your field?

Basically, the universe gave me an opportunity that I turned into a business, and the opportunity was to use my cultural and physical identity as a mixed-race Black lesbian born to immigrants, and everything I do is informed by that.

Who are some of your role models or mentors in the food space?

So many. Obviously Jessica Harris; Preeti Mistry; Charles Chen, I suppose. You [Klancy]. Tunde Wey; Julia Turshen; Ashtin Berry—anybody who works in food, and they're doing it with a conscious lens of moving the paradigm or breaking out of the status quo. Anybody doing that work is a mentor of mine.

What are you most proud of?

I'm still standing and I'm still creating.

What is an important lesson you've learned about money, compensation, or finance over the course of your career?

My big learning has been that money is energy, and that's a beautiful thing because that means it can come at anytime from anywhere, and that understanding—that knowledge has helped me break out of the scarcity mentality, which I've had my entire existence. Coming to understand what a scarcity mentality is has been useful. Coming to understand that a lot of my relationship with money has been based on my parents' relationship with money, and I've been able to navigate a new relationship with it with that insight.

Having a different kind of emotional, energetic relationship with it has been useful, but also understanding from a finance perspective that there just is so much money available, and that the routes to access it get less difficult. I guess what I'm trying to say is learning to have an abundance mindset has shifted my whole relationship with money—how I get it, and how I view people with it as well.

So shifting the mindset has brought me closer to money, but also having boundaries around it. Having a hard boundary about being paid for my time or resources— it's meant I've had to say no to lots of cool ideas and cool projects and publications, which I may or may not regret down the line. But in the present moment, it means I feel good about how I value myself.

How do you take care of your mental health and deal with the stresses of your work?

I've been very reliant on a morning routine that involves journaling and meditation and a lot of astrology. I literally check about five different astrology apps every morning—

"I think the most important part is to be yourself, to learn to love yourself. Everything starts with that."

"What's my day like?" But I have become more flexible about what that looks like and how it happens. The key, really, is just taking time every morning, whether it involves meditation, whether it involves journaling, whether it involves gratitude, whether it involves affirmations. It may or may not include any or all of those things, but it's taking time for myself and having a hard boundary around that.

Sometimes that's exercise. That morning routine can involve lots of things or just a couple of the things, but it's about having a couple of hours every morning that are just mine for me to breathe, to think, to contemplate, and to have space outside of the noise that will inevitably come throughout the day.

What advice would you offer to someone who wants to do what you do?

Don't! Don't do it. I don't know. It depends what part of what I do, I suppose. Actually, that's bullshit because all parts are the same thing. I mean, if what I do is cocreating toward a more conscious planet, which is my lofty ideal, then anyone can start anytime that they—they can start by doing a sixty-second meditation. They can start by changing their buying choices. They can start by practicing antiracism. They can buy my cookbook—you know what I mean?

It could be any number of things, but I think the most important part is to be yourself, to learn to love yourself. Everything starts with that. Learn to love yourself and your duality and celebrate yourself and your duality. Don't just be celebrating yourself for your high moments where you're the best version of yourself, but acknowledge and accept all parts and share all parts. So authenticity—that's the secret ingredient to everything that I do. It's like I wear it all out there. It's just all out there, and that is it. That's the source—authenticity.

What do you most enjoy about your career?

I want to say the struggle—because I think it speaks back to the journey. If the journey was smooth, I wouldn't have learned anything, and if I didn't learn anything, I wouldn't have grown. I wouldn't have much to say if any of this had been easy. What would I have to say? I wouldn't be able to share anything.

What's the most difficult aspect of your career?

I honestly think it's the lens that people throw on me or my business in terms of success. I'm constantly—I don't say this to be critical of it, but constantly people want my advice or time. I think people think that me and my business are a lot bigger than they are. I think people think that I'm really wealthy, that I have everything sorted, that I'm stable. So I think the hardest part is other people's assumptions and the expectation that I can—like charities and stuff, like, constantly trying to get me to do stuff. There's a limit to how much time I can donate to projects, as much as I care about them. I would love to mentor people more regularly, or I would love to coach people, but I have to pay my bills. So I think there's always this thing of people thinking that the number of followers you have means that you are therefore in a position to give more of yourself than you already are, and I think a lot of my work already gives a lot of myself— or I try to make it so anyway.

What are some of your favorite things to eat or drink?

It really depends on my mood and where I am. You know? So to drink, right now my favorite kind of drink is anything sparkling and nonalcoholic, so usually fruit based— pomegranate and cranberry or hibiscus. Like red or pink drinks that are sparkling but nonalcoholic. And to eat, I think, I've got a huge penchant for tacos right now.

Jollof Risotto
WITH PRAWNS

BY ZOE ADJONYOH / MAKES 2 SERVINGS

This recipe is my riff on the famous West African dish jollof, which is a rice dish. Within the diaspora there's a longstanding dispute about whose jollof is superior—the contention is especially legendary between Ghanaians and Nigerians, although the dish is also popular in other West African countries.

Making this recipe involves cooking a chalé sauce, which is a spicy tomato sauce. When I was a kid, I watched my dad cook his chalé sauce, and then he would add meat or fish. For this particular jolof risotto recipe I top the dish off with prawns. I regularly make a batch of chalé and store unused sauce for later use. For the spices, you can find baobab powder, jollof spice mix, and selim at zoesghanakitchen.com, on Amazon, or at your local African grocery store.

CHALÉ SAUCE

14 ounces canned tomatoes or 1½ cups fresh tomatoes, chopped

1 roasted and seeded red bell pepper (okay to use ½ cup jarred roasted bell pepper)

2 garlic cloves (optional)

1 tablespoon tomato puree

1 small white onion, chopped

1-inch piece fresh ginger, grated

½ teaspoon red pepper flakes

½ teaspoon chili powder

1 teaspoon extra hot Madras curry powder

½ small scotch bonnet pepper, seeded, or ½ teaspoon cayenne

Salt

PRAWNS

1 pound large prawns, peeled, deveined, and tails left on

1 tablespoon baobab powder

1 tablespoon olive oil

2 garlic cloves, minced

1 tablespoon grated lemon zest

1 tablespoon chopped fresh parsley

1 teaspoon sea salt

RISOTTO

2 tablespoons olive oil

1½ tablespoons unsalted butter

1 large white onion, diced

1 heaped tablespoon jollof spice mix

1 teaspoon extra hot Madras curry powder

1 teaspoon extra hot chili powder

1 clove garlic

1 tablespoon chopped thyme leaves

6 grains of selim pepper (guinea pepper), crushed or snapped open

1 tablespoon tomato puree

2 cups good-quality chicken stock, kept steaming hot

¾ cup arborio rice

1¼ cups chalé sauce

Chopped parsley and fresh lemon juice, for garnish

For the chalé sauce, combine the tomatoes, roasted pepper, garlic, tomato puree, onion, ginger, pepper flakes, chili powder, curry powder, and scotch bonnet pepper in a blender or food processor. Add salt to taste. Process until smooth. Refrigerate in an airtight container until ready to use, up to 2 weeks, and up to 1 month in the freezer.

For the prawns, combine them in a bowl with the baobab powder, olive oil, garlic, lemon zest, parsley, and salt. Toss to coat. Cover and refrigerate while you make the risotto.

For the risotto, heat the oil and butter in a wide, nonstick pan over medium-low heat. Sauté the onion with the spice mix, curry powder, and chili powder until soft, about 5 minutes. Stir in the garlic, thyme, and selim. Stir in the tomato puree and cook, stirring, until it turns a deep brick-red color.

Slowly stir in ¼ cup of the stock to deglaze the pan. Stir in the rice, making sure all the grains are covered in spice mix. Cook, stirring, for 3 to 4 minutes to open the grains. Stir in ½ cup chalé sauce and reduce until the pan is almost dry. Add ½ cup stock and cook, stirring, until the stock is absorbed and the pan is almost dry. Continue stirring in chalé sauce and stock ½ cup at a time until the rice is tender but still firm.

Add the prawns to the pan and cook, turning once, until they are pink and opaque, 4 to 5 minutes.

Serve immediately, garnished with parsley and a sprinkle of fresh lemon juice.

Lani Halliday

BAKER, ARTIST, FOUNDER
OF BRUTUS BAKESHOP
BROOKLYN, NEW YORK

How would you describe your work?

In terms of the work that people see that's on the physical plane (we are spiritual beings, in a physical body; the work I do that people see is very much on the physical plane), I do inclusive baked goods, which means that I hit as many of the big nos as possible: Everything I do is gluten-free. Most things I do are vegan. I like to make things that are delicious and delightful, that really take into consideration what everyone can eat. It's fun and that's how I would describe my work.

I also create content and digital media, and I'm also always just reading into other, different kinds of partnerships like catering or collaborations or recipe developing.

How did you begin in your field?

I started baking when I was nineteen. I was a little bit of a . . . I didn't really have a lot of direction. I had huge aspirations. But I didn't have a lot of direction, and I found myself putting myself through community college and working in a grocery store in the front end as a customer service clerk, wrangling carts and things like that. The guy who ran the bakery, he had been a baker for two and a half decades; he was incredibly talented. He ran this organic scratch-bread bakery inside of this very large grocery store. He saw me, he liked my energy, he pulled me in, and he was like, "You're going to be my apprentice. I'm going to teach you how to bake." I was like, "Oh, wow. Someone sees me. I'm seeable. Amazing."

He taught me everything about artisan bread, and I just really fell in love with—not even so much the bread baking, and that's where the whole spiritual part comes in. It wasn't about what I was making. It was the fact that I, for the first time in my life, felt like an expert at something. I felt like I had the power to see and be seen and have an impact on my community. I would show up to work, and I had these two hands and very basic things like flour, water, salt, grease. I was creating all these things that made people feel joy, and they were my community. I had never experienced anything like that before. I thought for a long time I was following a skill set, but I was really following that feeling of creating a community and feeling a part of something and feeling important.

What is an important lesson you've learned about money, compensation, or finance over the course of your career?

If you don't make it and you don't pay attention to it—if you're like, "I'm not a money person"—you've got to become a money person. It's a challenge for me. I identify very much as a creative, and I think that there's a misconception that the two things are diametrically opposed, you're one or the other. We all know whatever we pay attention to grows, so we want to pay attention to the money because we want the money to grow.

"If you're like, 'I'm not a money person,' you've got to become a money person."

And also I think on a spiritual and energetic level, I think that there's this conversation around abundance and desperation, two things that are opposed to each other—or maybe desperation is such a gross word, but abundance and lack. Examine your unconscious beliefs about money, because they really inform everything.

I got into a place where I was really fearful, that there are all these opportunities coming and if I say no, that the opportunities are going to stop. So I really overloaded myself doing things that were not necessarily compensating me in a way that I felt was worthy of my time. Maybe only half of them are paying what I really think I should be getting. What I should have done is said yes only to the things where I was happy with the compensation structure and just said, "No thank you," for those other things.

I think when I was first starting, I would do anything and everything to get my name out there and really build this brand recognition. Retrospectively if I would have actually just spent that time that I gave away for free working on something that would make money but was more behind the scenes, I'd probably be in a different place right now and not so burned out.

Those choices stemmed from my unconscious beliefs about money. As I evolved as an entrepreneur and really spent time unpacking what those things are, I feel a lot more in control of how I discern what activities I engage in as a business.

What advice would you offer to someone who wants to do what you do?

My advice is before you do what I do, figure out what it is that you *think* I'm creating by the things that I get up to and then figure out how to create those things in your life. I think that I would start there. Take those things that you see that I embody, and then figure out what your version of that looks like based on what brings you joy and what your desires are.

What are some of your favorite things to eat or drink?

Bitter sodas and water. Or also, I love these things called Hiball. Not a highball the cocktail, it's with caffeine. I'm not a huge coffee person, but I am a huge caffeine person. That is probably one of my favorite things to drink.

I've been on this mochi donut kick lately. There's this little tea spot down in Chinatown. I will ride my bike over the Manhattan Bridge and come back over every single bump on the Brooklyn Bridge to go get myself a mochi donut from the place downtown. I get two usually because they're just that delicious.

Spiced Oatmeal Cookie Cake

BY LANI HALLIDAY / MAKES 8 SERVINGS

CAKE

1½ cups gluten-free flour blend (I use Bob's Red Mill)

1 teaspoon baking soda

1 teaspoon kosher salt

1 teaspoon ground cinnamon

3 cup old-fashioned oats

1½ cups unsweetened flaked coconut

1 cup organic all-vegetable shortening (I use Spectrum)

1½ cups granulated sugar

¼ cup aquafaba (the drained juice from a can of chickpeas)

½ cup oat milk

2 tablespoons pomegranate molasses

3 tablespoons pure vanilla extract

FROSTING

1½ pounds (or 3½ cups) confectioners' sugar

12 ounces (or 1½ cups) organic all-vegetable shortening

1 teaspoon salt

2 tablespoons pure vanilla extract

4 tablespoons pomegranate molasses

4 drops pink gel food coloring

Oat milk as needed to thin

The thing I like about this recipe is it's made up of some of my favorite things—cookies and frosting. Put it all together and it's a beautiful gluten-free vegan cookie cake. Once you get to the frosting stage, remember it's a semi-naked cake because it's a cookie cake and the finished product is a picture of rustic perfection. The presentation is the fun part for me because I love making things look pretty. You can decorate this cookie cake anyway you want.

Make sure to put the frosted cake in the refrigerator for at least three hours, or even better overnight, before slicing into it.

For the cake, preheat the oven to 350°F with a rack in the middle. Coat three 9-inch round cake pans with nonstick cooking spray and line the bottoms with parchment paper.

In a large mixing bowl, whisk together the flour, soda, salt, and cinnamon. In another bowl, toss the oats and coconut to combine. Set aside.

In the bowl of a stand mixer, combine the shortening and sugar and beat with the whisk attachment on medium-high speed until light and fluffy, 5 minutes, stopping a couple of times to scrape down the bowl. With the mixer on low speed, gradually add the aquafaba, milk, molasses, and vanilla. Combine the wet and dry ingredients, mixing until well combined.

Divide the batter evenly among the pans and bake until golden brown, 15 to 19 minutes. Set the pans on a rack to cool. After about 10 minutes, run a table knife around the inside edges of the pans to release the cake layers and set them on the rack to cool completely. Transfer to a parchment-lined sheet pan set in the refrigerator to chill for about 20 minutes, while you make the frosting.

For the frosting, sift the confectioners' sugar through a sieve. (This step is crucial for smooth frosting.) In the bowl of a stand mixer, beat the sifted sugar and shortening with the whisk attachment, starting with pulses on low speed to avoid the sugar "floofing" out of the bowl and increasing to medium speed until combined.

With the mixer on low speed, gradually beat in the salt, vanilla, molasses, and food coloring, stopping a few times to scrape down the bowl. The color should be an even pink. Starting with a few tablespoons, add oat milk until you achieve a smooth, spreadable consistency. (Frosting may be made ahead and held, covered, at room temperature for a few hours.)

To assemble, dab a little frosting on a cake circle or serving plate and place the first cake layer on it. Top the layer with a large scoop of frosting and spread it evenly to the edges. Repeat with the second and third layers, topping the cake off with a generous slick of frosting and leaving the sides naked. Make certain the frosted cake spends at least 3 hours in the refrigerator, ideally overnight, before slicing into it. When you're ready to serve, add sprinkles! Celebrate and enjoy.

Jamila Robinson

PHILADELPHIA INQUIRER
FOOD EDITOR, FOOD
MEDIA LEADER
WASHINGTON, DC

How would you describe your work?

It's the essential part of journalism, which is public service, and how we think about living our lives better. And I think features journalists, lifestyle journalists—people who do food, art, and culture—really have a pulse on how to help people live their lives better because that is indeed a public service. So me thinking about journalism is thinking about how food helps build community, and if we can do that then we are doing a public service. We are helping to inform the public not only about the best places to eat, but how restaurants in the neighborhood anchor the community, and the ways—whether it's real estate or the economy—the ways that food intersects with every part of our lives. I think it's essential that we share that. So it's journalism, but it really is that public service piece.

When did you know that you wanted to be a journalist, and how did you begin?

It's the only thing I've ever wanted to do. The funny story is I was ten, and we were a newspaper family. We read a lot of newspapers. We probably got the two dailies of my hometown (which is Detroit, Michigan), and then we also got the *Michigan Chronicle* (which is the Black paper), and then we got *Time* and *Newsweek*.

When I was ten, I was obsessed with Michael Jackson, and I realized that during the height of *Thriller*, there were stories in the paper about Michael Jackson almost every day—and it hit me that the only people who actually got to talk to Michael Jackson were journalists, and I was like, "I need to do that." Part of it is because I didn't think that the questions were that interesting. A journalist would ask him, "I hear you're feuding with your brothers," and he'd say, "I love my brothers," and I'm like, "You're asking him the wrong question." Because I have brothers and my brothers annoy me, so I wanted to know what those things were, and I didn't think people were asking the right questions about his brothers.

Then, when the Pepsi commercial accident happened and they were sending him to a burn unit—well, I have a third-degree burn on my shoulder and that happened when I was five, so I was very aware of what it's like to go to a burn unit, what the process of healing is. And even at ten, I was like, "How are you going to go tour in six weeks? Dude, you've got to change those bandages every day, and this is your scalp, and this is his shoulder," and I wanted to hear more from him about that process of healing even as a ten-year-old, and I was like, "I would ask him totally different questions."

Every day I would think about the questions I would ask Michael Jackson that would probably elicit better responses that I wasn't reading in every single paper, so it's something that I started doing.

So it's the only thing that I've ever wanted to do, and I've always found a way to incorporate the arts.

In high school, I wrote about musical theater, I wrote about "Here's what you need to know before you take

your SATs," "Here are the Top 10 questions from our AP teachers." Those were the kinds of things that I'd like to do, and so I brought that along with me to all my internships, and I was very fortunate to be part of the inaugural High School Journalism Program at the *Detroit Free Press*, which was led by a man called Bob McGruder, one of the first Black managing editors at a major daily in the country, and he walked the talk. Because even at that time they were saying, "We need more Black journalists. We need more Black editors," and he's like, "Well, you know, you have to grow them," and he started this program that would do that. Some of the alumni include myself, people like Jemele Hill, John Eligon at the *New York Times*, and dozens and dozens of other journalists, many of whom are of color, who are now leading organizations. So it's a long answer, but it was Michael Jackson that got me here.

What advice would you offer to someone who wants to do what you do?

Well—so many things. One is read. Read a lot, write a lot. Some of the best advice I've ever received was: "Do what you want. Know what the rules are, but do what you want." People are so much freer now to speak up, to speak their minds, to say what they think now, and that is something that I really admire because I'm like, "Mmm, I don't know if I would say that out loud like that."

Also, so much of the business is relationship building. It is cultivating relationships, it's sustaining relationships, it's maintaining relationships, and it is building more. And if you aren't good at building relationships, then you aren't going to be good at this business, because not everything can be blasted on Twitter, and you have to know when to step back and sometimes let the bus crash or say, "You know what? Not my party."

Self-awareness is key, and that requires being able to take feedback. Every now and then I will encounter a writer who doesn't want to be edited and thinks like, "Oh, you're ruining my voice!" and I'm like, "Girl, you don't have a voice yet. You haven't established that. I'm trying to help you do that." Having a good relationship with an editor is only going to sharpen your work.

And I want to say this too, because I think it's important. A lot of Black women, especially, have this thing somebody decided to call "impostor syndrome," which I think is nonsense. When you feel as if you don't belong in a space, that is not "impostor." That's not being welcome. That's not being heard. That's not the same thing as like, "Ooh—I don't know. I'm not cool enough to be in this neighborhood." That

would be an impostor. What I need (and I think what a lot of Black women, especially, need) is somebody to believe in their ideas as much as we believe in them—and the magic that we bring. We need people to say, "Yes, that is magical. Go forth and do it." But you need those doors opened. You need that light filled. But the idea that you don't belong here—says who? Who made that decision? Who made that call? Taking up space is a matter of—it goes back to self-awareness and knowing who you are.

How do you take care of your mental health and deal with the stresses of your work?

I don't. You know, I have a funny story. I fired my therapist and hired a skating coach. Actually, it's so funny because we talk about therapy a lot now, and sometimes—like, for me, I don't always need therapy. What I need is a task.

I've been taking skating lessons for twenty-odd years, and I said, "I'm going to go spend some time at the ice rink." I would go skate off my day, and I was having a hard time with a particular turn—suddenly I couldn't do it anymore, and somebody asked me if I was working with a skating coach, and I was like, "No, because I'm not competing, and blah, blah, blah." And so she's like, "Well, you should just take a lesson or two," and I was like, "That's a good idea."

So I called this coach, and she says, "Oh, you're at this level, this and this and that." Her name is Aurora. She's Black, and I purposely hired a Black skating coach. She said, "Let me see your flying camel," and I was like, "Oh, I can't really do a flying camel anymore. I had this done, and blah, blah, blah," and she's like, "Did I ask you all of that?" She's like, "Go out there and let me see the jump."

So I go up, I do the jump, land the jump—but it doesn't spin. I was like, "See? I told you. I can't do a flying camel," and she's like, "No. What we need to do is work on your backspin. We need to work on your camel spin." She gave me these tasks, and then all of a sudden I was like, "Oh! Yeah," and then she's like, "When you take a jump, I need you to jump like you're reaching for the ancestors. Get your arms out and fly into it," and I was like that's what I needed to hear. I didn't need to hear about, like, "Oh, when I was twelve I didn't have enough . . ."

That's not my thing. What I needed was to see progress and to feel like I was accomplishing something, so I could do the jumps.

What are some of your favorite things to eat or drink?

It's always going to be a lemon tart for me. A lemon tart just reminds me of my grandmother.

Lemon Tart

BY JAMILA ROBINSON / MAKES 6–8 SERVINGS

TART SHELL

1½ cups all-purpose flour

3 tablespoons granulated sugar

½ teaspoon kosher salt

1 egg yolk

1 teaspoon grated lemon zest

1 stick (½ cup) unsalted butter, cubed and chilled

¼ cup ice water

LEMON CURD

1 cup granulated sugar

2 large eggs

2 large egg yolks

2 tablespoons grated lemon zest plus ¾ cup freshly squeezed lemon juice (from about 6 lemons)

6 tablespoons (3 ounces) unsalted butter, cut into pieces

For the tart shell, combine the flour, sugar, salt, yolk, and zest in a food processor, and pulse until just mixed. Add the butter and pulse until grainy. With the machine running, add the ice water, processing until the dough just comes together.

Press the dough into an 8-inch tart shell with a removable bottom, neatly trimming the sides. Cover with parchment paper and place in the refrigerator or freezer to chill while the oven heats.

Meanwhile, preheat the oven to 350°F.

When the oven is hot, place pie weights or a heavy dish in the chilled tart shell and bake until golden, 25 to 30 minutes. Set it aside on a wire rack to cool completely.

Keep the oven at 350°F.

In a small saucepan, whisk together the sugar, eggs, egg yolks, lemon zest, and juice. Cook over low heat, whisking constantly, until the curd is thickened, 7 to 8 minutes. (You should be able to draw a line down the back of a wooden spoon coated with the lemon mixture.)

Remove the pan from the heat and add the butter, 1 tablespoon at a time, stirring after each addition until the butter is almost melted.

Pour the curd through a fine wire-mesh strainer into the cooled tart shell. Bake until the curd is set but still slightly wobbly, 8 to 10 minutes. Set it on a rack to cool completely.

Osayi Endolyn

FOOD AND CULTURE
WRITER, PRODUCER
BROOKLYN, NEW YORK

How did you begin in your field?

I asked myself one evening what I would be doing if I could do anything. This came after years of feeling unfocused and unsure about what I wanted but having the sense there was a way I could be using my voice that I wasn't present to yet. The answer was "You'd be a writer." Once I gave myself permission to pursue it, things fell into place. I began by practicing living as a writer.

I bought books about writing careers. I subscribed to literary publications. I explored what I wanted to write about and researched how to pitch. I got rejected a lot. I started a blog. I started a writing group. And then eventually, those things led to more opportunities. I entered a graduate school program and I did an MFA in writing.

I didn't set out to become a food writer, per se. I didn't have a goal of "I want to work on cookbooks" or things like that. That all came later.

What pulled you into food?

I was starting to understand the things that felt good to write about were things that I already had an interest in personally, and at the time I was into craft beer. I lived in Atlanta, Georgia, and that scene was seeing explosive growth.

I was interning at *Atlanta* magazine, and I attended a meeting where there was an assignment they wanted to make, and the person they wanted to do it wasn't available. I later talked to the editor in chief, his name was Steve Fennessy, and got the assignment myself, which was a feature on one of the largest craft breweries to come out of Atlanta, and really the region. I did an oral history on them, and that was my first big, paid feature assignment. I think it was around four thousand words. Hefty! Lots of interviews and distilling separate narratives into one. That wasn't typical—interns don't get features. But I had a few clips and could demonstrate my familiarity with the subject, even though my editorial experience wasn't extensive. When you're starting out as a writer and you have a body of knowledge, that doesn't necessarily have to be the only thing that you work on, but it can be a great way to get a foothold.

The range of storytelling available in food writing became more apparent to me when I wrote an essay about seeking out Nigerian food in restaurants in the Atlanta area. It was a personal essay where I linked my father's Edo culture, my maternal heritage through the Great Migration, and my California upbringing with the Southern food that was around me. It also referenced the changing dynamics of the food scene in Atlanta. I hadn't seen a lot of work like that published in the magazine before, and it was, I think, making visible the kinds of dining experiences that we've only recently started to see in broader, popular publications. The response to that piece affirmed for me what I already felt, that cultural experiences like mine were not niche or exceptional. They represent millions of us who have not been centered in food storytelling for generations. I saw that writing about food could be a lens to explore immigration and labor and the history of how we talk about identity. All of that can come from driving around metro Atlanta looking for egusi soup.

What is the biggest lesson you've learned about money, compensation, or finance so far in your career?

The money you earn has nothing to do with worth, like what you earn does not correlate to your actual value. So using money as a metric for what you think you deserve is not useful.

The market is going to have a perception of what your value is that is different from what your internal metric is—and there should be a gap there because, especially in the book world, there is a delay between projects that you're negotiating right now versus projects that are on their way to being published. There's always a two- to three-year gap between what the perception of your value is versus what you know your value is.

I can set my price in a way I couldn't ten years ago; similarly opportunities that I would have jumped at a while back are not as appealing to me now. I've learned that choosing projects more selectively is a better use of creative energy and a better time-to-value exchange.

I've also learned to be more clear about what it is I'm being asked to do on projects, particularly collaborative ones where, because I work on a lot of projects that have not existed before, there is sometimes a truncated idea of what my role is or what it should become. I have sometimes been the last to realize, "Oh, the thing that I negotiated to do on this project isn't actually what I'm being asked to do every day."

For example, my cookbooks aren't like most of the ones that preceded me, where a restaurant menu is distilled into book form, or a TV personality collects a bunch of recipes around a theme like "quick dinners." That assignment is different than taking the cultural identity of a chef or the personal life experience of a chef combined with their cultural identity and using that as a foundation to create a cookbook that speaks to an expansive historic narrative, like with *Black Power Kitchen*, the book I wrote for Ghetto Gastro. Because now you're not just getting into the existing infrastructure of a restaurant (which is already telling a story—you just have to transfer it). You now have to figure out what elements of this person's life, career, work, culture, food heritage, food knowledge have impacted this person's cooking.

I've learned that sometimes, even though these projects come up as "work-for-hire," they're really not. I'm integral to the spine of the editorial project, which means that I'm investing a lot more time and resources and energy and creativity, and that has implications on the compensation side. It's also affected my sense of ownership. If you want my strategic brain and my bright ideas, I now understand you're gonna have to come off of some percentage points, and a good creative partner will be happy to do that. For a long time folks have told me that's not "how it works." Freedom for people who look like me wasn't "how it worked" once upon a time either, and that didn't make it correct. So don't call me, then!

In terms of my solo-authored work and projects where I advise media companies, or curate events, or produce stories across various platforms, we're definitely up against old ideas about compensation. It does feel like you have to educate people: "Yeah, if you want me to appear on your TV program that is going to be streaming in two hundred countries—I understand that you may not have an infinite budget, but the time that I spend on set that day and the time that I spend preparing for this interview or for this context you want me to bring to this TV show or whatever, that is worthy of payment. It's time."

So being clear about that is important, and being more transparent with friends and colleagues about what the rates are and what did you get paid. There are people who I feel really grateful to be able to ask, "Hey, I know you did this last year. What did they pay you? What should I ask for? What do you think?" Recognizing how much information can be gleaned from that kind of visibility is really useful.

Do you have a mission or motto, and if so, what is it?

I think right now, it's sort of more like a guiding light. I want my life to support me being joyful and me being at ease, and I think that sometimes (particularly in the United States) when we hear people talk like that, it sounds like you are saying you're going to disengage, like you're not going to live in the real world, because of course we know that we live in a world where there's a lot of dis-ease and lack of joy. But what I have come to understand is that—you really have to be understanding of your own flaws, your own shadow self, and your own capabilities, recognizing that, like, if I want to have this sense of playfulness in my life, then what do I need to establish so that that's possible?

What are some of your favorite things to eat or drink?

I love a Pinot Meunier Champagne, and I've almost never encountered seafood that I didn't love. Anything in the ocean is fair game.

"Choosing projects more selectively is a better use of creative energy and a better time-to-value exchange."

Amethyst Ganaway

CHEF, WRITER *CHARLESTON, SOUTH CAROLINA*

How would you describe your work?

Engaging, I guess. It's kind of the first thing I would say, it's engaging. Truthful. I try to just be as thoughtful and respectful to whatever it is that I'm either writing about or cooking. And I try to be as informative as possible as well. And like I said, as truthful as I possibly can.

How did you begin in your field?

Out of necessity. In college, I needed to work to pay bills and pay tuition. And that's how I got into food. I mean, food's always been a part of the culture, obviously, where I'm from [South Carolina]. So it's always been a part of who I am and what I do. But as a professional, it didn't really start until college.

Who are some of your role models or mentors in the food and hospitality space?

First would be my granny, even though she's not technically, right? But I mean, she's a pro in my book, obviously. Mashama Bailey, Nina Compton, Charise Multon, you [Klancy], Vertamae, of course, Ms. Sallie Ann Robinson. I think that's a good start to my list.

What is the biggest lesson you've learned so far about money, negotiation, or finance in your career?

To be honest and up front, I would say know your worth, but saying that is easier than doing it, I guess. Right? Because a lot of times, it's not necessarily that you don't know what you're worth, it's literally knowing how to put a dollar amount to that and feeling comfortable and feeling confident and going to whoever it is that's cutting that check and saying, "Well, this is what it's going to be." And to just stand firm in whatever that number might look like. I would also say, learn how to budget realistically. Regardless of what kind of path you take, this is not a career field where you are going to make a lot of money.

I mean, there are people who do, of course. But for the average Joe Schmo, it's just being smart but also enjoying yourself because it is a hard job, whatever that may be that you're doing. It's a hard job so you deserve to get paid well for it and you should be able to have time to actually enjoy that.

Tell me about how where you're from has influenced your approach to food and cooking. What are some of the most formative foods and food memories and experiences?

Where I'm from and the culture, a lot of people, we don't have a lot. But we have one another and we got good food. It's kind of how I approach a lot of things in life generally. You can make something good out of that. Especially if I'm cooking or even if I'm writing, I just kind of keep in mind that this is not something that's supposed to be frilly and fancy and perfect and tweezered on and have this particular

"I would say know your worth, but saying that is easier than doing it."

look about it that looks good to whoever in particular. It's food that's going to make you feel. It's going to make you feel good and it's going to be fresh and it's going to be grown in somebody's grandma's backyard.

I talk about crab boils and stuff like that a lot. I mean, it's a Southern thing for sure. Those things remind me that whatever I'm doing, it's more than just about me in this moment doing this one thing. This is about all of the people who are involved, who are a part of this, whether it's literally or just a part of the culture, the community. I'm from the South. I'm from Charleston, so that's always something that's kind of in me.

[When I write], it's just something that my grandma can read. Is this something she wants to read? Is this something that she's going to see herself in? Is this something that my friends can go home and make? I try to be mindful of that and just think about my community more than just myself.

How do you take care of your mental health and deal with the stresses of your work?

I really am learning to set boundaries and learning that my boundaries may not always be the best for other people, but they're what's best for me. That's what I'm learning about how to handle stress now, especially moving out of having to work in kitchens where that's a completely different level of stress. That's: I got to know how to handle stress on the fly. In the moment. But there are certain stresses that are just kind of constant. So it's just setting boundaries, setting routine. I'm a person who if I don't have a routine, I will sit here all day and nothing will get done. And then I have anxiety because I didn't get anything done. Right?

And taking time for myself, however that might look. So my phone is always on do not disturb.

What are some of your favorite things to eat or drink?

Drink? Always going to be bourbon or whiskey.

And then to eat, crab. Just some blue crab.

Pickled Eggs

BY AMETHYST GANAWAY / MAKES 4–6 SERVINGS

1 cup distilled white vinegar

1 cup red wine vinegar

½ cup water

3 tablespoons sugar

1 tablespoon kosher salt

1 small habanero or scotch bonnet pepper

1 large garlic clove, smashed

2 scallions, trimmed and thinly sliced

4–6 medium or large eggs, hard-cooked, cooled, and peeled

1 thin slice raw beet or red cabbage (optional)

Every part of my life and career comes back to where I'm from and the foods I ate growing up in North Charleston, South Carolina. Because of the community I grew up in, hospitality is ingrained in who I am, and so is sharing and passing down the history of the people who came before me. Hotlinks, souse, pickled eggs, smothered shrimp, okra, and greens of all kinds are dishes I see on menus everywhere now, but I know they have been made for hundreds of years by people who look and sound like me. This recipe for pickled eggs is one of my favorite things and reminds me of home.

You will need a 16-ounce mason jar with lid. A slice of beet or red cabbage gives the eggs a vibrant pink hue.

In a small pot, combine the vinegars, water, sugar, and salt, and heat over low just until the salt and sugar dissolve. Remove from the heat and let cool to room temperature.

For moderately spicy eggs, place the whole habanero in a clean, dry, quart-size mason jar; for more heat, halve and seed the pepper first. Add the garlic, scallions, and eggs.

Pour the cooled brine into the jar, submerging the ingredients and filling the jar completely (discard any unused brine). Tighten the lid on the jar and shake it gently. Refrigerate at least five days and up to 2 weeks before serving.

Klancy Miller

WRITER, AUTHOR, FOUNDER OF *FOR THE CULTURE: A MAGAZINE CELEBRATING BLACK WOMEN AND FEMMES IN FOOD & WINE* BROOKLYN, NEW YORK

How would you describe your work?

I am a writer, an editor, a home cook, a cookbook author, and the founder of *For the Culture: A Magazine Celebrating Black Women and Femmes in Food and Wine.*

How did you begin in your field?

I got my first job in food as a dishwasher at a gourmet grocery store. It was a summer job and I was fifteen and saving up money for a trip to Sweden and Denmark to meet up with a friend. My next food job was in college as a stir-fry cook in one of the cafeterias on campus. After I graduated from college at Columbia University I didn't know what I wanted to do so figured I would embark on an adventure of exploring my interests and doing a process of elimination until I found something I felt passionate about. I got a job in an international nongovernmental organization, and then in my spare time, after work and on weekends, I took cooking classes, filmmaking classes, dance classes, acting classes. The cooking classes stuck. Soon I was looking for a way to try to cook in a professional setting. I tried to get a job in a restaurant but had no real experience, but the chef offered me an apprenticeship as a prep cook on the weekends. I loved it! It was the first time I ever showed up on time for work. I decided to go to culinary school after that because my chef said, "You don't need to go to culinary school to become a chef, but you need to if you're going to become a pastry chef. I wanted to go to some kind of school, and I love sweets and Paris, so I decided I would go to Le Cordon Bleu for their pastry program. I got an extra job, saved money, and went. That was the beginning. Eventually, after working in Paris in bakeries and restaurants, I realized that I might not have the speed to work in a professional kitchen, so I started to look at other options to work with food. I got a job at Le Cordon Bleu in their recipe development department and then started writing about food on the side, on blogs, for free. When I got back to the States I did a series of informational interviews with editors and chefs and food publicists to figure out next steps, and I ended up doing food PR briefly and then freelance writing and starting a supper club and then ghostwriting, eventually writing my own cookbook, *Cooking Solo.* It's all a work in progress. My career is a quilt.

Who are some of your role models or mentors in the food, farming, and hospitality space?

Every single person in this book is a role model to me. Also Ellen Yin, Marcus Samuelsson, Bryant Terry, and Stephen Satterfield.

What are you most proud of?

I'm proud of myself for not giving up and for being committed to figuring things out the best I can. I'm proud of myself for always following my curiosity. I'm proud of myself for not being afraid to make mistakes or take risks. And I'm proud of the people in my life.

What is the greatest regret in your career?

I regret not staying in Paris longer than four years, but I guess I can always go back.

What is an important lesson you've learned about money, compensation or finance over the course of your career?

If you're a person who is not relying on a trust fund or a wealthy spouse, you may need a day job (possibly in another field) to gain some financial stability and take care of your bills as you start out or switch lanes. Try to learn from people who are "good with money" or who make more money than you do. Have an accountant. Ask questions. Save money. Get good at budgeting. Figure out what your goals are and what you want or need financially. Get really good at asking for what you want. If you're brave and willing, ask your peers what they make. Don't feel bad about your situation if you're broke—most people live in quiet desperation (or deep anxiety) at least sometimes when it comes to money. Don't get cocky if you start making a lot of money—it's not cute and money comes and goes. Know your worth and know what that looks like in terms of contracts you might sign; find a lawyer or agent who can really help explain what the contract you might sign means. Understand that at different phases of your career you will have more to learn about money.

How do you take care of your mental health and deal with the stresses of your work?

I speak to a therapist. I take walks in the morning to clear my mind. I try to laugh. I try to do the things that I know bring me joy, like going to concerts, going to the movies, hanging out with family and friends, traveling, going to the beach, taking naps, getting massages, taking long baths, eating delicious food, listening to my favorite artists, spending time in nature, taking vacations. Sometimes meditating. If I'm feeling down I sometimes have to remind myself what I've done in the past to create some joy. I also just sit with my feelings sometimes and let them run their course.

How have you approached creating a team for the work you do?

I'm still figuring out how to build a team.

What advice would you offer to someone who wants to do what you do?

Think about what you want to do. Write it down on paper. Write down the baby steps that you think might be required to do what you want to do. Take time to imagine yourself doing the things you want to do. Hang out with people who are doing things similar to what you want to do. Do what you want to do. Have a deep well of patience. Don't be in a rush to do anything. Occasionally, reevaluate what it is you would like to do. We change as we grow, and your work and goals might change too.

Do you have a mission or motto, and if so, what is it?

Fuck it. As my Dad says, the only two words you need. To me it can mean either "just do it" or "let it go."

What do you most enjoy about your work?

I love listening to peoples' stories. I love meeting people. I really enjoy the perks of good food and wine and the social aspect of food media and hospitality. At its best, working in food feels like being in a lively community.

What's the most difficult aspect of your career?

Writing. Managing my time. Dealing with administrative things like submitting invoices or responding to emails. Being overwhelmed and juggling too much. Really wondering if I'm being paid well. Feeling like I have to do everything myself.

What brings you joy and what would you like to experience more of?

Spending days on the beach with friends or family. Going to concerts, dancing, having picnics, the first weeks of a new or rekindled love.

What are some of your favorite things to eat or drink?

Champagne, green juices, passion fruit, cannoli, cookies, cakes, mangoes, salads, nuts, pizza, fish.

Parisian Chestnut Mini Cakes

BY KLANCY MILLER / MAKES 3 SERVINGS

2 tablespoons plus 1 teaspoon butter

1 cup chestnut cream

1 candied chestnut, diced (optional)

2 large eggs

2 ounces bittersweet chocolate (optional)

I learned how to make these mini chestnut cakes when I was an apprentice at Taillevent in Paris. I like to eat this rich cake with vanilla ice cream or with melted chocolate on top. Similar in consistency to flourless chocolate cake, these cakes keep well, so if you end up with extras, wrap them in plastic and put them in the refrigerator for up to three days. The main ingredient, chestnut cream, is a sweetened chestnut puree and it's available, as are candied chestnuts (marrons glacés), from gourmet shops and online sources like lepicerie.com.

Preheat the oven to 350°F. Use 1 teaspoon of the butter to grease three 3-inch ramekins or shallow tart molds. Set them aside.

In a small saucepan over medium heat, melt the remaining butter. Set it aside to cool slightly.

In a medium bowl, whisk the chestnut cream, melted butter, and candied chestnut, if using, until well combined. Whisk in the eggs one at a time.

Place the prepared molds on a sheet pan and divide the batter evenly among them. Place the pan in the oven and bake the cakes for 30 to 35 minutes, until firm and lightly browned. Set aside on a rack to cool for 10 minutes before unmolding.

Meanwhile, chop the chocolate, if using, and add it to the top of a double boiler or a metal bowl set on top of a saucepan that's half full of water. (The water should not touch the bottom of the bowl.) Heat over medium-high, stirring after 5 minutes, until the chocolate is completely melted.

To serve, unmold the cakes onto dessert plates and drizzle with the melted chocolate. Serve warm. (Or eat it straight from the ramekin!)

Raspberry Shortcake

BY KLANCY MILLER / MAKES 1 SERVING

2 tablespoons unsalted butter, melted, plus 1 teaspoon for the pan

¼ cup plus 1 teaspoon all-purpose flour

1 large egg white

2 tablespoons light brown sugar

1½ tablespoons whole milk

¼ teaspoon vanilla extract

¼ teaspoon baking powder

⅓ cup heavy whipping cream

1½ teaspoons confectioners' sugar

18 to 20 fresh raspberries

This is actually a take on a strawberry shortcake recipe from my book Cooking Solo: The Fun of Cooking for Yourself, *and the other twist is that it's a dessert for one. I'm a fan of the individual dessert for one because it feels like an elaborate treat, a decadent reward just because you're worth it. The base is a mini cake that gets sliced horizontally so that you can layer it with whipped cream and berries. If you want to make the recipe for several people you can multiply the ingredients by the number of guests, but I still recommend baking the cakes in individual ramekins.*

Preheat the oven to 350°F. Use 1 teaspoon of the butter to grease the inside of a 4-inch ramekin. Add 1 teaspoon of the flour, rotating the ramekin to coat it evenly, and shake out the excess.

In a small mixing bowl, whisk the egg white with the brown sugar until the sugar dissolves. Stir in the remaining flour and butter, the milk, vanilla, and baking powder, beating until smooth.

Pour the batter into the prepared ramekin, set it on a baking sheet, and place it in the oven. Bake for 24 to 26 minutes, until the cake is golden on top and a toothpick inserted in the center comes out clean. Set it aside on a rack to cool completely, about 30 minutes.

Shortly before serving, whisk the cream in a medium bowl until soft peaks form. Whisk in the confectioners' sugar, tasting and adding more if desired.

For a tower, remove the cake from the ramekin and cut it horizontally into three rounds of equal size. Place one round on a dessert plate and top with a third of the whipped cream and a third of the raspberries. Stack the second disk on top and layer it with a third of the whipped cream and a third of the berries. Place the final disk on top and garnish with the remaining whipped cream and raspberries.

For a low-rise dessert, arrange the cake rounds on a plate and top with the raspberries and whipped cream. Serve immediately.

Appendix

Zoe Adjonyoh
@zoeadjonyoh

Mennlay Golokeh Aggrey
@mennlay

Salimatu Amebebe
@salimatuamabebe

Myriam Babel
@odetobabel

Marva Babel
@odetobabel

Mashama Bailey
@mashamabailey

Ashtin Berry
@thecollectress

Lisa Binns
@stushinthebush

Fatmata Binta
@chef_binta

Rahanna Bisseret Martinez
@rahanna.bisseret.martinez

Michelle Braxton
@supperwithmichelle

Ardenia Brown
@therealchefbutta

Adrienne Cheatham
@chefadriennecheatham

Julia Coney
@juliaconey

Janine Copeland
@gojnine

Jessica Craig
@dachocolatechef84

Ayesha Curry
@ayeshacurry

Kia Damon
@kiacooks

Kyisha Davenport
@barnoirboston

Devita Davison
@DevitaDavison [on Twitter]

Cheryl Day
@cherylday

Gabrielle E. W. Carter
@gabrielle_eitienne

Osayi Endolyn
@osayiendolyn

Amethyst Ganaway
@thizzg

Jacqueline Greaves
@jacquiesfoodfortalk

Jerrelle Guy
@chocolateforbasil

Carla Hall
@carlaphall

Lani Halliday
@lanihalliday

Shanika Hillocks
@shanikahillocks

Dr. Jessica B. Harris
@drjessicabharris

Karis Jagger
@karisjagger

Sicily Johnson
@sicilysierra

Adjoa Kittoe
@seulful

Jillian Knox
@jjoules

Yewande Komolafe
@yewande_komolafe

Adrian Lipscombe
@adie_eats

Vallery Lomas
@foodieinnewyork

Wendy Lopez
@foodheaven

Merryanne Loum-Martin
@jnanetamsna

Krystal Mack
@krystalcmack

Cha McCoy
@cha_squared

Klancy Miller
@klancycooks

Kelly Mitchell
@kells01

Shannon Mustipher
@shannonmustipher

Thérèse Nelson
@blackculinary

Zella Palmer
@maisonzella

Leah Penniman
@leahpenniman

Anya Peters
@dawt.a

Rasheeda Purdie
@ramenbyra

Jamila Robinson
@jamilarobinson

Sophia Roe
@sophia_roe

Michelle Rousseau
@jasisters

Suzanne Rousseau
@suziequrious

Tiffani Rozier
@cheftiffanirozier

Elle Simone Scott
@elle_simone_scott

Georgia Silvera Seamans
@notesontea

Jacqui Sinclair
@juicycheffoodie

Joy Spence
@thejsaere

Nicole Taylor
@foodculturist

Kaylah Thomas
@_killahkaythomas

Sarah Thompson
@tri_sarah_thomps

Toni Tipton-Martin
@tonitiptonmartin

Fabienne Toback
@savyfaby

Paola Velez
@smallorchids

Korsha Wilson
@korshawilson

Amanda Yee
@paramette.ic

Index